YOUR VOICE AND MINE 4

~

HILKER LITTLE PROTHEROE

Holt, Rinehart and Winston of Canada, Limited

Douglas Hilker,
Head of English, Runnymede Collegiate Institute,
York Board of Education

Natalie Little,
Principal, Nelson A. Boylen Secondary School, North York
Board of Education

Brenda Protheroe,
Vice-Principal, York Memorial Collegiate Institute, York
Board of Education

Holt, Rinehart and Winston of Canada, Limited is grateful
for the evaluations and suggestions of these educators:

Neil Andersen
Scarborough Board of
Education
Scarborough, Ontario

Bil Chinn
Edmonton Public Schools
Edmonton, Alberta

Project Editor: Pam Young
Director, Art and Design: Mary Opper
Art Director: Julia Naimska
Designer: Julia Naimska
Assistant Art Director: Arnold Winterhoff
Cover Photo: Jon Amsterdam/Focus Stock Photo

Canadian Cataloguing in Publication Data
Hilker, Douglas
  Your voice and mine 4

For use in high schools.
Includes bibliographical references.
ISBN 0-03-921797-3

1. English literature – 20th century. 2. Canadian literature
(English) – 20th century.* 3. Readers (Secondary).
I. Little, Natalie. II. Protheroe, Brenda. III. Title.

PE1121.H56 1989   820'.8   C88-095248-2

Printed in Canada   3 4 5   93 92 91

CONTENTS

~❧~

STUDENT HANDBOOK

Checklists • Debating • Holding Conferences • Interviewing
Techniques • Keeping a Journal • Media Review: Film
• Media Review: Television • Oral Presentation Skills
• The Personal Usage Sheet • Planning and Organizing
Outline • Record of Individual Participation in a Group
and Self-evaluation Form • Research Skills: Notemaking
Format • Using Language to Learn • Vocabulary • Voices
• Word Processors • Working in Groups • The Writing
Folder • Whole-Book Activities • Glossary

PARENTING

INTRODUCTION

~

Sometimes students wonder about the selections and activities in a textbook like this. What good is it to read and talk and write about all these things?

We hope that this book will help you to become a success. When you graduate from secondary school, you might go on to college or you might join the workforce. In either case, you will be required to read, to write, to speak, to listen, to think, to communicate your ideas, and to use language effectively. Some of you will do more writing than others and some of you will listen more; what is important is that you acquire a level of language proficiency that enables you to be successful at anything you want to do.

This textbook is designed to engage you in interesting language activities that will develop your awareness of ideas and values in our society. It will assist you in developing skills that post-secondary institutions and employers value, such as team work, articulateness, organization of ideas and time, taking pride in your work, following instructions, careful reading, and comprehension.

Your high-school English program and this textbook will be successful only if they encourage and develop in you a level of language skill and confidence that allows you to read and write successfully in your future endeavours.

Enjoy the book.

And good luck developing your own voice.

PERMANENT
RELATIONSHIPS

VOICES

I'M BLACK, SHE'S WHITE COULD OUR LOVE SURVIVE?

DAVID MCKIE

When I think back to when I first met my wife seven and a half years ago, my mind races through an emotional scale ranging from regret to utter joy. Our love was tested from the start. As far as her parents were concerned, our relationship had one major flaw: I was black, and she was white.

Deirdre and I never perceived the colour difference. When my roommate introduced us in the fall of 1978, we were first-year students living in a residence at Carleton University in Ottawa. I was 19 and from Toronto, and one of my major preoccupations was playing football on the university team. Of less importance to me were my journalism studies. Deirdre, 18, and from a small town in British Columbia, was an intense A student majoring in French and planned to get a teaching degree.

Deirdre possessed one of the kindest smiles I had ever seen, exuding charm and grace. The cliché of love at first sight was the only way to describe my emotional state. I knew the feeling was mutual—I could see it in her eyes. Within weeks, Deirdre and I began seeing each other, and the first period of our courtship was innocent. We visited each other twice a day and philosophized while reading song lyrics. We were uninterested in many of the sexual exploits that seemed to characterize other teen-age couples. Christmas vacation soon arrived, and we said goodbye after many long embraces. Two weeks couldn't pass soon enough.

Little did we know that Christmas would mark the beginning of our worries, which would later cause us to reevaluate our love. The events that unfolded at Deirdre's home that Christmas, and during her visits thereafter, could only be explained to me years later when she was able to verbalize the struggles without bursting into tears.

FRIENDS

SHARON NEWMAN

This song was written by a high school student to be performed at her graduation.

This is a special time tonight
A time for us to share;
With friends we may not see again
'Though the love will always be there.

Thanks for the friendships
The deep warmth, the care;
Whenever someone was in need
A friend was always there.

Thank you for the laughter
And even for the tears;
The times we've spent together
Will be remembered throughout the years.

It was friends who made it all worthwhile
Through the struggles and the fears
They're the ones who were always there
To wipe away the tears.

Together we have made it through;
As friends we will remain;
Let us join together in our hearts
Until we meet again.

CHORUS:
And it's the bond we have
With our special friends
That will never be broken
No matter what the cost.

We'll keep all these memories
Forever in our hearts
Where they'll always be held safe
And never lost.

GRETA

I can never remember feeling good about myself. From the time I was a little kid I always felt nobody liked me—not my parents, my brothers, my sister, nobody. I never had any friends, someone I could tell everything to. I tried to make friends, but nobody seemed to care for me. They'd always go back with their other friends and leave me.

I also had a lot of problems with my appearance. Until grade nine I was a head taller than everybody else. The kids always called me names like Stretch and Daddy Long-Legs. I felt the other kids were always laughing at me.

Things weren't much better at home. The only way I could deal with my problems when I was a little kid—and even now—was to cry a lot. My mother wasn't very sympathetic. The crying bothered her; it got on her nerves.

Nobody in the family ever made an effort to understand me or even to talk to me. My family isn't exactly what you'd call warm. There's never any expressions of love or any feeling. It's a bunch of people living together under the same roof. That's about the size of it because none of us really like each other. I'm eighteen and I can't remember my mother or father ever hugging or kissing us.

Things started getting really bad in high school. I changed schools. In the old school even though I didn't have any friends I still had kids to hang around with; in the new school I had no one. At that age everybody's in groups. I felt out of it. I tried, but I couldn't get along with the others. I didn't like them; they were mostly into parties and drinking. I wasn't into that sort of thing and I felt really strange. I thought something was wrong with me. They thought I was weird. I tried to find kids with my interests and I did try to hang around in this other group. But I didn't have self-confidence and I felt like I was forcing myself on them and they didn't really want me.

High school was pretty much a waste. I felt totally useless. I was bored and depressed and always putting myself down. I figured I've got to stop being the way I am and try to change so that I'll find somebody who would like me. I knew I couldn't let anyone see what I was really like. So I went on a wilderness course and I met one girl that I really liked. Randy. We continued the friendship at home.

Mom Always There When I Need Her
DONNA YAWCHING

During a recent crisis in my life, I received a letter from my mother. She knew of my dilemma and, as mothers will inevitably do, was offering advice.

"Do whatever feels right to you," she wrote, after a preliminary page and a half of philosophizing over the problem. "You'll probably weep either way you decide, since life is like that. I'll supply the handkerchiefs and the shoulder."

That, I have decided, is what motherhood is all about. I'm not a mother and cannot pretend to have any great leanings in that direction, but I've come to this conclusion after long years of testing and pondering. From crisis to crisis, boyfriend to boyfriend (which is generally the same thing), through moments of hope, disappointment, despair, my mother (like most mothers) has always been there, handkerchiefs and shoulder at the ready. In time of triumph, she exults almost more than I do; in times of tragedy, she is a rock.

ACTIVITIES

Voices
pp. 14—17

1. In a group of four assign each member one of the monologues to read aloud to the group. Take a moment to read the monologues over silently before reading aloud. Discuss which monologue you found the most moving.

2. As a group, make a list of the qualities you value most in each of the following relationships:
- same-sex friends
- male-female: romantic
- male-female: platonic
- siblings
- parent-child
- employee-employer

Beside the first list make another list of the most common things people do that strain or destroy these relationships.

3. Write a journal entry patterned on one of the monologues in this unit, but use your own personal experience or that of someone you know well.

To Be in Love

GWENDOLYN BROOKS

To be in love
Is to touch things with a lighter hand.

In yourself you stretch, you are well.
You look at things
Through his eyes.
     A Cardinal is red.
     A sky is blue.
Suddenly you know she knows too.
She is not there but
You know you are tasting together
The winter, or light spring weather.

His hand to take your hand is overmuch.
Too much to bear.

You cannot look in his eyes
Because your pulse must now say
What must not be said.

When she
Shuts a door—
Is not there—
Your arms are water.

And you are free
With a ghastly freedom.

You are the beautiful half
Of a golden hurt.

You remember and covet his mouth,
To touch, to whisper on.

Oh when to declare
Is certain Death!

Oh when to apprize
Is to mesmerize,

To see fall down, the Column of Gold,
Into the commonest ash.

WORDS

WARING CUNEY

There
Are no words
To trace
The beauty
Of her face.

There
Are no words
To hold the rush
Of her blood
Into a blush.

Now
That our love
Has come to this
There are no words
For her kiss.

Now That Our Love

WARING CUNEY

Now that our love has drifted
To a quiet close,
Leaving the empty ache
That always follows when beauty goes—
Now that you and I,
Who stood tip-toe on earth
To touch our fingers to the sky,
Have turned away
To allow our little love to die—
Go dear, seek again the magic touch.
But if you are wise,
As I shall be wise,
You will never again
Love over much.

AT SEVENTEEN

JANIS IAN

I learned the truth at seventeen
That love was meant for beauty queens
—And high school girls with clear skinned smiles
Who married young and then retired.
The valentines I never knew,
The Friday night charades of youth
Were spent on one more beautiful—
At seventeen I learned the truth.

And those of us with ravaged faces
Lacking in the social graces,
Desperately remained at home
Inventing lovers on the phone
Who called to say, "Come dance with me,"
And murmured vague obscenities.
It isn't all it seems,
At seventeen.

A brown-eyed girl in hand-me downs
Whose name I never could pronounce
Said, "Pity, please, the ones who serve,
They only get what they deserve.
The rich relationed home-town queen
Marries into what she needs
A guarantee of company
And haven for the elderly."

Remember those who win the game
Lose the love they sought to gain
In debentures of quality
And dubious integrity.
Their small town eyes will gape at you
In dull surprise when payment due
Exceeds accounts received,
At seventeen.

    To those of us who know the pain
    Of valentines that never came,
    And those whose names were never called
    When choosing sides for basketball.
    It was long ago and far away,
    The world was younger than today,
    And dreams were all they gave for free
    To ugly duckling girls like me.

We all play the game and when we dare
To cheat ourselves at solitaire
Inventing lovers on the phone
Repenting other lives unknown,
That call and say, "Come dance with me,"
And murmur vague obscenities
At ugly girls like me
At seventeen.

HOW DO I LOVE THEE?

~

ELIZABETH BARRETT BROWNING

How do I love thee? Let me count the ways.
I love thee to the depth and breadth and height
My soul can reach, when feeling out of sight
For the ends of Being and ideal Grace.
I love thee to the level of every day's
Most quiet need, by sun and candlelight.
I love thee freely, as men strive for Right;
I love thee purely, as they turn from Praise.
I love thee with the passion put to use
In my old griefs, and with my childhood's faith.
I love thee with a love I seemed to lose
With my lost saints—I love thee with the breath,
Smiles, tears of all my life!—and, if God choose,
I shall but love thee better after death.

FOR ANNE

LEONARD COHEN

With Annie gone,
Whose eyes compare
With the morning sun?

Not that I did compare,
But I do compare
Now that she's gone.

ACTIVITIES

To Be in Love
pp. 19–25

1. Work in a small group, reread "To Be in Love," and decide what the speaker has to say about being in love. List the images the poet used to express this feeling. Reread "Words," "Now That Our Love," and "For Anne," and describe the images used and the feelings experienced after love has ended. Write a paragraph in your journal explaining which touched you the most—the poem about being in love or the poems on love ending.

2. "At Seventeen" is written from a girl's point of view. Write a similar version of "At Seventeen" from a boy's point of view. Read aloud your poem to other students who have written new versions.

3. Discuss with two other people what the speaker is saying in "How Do I Love Thee?" Write your own poem titled "How Do I Love Thee?" to someone you care for.

4. Collect several pictures and make a collage. Your collage may be based on one of the poems in this part of the unit, on another love poem that you like, or on one of your own. Put your collage on the bulletin board and explain it to another student or to the class.

BENNY, THE WAR IN EUROPE, AND MYERSON'S DAUGHTER BELLA

~

M O R D E C A I   R I C H L E R

When Benny was sent overseas in the autumn of 1941 his father, Mr. Garber, thought that if he had to give up one son to the army, it might as well be Benny who was a quiet boy, and who wouldn't push where he shouldn't; and Mrs. Garber thought: "My Benny, he'll take care, he'll watch out"; and Benny's brother Abe thought "when he comes back, I'll have a garage of my own, you bet, and I'll be able to give him a job." Benny wrote every week, and every week the Garbers sent him parcels full of good things that a Jewish boy should always have, like salami and pickled herring and *shtrudel*. The food parcels were always the same, and the letters—coming from Camp Borden and Aldershot and Normandy and Holland—were always the same too. They began—"I hope you are all well and good"—and ended—"don't worry, all the best to everybody, thank you for the parcel."

When Benny came home from the war in Europe, the Garbers didn't make much of a fuss. They met him at the station, of course, and they had a small dinner for him.

Abe was thrilled to see Benny again. "Atta boy," was what he kept saying all evening, "Atta boy, Benny."

"You shouldn't go back to the factory," Mr. Garber said. "You don't need the old job. You can be a help to your brother Abe in his garage."

"Yes," Benny said.

"Let him be, let him rest," Mrs. Garber said, "What'll happen if he doesn't work for two weeks?"

"Hey, when Artie Segal came back," Abe said, "he said

"... if he had to give up one son to the army, it might as well be Benny ..."

that in Italy there was nothing that a guy couldn't get for a couple of Sweet Caps. Was he shooting me the bull, or what?"

Benny had been discharged and sent home, not because the war was over, but because of the shrapnel in his leg, but he didn't limp too badly and he didn't talk about his wound or the war, so at first nobody noticed that he had changed. Nobody, that is, except Myerson's daughter Bella.

Myerson was the proprietor of Pop's Cigar & Soda, on Laurier Street, and any day of the week, you could find him there seated on a worn, peeling kitchen chair playing poker with the men of the neighbourhood. He had a glass eye and when a player hesitated on a bet, he would take it out and polish it, a gesture that never failed to intimidate. His daughter, Bella, worked behind the counter. She had a club foot and mousy hair and some more hair on her face, and although she was only twenty-six, it was generally supposed that she would end up an old maid. Anyway she was the one—the first one—who noticed that the war in Europe had changed Benny. And, as a matter of fact, the very first time he came into the store after his homecoming she said to him: "What's wrong, Benny? Are you afraid?"

"I'm all right," he said.

Benny was a quiet boy. He was short and skinny with a long narrow face, a pulpy mouth that was somewhat crooked, and soft black eyes. He had big, conspicuous hands, which he preferred to keep out of sight in his pockets. In fact, he seemed to want to keep out of sight altogether and whenever possible, he stood behind a chair or in a dim light so that people wouldn't notice him—and, noticing him, chase him away. When he had failed the ninth grade at Baron Byng High School, his class-master, a Mr. Perkins, had sent him home with a note saying: "Benjamin is not a student, but he has all the makings of a good citizen. He is honest and attentive in class and a hard worker. I recommend that he learn a trade."

And when Mr. Garber had read what his son's teacher had written, he had shaken his head and crumpled up the bit of paper and said—"A trade?"—he had looked at his boy and shaken his head and said—"A trade?"

Mrs. Garber had said stoutly, "Haven't you got a trade?"

"Shapiro's boy will be a doctor," Mr. Garber had said.

"Shapiro's boy," Mrs. Garber had said.

And afterwards, Benny had retrieved the note and smoothed out the creases and put it in his pocket, where

> ". . . he didn't talk about his wound or the war, so at first nobody noticed that he had changed."

28

it had remained. For Benny was sure that one day a policeman, or perhaps even a Mountie, would try to arrest him, and then the paper that Mr. Perkins had written so long ago might prove helpful.

Benny figured that he had been lucky, truly lucky, to get away with living for so long. Oh, he had his dreams. He would have liked to have been an aeroplane pilot, or still better, to have been born rich or intelligent. Those kind of people, he had heard, slept in mornings until as late as nine o'clock. But he had been born stupid, people could tell that, just looking at him, and one day they would come to take him away. They would, sure as hell they would.

The day after his return to Montreal, Benny showed up at Abe's garage having decided that he didn't want two weeks off. That pleased Abe a lot. "I can see that you've matured since you've been away," Abe said. "That's good. That counts for you in this world."

Abe worked very hard, he worked night and day, and he believed that having Benny with him would give his business an added kick. "That's my kid brother Benny," Abe used to tell the cabbies. "Four years in the infantry, two of them up front. A tough hombre, let me tell you."

For the first few weeks Abe was very pleased with Benny. "He's slow," he thought, "no genius of a mechanic, but the customers like him and he'll learn." Then Abe began to notice things. When business was slow, Benny—instead of taking advantage of the lull to clean up the shop—used to sit shivering in a dim corner, with his hands folded tight on his lap. The first time Abe noticed his brother behaving like that, he said: "What's wrong? You got a chill?"

"No. I'm all right."

"You want to go home, or something?"

"No."

Then, when Abe began to notice him sitting like that more and more, he pretended not to see. "He needs time," he thought. But whenever it rained, and it rained often that spring, Benny was not to be found around the garage, and that put Abe in a bad temper. Until one day during a thunder shower, Abe tried the toilet door and found that it was locked. "Benny," he yelled, "come on out, I know you're in there."

Benny didn't answer, so Abe got the key. He found Benny huddled in a corner, his head buried in his knees, trembling, with sweat running down his face in spite of the cold.

"Benny figured he had been lucky, truly lucky, to get away with living for so long."

"It's raining," Benny said.

"Benny, get up. What's wrong?"

"Go away," Benny said. "It's raining."

"I'll get a doctor, Benny. I'll . . . ."

"Don't—you musn't. Go away. Please, Abe."

"But Benny . . . ."

A terrible chill must have overcome Benny just then for he began to shake violently, just as if an inner whip had been cracked. Then, after it had passed, he looked up at Abe dumbly, his mouth hanging open. "It's raining," he said.

His discovery that afternoon gave Abe a good scare, and the next morning he went to see his father. "It was awful spooky, Paw," Abe said. "I don't know what to do with him."

"The war left him with a bad taste," Mrs. Garber said. "It made him something bad."

"Other boys went to the war," Abe said.

"Shapiro's boy," Mr. Garber said, "was an officer."

"Shapiro's boy," Mrs. Garber said. "You give him a vacation, Abe. You insist. He's a good boy. From the best. He'll be all right."

Benny did not know what to do with his vacation, so he tried sleeping in late like the rich and the intelligent, but in the late morning hours he dreamed bad dreams and that made him very frightened so he gave up that kind of thing. He did not dare go walking because he was sure that people could tell, just looking at him, that he was not working, and he did not want others to think that he was a bum. So he began to do odd jobs for people in the neighbourhood. He repaired bicycles and toasters and lamps. But he did not take any money for his work and that made people a little afraid. "Isn't our money good enough for him? All right, he was wounded, so maybe *I* was the one who shot him?"

Benny began to hang around Pop's Cigar & Soda.

"I don't like it, Bella," Mr. Myerson said, admiring the polish of his glass eye against the light. "I need him here like I need a cancer."

"Something's wrong with him psychologically," one of the card players said.

But obviously Bella liked having Benny around, and after a while Mr. Myerson stopped complaining. "Maybe the boy is serious," he thought, "and what with her club-foot and all that stuff on her face, I can't start picking and choosing. Beside, it's not as if he was a crook!"

"I need him here like I need a cancer."

Bella and Benny did not talk much when they were together, afraid, perhaps, that whatever it was that was "starting" up between them, was rich in delicacy, and would be soiled by ordinary words. She used to knit, he used to smoke. He would watch silently as she limped about the store, silently, with longing, and burning hope and consternation. The letter from Mr. Perkins was in his pocket. He wanted to tell her about the war—about things.

"I was walking with the sergeant. He reached into his pocket to show me a letter from his wife when . . . ."

There he would stop. A twitching would start around his eyes and he would swallow hard and stop.

Bella would look up from her knitting, waiting for him the way a mother waits for a child to be reasonable, knowing that it is only a question of time. But Benny would begin to shiver, and, looking down at the floor, grip his hands together until the knuckles went white. Around five in the afternoon he would get up and leave without saying a word. Bella would give him a stack of magazines to take home and at night he would read them all from cover to cover and the next morning he would bring them back as clean as new. Then he would sit with her in the store again, looking down at the floor or at his hands, as though he were in great pain. Time passed, and one day instead of going home around five in the afternoon he went upstairs with her. Mr. Myerson, who was watching, smiled happily. He turned to Mr. Shub and said: "If I had a boy of my own, I couldn't wish for a better one than Benny."

"Look who's counting his chickens already," Mr. Shub said.

Benny's vacation continued for several weeks and every morning he sat down in the store and stared at his hands, as if he expected them to have changed overnight, and every evening he went upstairs with Bella pretending not to have heard the remarks, the good-natured observations that had been made by the card-players as they passed.

Until, one afternoon she said to him: "I'm going to have a baby."

"All right," Benny said.

"Aren't you even going to say luck or something?"

Benny got up and bit his lower lip and gripped his hands together hard. "If you only knew what I have seen," he said.

They had a very simple wedding without speeches in a small synagogue and after the ceremony was over Abe slapped his younger brother's back and said: "Atta boy,

> "He wanted to tell her about the war—about things."

Benny. Atta boy."

"Can I come back to work?"

"Sure, of course you can. You're the old Benny again,"
Abe said. "I can see that."

And when Mr. Garber got home, without much more to
expect but getting older, and more tired earlier in the day,
he turned to his wife and said: "Shapiro's boy married
into the Segals."

"Shapiro's boy," Mrs. Garber said.

Benny went back to the garage but this time he settled
down to work hard and that pleased Abe a good deal.
"That's my kid brother, Benny," Abe used to tell the cabbies, "married six weeks and he's already got one in the
oven. A quick worker, I'll tell you."

Benny settled down to work hard and when the baby
was born he even laughed a little and began to save money
and plan things, but every now and then, usually when
there was a slack period at the garage, Benny would shut
up tight and sit in a chair in a dark corner and stare at
his hands. Bella was good with him. She never raised her
voice to say an ugly thing, and when he woke up screaming
from a dream about the war in Europe she would stroke
his neck and say tender things. He, on the other hand,
began to speak to her confidentially.

> "... when he woke up
> screaming from a dream
> about the war in
> Europe, she would
> stroke his neck ..."

"Bella?"

"Yes."

"I killed a man."

"What? You what? When did you . . . ."

"In the war."

"Oh in the war. For a moment I—a German you
mean . . . ."

"Yes, a German."

"If you ask me it's too bad you didn't kill a dozen. Those
Germans I . . . ."

"I killed him with my hands."

"Go to sleep."

"Bella?"

"Yes."

"Are you ashamed that I . . . ."

"Go to sleep."

"I saw two babies killed," he said. "What if . . . ."

"There won't be another war. Don't worry about our
baby."

"But . . . ."

"Sleep. Go to sleep."

The baby grew into a fine, husky boy, and whenever

there was a parade Benny used to hoist him on his shoulders so that he could see better. He was amazed, truly amazed, that he could have had such a beautiful child. He hardly had nightmares at all any more and he became talkative and somewhat shrewd. One night he came home and said: "Abe is going to open a branch on Mount Royal Street. I'm going to manage it. I'm going to be a partner in it."

So Benny finally threw away the paper that Mr. Perkins had written for him so long ago. They bought a car and planned, the following year, to have enough money saved so that Bella could go to a clinic in the United States to have an operation on her club foot. "I can assure you that

I'm not going to spend such a fortune to make myself beautiful," Bella said, "and plainly speaking I'm not doing it for you. But I don't want that when the boy is old enough to go to school that he should be teased because his mother is a cripple."

Then, a month before Bella was to go to the clinic, they went to see their first cinemascope film. Now, previous to that evening, Bella had made a point never to take Benny along to see a war film, no matter who was playing in it. So as soon as the newsreel came on—it was that special one about the hydrogen bomb tests—she knew that she had made a mistake in bringing Benny with her, cinemascope or no cinemascope. She turned to him quickly. "Don't look," she said.

But Benny was enthralled. He watched the explosion, and he watched as the newsreel showed by means of diagrams what a hydrogen bomb could do to a city the size of New York—never mind Montreal.

Then he got up and left.

When Bella got home that night she found Benny huddled up in a dark corner with his head buried in his knees, trembling, with sweat running down his face. She tried to stroke his neck but he moved away from her.

"Should I send for a doctor?"

"Bella," he said. "Bella, Bella."

"Try to relax," she said. "Try to think about something pretty. Flowers, or something. Try for the boy's sake."

"Bella," he said. "Bella, Bella."

When she woke up the next morning he was still crouching there in that dark corner gripping his hands together tight, and he wouldn't eat or speak—not even to the boy.

The living-room was in a mess, papers spilled everywhere, as if he had been searching for something.

Finally—it must have been around noon—he put on his hat and walked out of the house. She knew right then that she should have stopped him. That she shouldn't have let him go. She knew.

Her father came around at five o'clock and she could tell from the expression on his face that she had guessed right. Mr. and Mrs. Garber were with him.

"He's dead?" Bella asked.

"Shapiro's boy, the doctor," Mr. Garber said, "said it was quick."

"Shapiro's boy," Mrs. Garber said.

"It wasn't the driver's fault," Mr. Myerson said.

"I know," Bella said.

> "... she found Benny huddled up in a dark corner with his head buried in his knees, ..."

ACTIVITIES

Benny, the War in Europe, and Myerson's Daughter Bella pp.27–35

1. Before reading the story, write in your journal about:
   a) how your parents or guardians view you (i.e., smart, loving, a trouble-maker);
   b) what expectations they have of you;
   c) whether they compare you to others such as an older or younger brother or sister, a neighbour, a cousin, and, if so, how you feel about it; and
   d) your identity (how you see yourself, how you would describe or define yourself, how you feel about yourself).

   With a partner you trust share as many of these thoughts as you feel comfortable with.

2. After reading "Benny, the War in Europe, and Myerson's Daughter Bella," write the journal entry Benny would have written if he had been given activity #1 to complete. Read your entry to others in a small group.

3. a) Discuss with a partner the significance of the note Benny's teacher had given him, why he carried it with him, and how, in combination with other factors, it might have contributed to his suicide many years later.
   b) Discuss with your partner occasions when you received positive and negative feedback and how it made you feel. Have you received negative feedback? Talk also about occasions when you have given positive feedback to your peers, parents, or teachers.
   c) Write an encouraging, affirming note to someone in your life and give it to him or her.

4. Invite a psychologist or guidance counsellor to your class to talk about identity, self-image, and self-esteem. In small groups prepare several questions before your guest comes to the class.

THANKS FOR THE RIDE

~

A L I C E   M U N R O

My cousin George and I were sitting in a restaurant called Pop's Cafe, in a little town close to the Lake. It was getting dark in there, and they had not turned the lights on, but you could still read the signs plastered against the mirror between the fly-speckled and slightly yellowed cutouts of strawberry sundaes and tomato sandwiches.

"Don't ask for information," George read. "If we knew anything we wouldn't be here" and "if you've got nothing to do, you picked a hell of a good place to do it in." George always read everything out loud—posters, billboards, Burma-Shave signs, "Mission Creek. Population 1700. Gateway to the Bruce. We love our children."

I was wondering whose sense of humour provided us with the signs. I thought it would be the man behind the cash register. Pop? Chewing on a match, looking out at the street, not watching for anything except for somebody to trip over a crack in the sidewalk or have a blowout or make a fool of himself in some way that Pop, rooted behind the cash register, huge and cynical and incurious, was never likely to do. Maybe not even that; maybe just by walking up and down, driving up and down, going places, the rest of the world proved its absurdity. You see that judgment on the faces of people looking out of windows sitting on front steps in some little towns; so deeply, deeply uncaring they are, as if they had sources of disillusionment which they would keep, with some satisfaction, in the dark.

There was only the one waitress, a pudgy girl who leaned over the counter and scraped at the polish on her fingernails. When she had flaked most of the polish off her thumbnail she put the thumb against her teeth and rubbed the nail back and forth absorbedly. We asked her what her name was and she didn't answer. Two or three minutes later the thumb came out of her mouth and she said, inspecting it: "That's for me to know and you to find out."

"All right," George said. "Okay if I call you Mickey?"

"I don't care."

"Because you remind me of Mickey Rooney," George said. "Hey, where's everybody go in this town? Where's everybody go?" Mickey had turned her back and begun to drain out the coffee. It looked as if she didn't mean to talk any more, so George got a little jumpy, as he did when he was threatened with having to be quiet or be by himself. "Hey, aren't there any girls in this town?" he said almost plaintively. "Aren't there any girls or dances or anything? We're strangers in town," he said. "Don't you want to help us out?"

"Hey, aren't there any girls in this town?"

"Dance hall down on the beach closed up Labour Day," Mickey said coldly.

"There are other dance halls?"

"There's a dance tonight out at Wilson's *school*," Mickey said.

"That old-time? No, no, I don't go for that old-time. *All-a-man left* and that, used to have that down in the basement of the church. Yeah, *ever'body swing*—I don't go for that. Inna basement of the *church*," George said, obscurely angered. "You don't remember that," he said to me. "Too young."

I was just out of high-school at this time, and George had been working for three years in the Men's Shoes in a downtown department store, so there was that difference. But we had never bothered with each other back in the city. We were together now because we had met unexpectedly in a strange place and because I had a little money, while George was broke. Also I had my father's car, and George was in one of his periods between cars, which made him always a little touchy and dissatisfied. But he would have to rearrange these facts a bit, they made him uneasy. I could feel him manufacturing a sufficiency of good feeling, old-pal feeling, and dressing me up as Old Dick, good kid, real character—which did not matter one way or the other, though I did not think, looking at his tender blond piggish handsomeness, the nudity of his pink mouth, and the surprised, angry creases that frequent puzzlement was beginning to put into his forehead, that I would be able to work up an Old George.

I had driven to the Lake to bring my mother home from a beach resort for women, a place where they had fruit juice and cottage cheese for reducing, and early-morning swims in the Lake, and some religion, apparently, for there was a little chapel attached. My aunt, George's mother, was staying there at the same time, and George arrived about an hour or so after I did, not to take his mother home, but to get some money out of her. He did not get along well with his father, and he did not make much money working in the shoe department, so he was very often broke. His mother said he could have a loan if he would stay over and go to church with her the next day. George said he would. Then George and I got away and drove half a mile along the lake to this little town neither of us had seen before, which George said would be full of bootleggers and girls.

It was a town of unpaved, wide, sandy streets and bare yards. Only the hardy things like red and yellow nasturtiums, or a lilac bush with brown curled leaves, grew out of that cracked earth. The houses were set wide apart, with their own pumps and sheds and privies out behind; most of them were built of wood and painted green or grey or yellow. The trees that grew there were big willows or poplars, their fine leaves greyed with the dust. There were no trees along the main street, but spaces of tall grass and dandelions and blowing thistles—open country between the store buildings. The town hall was surprisingly large, with a great bell in a tower, the red brick rather glaring in the midst of the town's walls of faded, pale-painted wood. The sign beside the door said that it was a memorial to the soldiers who had died in the First World War. We had a drink out of the fountain in front.

We drove up and down the main street for a while, with George saying: "What a dump! Jesus, what a dump!" and "Hey, look at that! Aw, not so good either." The people on the street went home to supper, the shadows of the store buildings lay solid across the street, and we went into Pop's.

"Hey," George said, "is there any other restaurant in this town? Did you see any other restaurant?"

"No," I said.

"Any other town I ever been," George said, "pigs hangin' out the windows, practically hangin' off the trees. Not here. Jesus! I guess it's late in the season," he said.

"You want to go to a show?"

The door opened. A girl came in, walked up and sat on a stool, with most of her skirt bunched up underneath her. She had a long somnolent face, no bust, frizzy hair; she

"Any other town I ever been . . . pigs hangin' out the windows, practically hangin' off the trees."

was pale, almost ugly, but she had that inexplicable aura of sexuality. George brightened, though not a great deal. "Never mind," he said. "This'll do. This'll do in a pinch, eh? In a pinch."

He went to the end of the counter and sat down beside her and started to talk. In about five minutes they came back to me, the girl drinking a bottle of orange pop.

"This is Adelaide," George said. "Adelaide, Adeline— Sweet Adeline. I'm going to call her Sweet A, Sweet A."

Adelaide sucked at her straw, paying not much attention.

"She hasn't got a date," George said. "You haven't got a date have you, honey?"

Adelaide shook her head very slightly.

"Doesn't hear half what you say to her," George said. "Adelaide, Sweet A, have you got any friends? Have you got any nice, young little girl friend to go out with Dickie?

You and me and her and Dickie?"

"Depends," said Adelaide. "Where do you want to go?"

"Anywhere you say. Go for a drive. Drive up to Owen Sound, maybe."

"You got a car?"

"Yeah, yeah, we got a car. C'mon, you must have some nice little friend for Dickie." He put his arm around this girl, spreading his fingers over her blouse. "C'mon out and I'll show you the car."

Adelaide said: "I know one girl might come. The guy she goes around with, he's engaged, and his girl came up and she's staying at his place up the beach, his mother and dad's place, and—"

"Well that is certainly int-er-esting," George said. "What's her name? Come on, let's go round and get her. You want to sit around drinking pop all night?"

"I'm finished," Adelaide said. "She might not come. I don't know."

"Why not? Her mother not let her out nights?"

"Oh, she can do what she likes," said Adelaide. "Only there's times she don't want to. I don't know."

We went out and got into the car, George and Adelaide in the back. On the main street about a block from the cafe we passed a thin, fair-haired girl in slacks and Adelaide cried: "Hey stop! That's her! That's Lois!"

I pulled in and George stuck his head out of the window, whistling. Adelaide yelled, and the girl came unhesitatingly, unhurriedly to the car. She smiled, rather coldly and politely, when Adelaide explained to her. All the time George kept saying: "Hurry up, come on, get in! We can talk in the car." The girl smiled, did not really look at any of us, and in a few moments, to my surprise, she opened the door and slid into the car.

"I don't have anything to do," she said. "My boy friend's away."

"That so?" said George, and I saw Adelaide, in the rear-vision mirror, make a cross warning face. Lois did not seem to have heard him.

"We better drive around to my house," she said. "I was just going down to get some Cokes, that's why I only have my slacks on. We better drive around to my house and I'll put on something else."

"Where are we going to go," she said, "so I know what to put on?"

I said: "Where do you want to go?"

"Okay, okay," George said. "First things first. We gotta get a bottle, then we'll decide. You know where to get one?" Adelaide and Lois both said yes, and then Lois said to me: "You can come in the house and wait while I change, if you want to." I glanced in the rear mirror and thought that there was probably some agreement she had with Adelaide.

Lois's house had an old couch on the porch and some rugs hanging down over the railing. She walked ahead of me across the yard. She had her long pale hair tied at the back of her neck; her skin was dustily freckled, but not tanned; even her eyes were light-coloured. She was cold and narrow and pale. There was derision, and also great gravity, about her mouth. I thought she was about my age or a little older.

She opened the front door and said in a clear, stilted voice: "I would like you to meet my family."

"She was cold and narrow and pale."

The little front room had linoleum on the floor and flowered paper curtains at the windows. There was a glossy chesterfield with a Niagara Falls and a To Mother cushion on it, and there was a little black stove with a screen around it for summer, and a big vase of paper apple blossoms. A tall, frail woman came into the room drying her hands on a dishtowel, which she flung into a chair. Her mouth was full of blue-white china teeth, the long cords trembled in her neck. I said how-do-you-do to her, embarrassed by Lois's announcement, so suddenly and purposefully conventional. I wondered if she had any misconceptions about this date, engineered by George for such specific purposes. I did not think so. Her face had no innocence in it that I could see; it was knowledgeable, calm, and hostile. She might have done it, then, to mock me, to make me into this caricature of The Date, the boy who grins and shuffles in the front hall and waits to be presented to the nice girl's family. But that was a little far-fetched. Why should she want to embarrass me when she had agreed to go out with me without even looking into my face? Why should she care enough?

> "Why should she want to embarrass me when she had agreed to go out with me . . ."

Lois's mother and I sat down on the chesterfield. She began to make conversation, giving this the Date interpretation. I noticed the smell in the house, the smell of stale small rooms, bedclothes, frying, washing, and medicated ointments. And dirt, though it did not look dirty. Lois's mother said: "That's a nice car you got out front. Is that your car?"

"My father's."

"Isn't that lovely! Your father has such a nice car. I always think it's lovely for people to have things. I've got no time for these people that's just eaten up with malice 'n envy. I say it's lovely. I bet your mother, every time she wants anything, she just goes down to the store and buys it—new coat, bedspread, pots and pans. What does your father do? Is he a lawyer or doctor or something like that?"

"He's a chartered accountant."

"Oh. That's in an office, is it?"

"Yes."

"My brother, Lois's uncle, he's in the office of the CPR in London. He's quite high up there, I understand."

She began to tell me about how Lois's father had been killed in an accident at the mill. I noticed an old woman, the grandmother probably, standing in the doorway of the room. She was not thin like the others, but as soft and shapeless as a collapsed pudding, pale brown spots melt-

ing together on her face and arms, bristles of hairs in the moisture around her mouth. Some of the smell in the house seemed to come from her. It was a smell of hidden decay, such as there is when some obscure little animal has died under the verandah. The smell, the slovenly, confiding voice—something about this life I had not known, something about these people. I thought: my mother, George's mother, they are innocent. Even George, George is innocent. But these others are born sly and sad and knowing.

I did not hear much about Lois's father except that his head was cut off.

"Clean off, imagine, and rolled on the floor! Couldn't open the coffin. It was June, the hot weather. And everybody in town just stripped their gardens, stripped them for the funeral. Stripped their spirea bushes and peenies and climbin' clemantis. I guess it was the worst accident ever took place in this town.

"Lois had a nice boy friend this summer," she said. "Used to take her out and sometimes stay here overnight when his folks weren't up at the cottage and he didn't feel like passin' his time there all alone. He'd bring the kids candy and even me he'd bring presents. That china elephant up there, you can plant flowers in it, he brought me that. He fixed the radio for me and I never had to take it into the shop. Do your folks have a summer cottage up here?"

I said no, and Lois came in, wearing a dress of yellow-green stuff—stiff and shiny like Christmas wrappings—high-heeled shoes, rhinestones, and a lot of dark powder over her freckles. Her mother was excited.

"You like that dress?" she said. "She went all the way to London and bought that dress, didn't get it anywhere round here!"

We had to pass by the old woman as we went out. She looked at us with sudden recognition, a steadying of her pale, jellied eyes. Her mouth trembled open, she stuck her face out at me.

"You can do what you like with my gran'daughter," she said in her old, strong voice, the rough voice of a country woman. "But you be careful. And you know what I mean!"

Lois's mother pushed the old woman behind her, smiling tightly, eyebrows lifted, skin straining over her temples. "Never mind," she mouthed at me, grimacing distractedly. "Never mind. Second childhood." The smile stayed on her face; the skin pulled back from it. She seemed to be listening all the time to a perpetual din and racket in her head. She grabbed my hand as I followed Lois out. "Lois is a nice girl," she whispered. "You have a nice time, don't let her mope!" There was a quick, grotesque, and, I suppose, originally flirtatious, flickering of brows and lids. "Night!"

Lois walked stiffly ahead of me, rustling her papery skirt. I said: "Did you want to go to a dance or something?"

"No," she said. "I don't care."

"Well you got all dressed up—"

"I always get dressed up on Saturday night," Lois said, her voice floating back to me, low and scornful. Then she began to laugh, and I had a glimpse of her mother in her, that jaggedness and hysteria. "Oh, my God!" she whispered. I knew she meant what had happened in the house, and I laughed too, not knowing what else to do. So we went back to the car laughing as if we were friends, but we were not.

> "There was a quick, grotesque, and, . . . flirtatious flickering of brows and lids."

We drove out of town to a farmhouse where a woman sold us a whisky bottle full of muddy-looking homemade liquor, something George and I had never had before. Adelaide had said that this woman would probably let us use her front room, but it turned out that she would not, and that was because of Lois. When the woman peered up at me from under the man's cap she had on her head and said to Lois, "Change's as good as a rest, eh?" Lois did not answer, kept a cold face. Then later the woman said that if we were so stuck-up tonight her front room wouldn't be good enough for us and we better go back to the bush. All the way back down the lane Adelaide kept saying: "Some people can't take a joke, can they? Yeah, stuck-up is right—" until I passed her the bottle to keep her quiet. I saw George did not mind, thinking this had taken her mind off driving to Owen Sound.

We parked at the end of the lane and sat in the car drinking. George and Adelaide drank more than we did. They did not talk, just reached for the bottle and passed it back. This stuff was different from anything I had tasted before; it was heavy and sickening in my stomach. There was no other effect, and I began to have the depressing feeling that I was not going to get drunk. Each time Lois handed the bottle back to me she said "Thank you" in a mannerly and subtly contemptuous way. I put my arm around her, not much wanting to. I was wondering what was the matter. This girl lay against my arm, scornful, acquiescent, angry, inarticulate and out-of-reach. I wanted to talk to her then more than to touch her, and that was out of the question; talk was not so little a thing to her as touching. Meanwhile I was aware that I should be beyond this, beyond the first stage and well into the second (for I had a knowledge, though it was not every comprehensive, of the orderly progression of stages, the ritual of back- and front-seat seduction). Almost I wished I was with Adelaide.

"Do you want to go for a walk?" I said.

"That's the first bright idea you've had all night," George told me from the back seat. "Don't hurry," he said as we got out. He and Adelaide were muffled and laughing together. "Don't hurry back!"

Lois and I walked along a wagon track close to the bush. The fields were moonlit, chilly and blowing. Now I felt vengeful, and I said softly, "I had quite a talk with your mother."

"I can imagine," said Lois.

"She told me about that guy you went out with last summer."

"This summer."

"It's last summer now. He was engaged or something, wasn't he?"

"Yes."

I was not going to let her go. "Did he like you better?" I said. "Was that it? Did he like you better?"

> "I was not going to let her go. Did he like you better? . . . Was that it?"

"No, I wouldn't say he liked me," Lois said. I thought, by some thickening of the sarcasm in her voice, that she was beginning to be drunk. "He liked Momma and the kids okay but he didn't like me. *Like me*," she said, "What's that?"

"Well, he went out with you—"

"He just went around with me for the summer. That's what those guys from up the beach always do. They come down here to the dances and get a girl to go around with. For the summer. They always do.

"How I know he didn't *like* me," she said, "he said I was always bitching. You have to act grateful to those guys, you know, or they say you're bitching."

I was a little startled at having loosed all this. I said: "Did you like him?"

"Oh, sure! I should, shouldn't I? I should just get down on my knees and thank him. That's what my mother does. He brings her a cheap old spotted elephant—"

"Was this guy the first?" I said.

"The first steady. Is that what you mean?"

It wasn't. "How old are you?"

She considered. "I'm almost seventeen. I can pass for eighteen or nineteen. I can pass in a beer parlour. I did once."

"What grade are you in at school?"

She looked at me, rather amazed. "Did you think I still went to school? I quit that two years ago. I've got a job at the glove-works in town."

"That must have been against the law. When you quit."

"Oh, you can get a permit if your father's dead or something."

"What do you do at the glove-works?" I said.

"Oh, I run a machine. It's like a sewing machine. I'll be getting on piecework soon. You make more money."

"Do you like it?"

"Oh, I wouldn't say I loved it. It's a job—you ask a lot of questions," she said.

"Do you mind?"

"I don't have to answer you," she said, her voice flat and small again. "Only if I like." She picked up her skirt and spread it out in her hands. "I've got burrs on my skirt," she said. She bent over, pulling them one by one. "I've got burrs on my dress," she said. "It's my good dress. Will they leave a mark? If I pull them all—slowly—I won't pull any threads."

"You shouldn't have worn that dress," I said. "What'd you wear that dress for?"

She shook the skirt, tossing a burr loose. "I don't know," she said. She held it out, the stiff, shining stuff, with faintly drunken satisfaction. "I wanted to show you guys!" she said, with a sudden small explosion of viciousness. The drunken, nose-thumbing, toe-twirling satisfaction could not now be mistaken as she stood there foolishly, tauntingly, with her skirt spread out. "I've got an imitation cashmere sweater at home. It cost me twelve dollars," she said. "I've got a fur coat I'm paying on, paying on for next winter. I've got a fur coat—"

"That's nice," I said. "I think it's lovely for people to have things."

She dropped the skirt and struck the flat of her hand on my face. This was a relief to me, to both of us. We felt a fight had been building in us all along. We faced each other as warily as we could, considering we were both a little drunk, she tensing to slap me again and I to grab her or slap her back. We would have it out, what we had against each other. But the moment of this keenness passed. We let out our breath; we had not moved in time. And the next moment, not bothering to shake off our enmity, nor thinking how the one thing could give way to the other, we kissed. It was the first time, for me, that a kiss was accomplished without premeditation, or hesitancy, or over-haste, or the usual vague ensuing disappointment. And laughing shakily against me, she began to talk again, going back to the earlier part of our conversation as if nothing had come between.

"Isn't it funny?" she said. "You know, all winter all the girls do is talk about last summer, talk and talk about those guys, and I bet you those guys have forgotten even what their names were—"

But I did not want to talk any more, having discovered another force in her that lay side by side with her hostility, that was, in fact, just as enveloping and impersonal. After a while I whispered: "Isn't there some place we can go?"

"Afterwards I wished that I had told her. She would have known what it meant."

And she answered: "There's a barn in the next field."

She knew the countryside; she had been there before.

We drove back into town after midnight. George and Adelaide were asleep in the back seat. I did not think Lois was asleep, though she kept her eyes closed and did not say anything. I had read somewhere about *Omne animal*, and I was going to tell her, but then I thought she would not know Latin words and would think I was being—oh, pretentious and superior. Afterwards I wished that I had told her. She would have known what it meant.

Afterwards the lassitude of the body, and the cold; the separation. To brush away the bits of hay and tidy ourselves with heavy unconnected movements, to come out of the barn and find the moon gone down, but the flat stubble fields still there, and the poplar trees, and the stars. To find our same selves, chilled and shaken, who had gone that headlong journey and were here still. To go back to the car and find the others sprawled asleep. That is what it is: *triste. Triste est.*

That headlong journey. Was it like that because it was the first time, because I was a little, strangely drunk? No. It was because of Lois. There are some people who can go only a little way with the act of love, and some others who can go very far, who can make a greater surrender, like the mystics. And Lois, this mystic of love, sat now on the far side of the car-seat, looking cold and rumpled, and utterly closed up in herself. All the things I wanted to say to her went clattering emptily through my head. *Come and see you again—Remember—Love*—I could not say any of these things. They would not seem even half-true across the space that had come between us. I thought: I will say something to her before the next tree, the next telephone pole. But I did not. I only drove faster, too fast, making the town come nearer.

The street lights bloomed out of the dark trees ahead; there were stirrings in the back seat.

"What time is it?" George said.

"Twenty past twelve."

"We musta finished that bottle. I don't feel so good. Oh, Christ, I don't feel so good. How do you feel?"

"Fine."

"Fine, eh? Feel like you finished your education tonight, eh? That how you feel? Is yours asleep? Mine is."

"I am not," said Adelaide drowsily. "Where's my belt? George—oh. Now where's my other shoe? It's early for Saturday night, isn't it? We could go and get something to eat."

"I don't feel like food," George said. "I gotta get some sleep. Gotta get up early tomorrow and go to church with my mother."

"Yeah, I know," said Adelaide, disbelieving, though not too ill-humoured. "You could've anyways bought me a hamburger!"

I had driven around to Lois's house. Lois did not open her eyes until the car stopped.

She sat still a moment, and then pressed her hands down over the skirt of her dress, flattening it out. She did not look at me. I moved to kiss her, but she seemed to draw slightly away, and I felt that there had after all been something fraudulent and theatrical about this final gesture. She was not like that.

George said to Adelaide: "Where do you live? You live near here?"

"Yeah. Half a block down."

"Okay. How be you get out here too? We gotta get home sometime tonight."

He kissed her and both the girls got out.

I started the car. We began to pull away, George settling down on the back seat to sleep. And then we heard the female voice calling after us, the loud, crude, female voice, abusive and forlorn:

"Thanks for the ride!"

It was not Adelaide calling; it was Lois.

"Feel like you finished your education tonight, eh? That how you feel?"

ACTIVITIES

1. Before reading the story, complete the following activities:

Thanks for the Ride
pp. 37–50

    a) In your journal write about your views on dating. You might want to explore such topics as the first date ever, the first date with a certain person, expectations of men and women, who should ask whom for a date, etc.

    b) In a small group discuss your views on the topics listed above.

2. The editor of an anthology of short stories is considering hiring you to illustrate a scene from this story. Write a proposal for the editor that includes your illustration and a brief explanation of why you consider the scene to be important to the story.

3. Imagine the kinds of lives the narrator, George, Adelaide, and Lois will be leading ten years after the events in the story. What education and jobs will they have? Where will they be living? Will they be single, married, divorced, etc? Will they be happy? With a partner make notes about the four lives and, before you present your ideas to another pair of students, discuss what information in the story supports your ideas.

Man-Woman Talk

DEBORAH TANNEN

R iding home in a car, a woman asks, "Are you thirsty? Would you like to stop for a drink?" The man answers, "No," and they do not stop.

The man is later surprised to learn that the woman is displeased: she wanted to stop. He wonders why she didn't just tell him what she wanted.

The woman is disgruntled, not because she didn't get her way but because she felt her opinion wasn't sought and wasn't considered.

When she asked, "Would you like to stop?" she did not expect a yes-no answer. She expected a counter-question: "I don't know. Would you like to?"

She could then respond, "Well, I'd kind of like to. How tired are you?"

The woman must realize that when he answers "yes" or "no," he is not making a non-negotiable demand. If she has other ideas, he expects she will state them without being invited to do so.

A woman who led workshops with a male colleague was distressed because he did all the talking. When anyone asked a question, he answered before she had a chance to speak.

She blamed him for dominating her.

One common way of understanding this situation would be to suggest that men are chauvinists and think nothing of interrupting women. Another would be to look for psychological motives in one or both parties: She is passive; he is narcissistic.

But another, more elegant explanation is possible: a linguistic one.

Linguistics could tell us that these two individuals have different timing habits for when they take turns. She expects a slightly longer pause between speaking turns than he does.

So while she was waiting for what seemed to her the proper pause, he became restless. The appropriate pause to him had come and gone.

To avoid what he thought would be an uncomfortable silence and the appearance that neither of them had anything to say, the man began to answer . . . .

Another example: A man fixes himself a snack and is about to eat it when he notices that his wife looks hurt. He asks what's wrong and is told, "You didn't offer me any."

"I'm sorry," he says, "I didn't know you were hungry. Here, have this."

She declines: "You didn't make it for me."

He is confused, because he regards the snack as a matter of food: the message. But she is concerned with the metamessage: Does he think of her as she would think of him?

Yet another example is a conversation in which a man asks a woman, "How was your day?"

She responds with a 20-minute answer, full of details about whom she met, what was said and what she thought—regardless of whether she spent her day at home with the children or in an executive office.

Then she asks him, "How was your day?" and he responds, "Same old rat race."

Conversations like this lead women to

complain that men don't tell them anything and lead men to complain that they don't understand what women want . . . .

Linguistic signals include shifts in pitch, loudness, pacing, tone of voice, and intonation, and linguistic devices such as storytelling and relative indirectness . . . .

Issues of male-female communication strike at the heart of everyone's everyday experience, at home and at work . . . .

A frequent complaint of women about men is that they don't listen to them. Men frequently protest, "I was listening!"

The question of listenership reflects the core of relationships: "Are you listening?" means "Are you interested?" which means "Do you love me?" The questions, "Are you listening?" and "Are you interested?" lie at the center of most conversations, including, for example, job interviews and business negotiations.

There may be instances in which people actually are not listening, but these are far fewer than people think.

A linguistic approach suggests that many of these misunderstandings can be traced to habits for displaying listenership.

For example, research has shown that, on the average, women give more frequent overt signs of listening: "mhm," "uhuh," "yeah," head nods, changing facial expressions.

Expecting the same show of responsiveness, women see men who listen quietly and attentively as not really listening at all, like the spectre of silence on a telephone line that causes one to inquire, "Are you still there?"

Conversely, a man who expects a woman to show she's listening simply by fixing her eyes on his face, feels she is over-reacting when she keeps up a steady stream of "mhms" and "uhuhs."

Whereas women tend to say "yeah" to mean "I'm listening and following," men tend to say it to mean "I agree." So part of the reason women offer more of these listening noises, according to anthropologists Daniel Maltz and Ruther Borker, is that women are listening more often than men are agreeing.

Maltz and Borker report extensive research that shows that men and women develop assumptions about the role of language in close relationships from their childhood friends.

Little girls play with other girls, and the center of their social life is a best friend with whom they share secrets. It is the telling of secrets that makes them best friends.

Boys, in contrast, tend to play in groups, so their talk is less likely to be private. Rather, it is competitive talk about who is best at what, or performance talk that places the speaker at center stage, like Othello telling about his travels.

What makes boys friends is not what they say to each other but what they do together. So when a man is close to a woman, doing things together makes them close; nothing is missing for him if they don't talk about personal details. But she is missing what, for her, is the definitive element in intimacy.

Neither of these styles is right or wrong; they are just different. The frustration that both feel comes from the conviction that his or her own way is logical and self-evident . . . .

A C T I V I T I E S

Man-Woman Talk
pp. 52–53

1. In a group, discuss the examples of differences between man-talk and woman-talk in the essay and, in each case, what caused the misunderstanding. Discuss whether anyone in the group ever experienced or witnessed a misunderstanding similar to the ones in the examples.

2. With a partner define what is meant by the following linguistic signals mentioned in the essay: pitch, loudness, pacing, tone, intonation, and pauses. Prepare a reading for the class of the opening paragraph of *A Tale of Two Cities*, reprinted here. Be ready to explain how you have varied your linguistic signals to ensure that those hearing your reading understand the ideas being expressed.

> *It was the best of times, it was the worst of times, it was the age of wisdom, it was the age of foolishness, it was the epoch of belief, it was the epoch of incredulity, it was the season of Light, it was the season of Darkness, it was the spring of hope, it was the winter of despair, we had everything before us, we had nothing before us, we were all going direct to Heaven, we were all going direct the other way—in short, the period was so far like the present period, that some of its noisiest authorities insisted on its being received, for good or for evil, in the superlative degree of comparison only.*

3. a) Although the English language doesn't give genders to every noun as many other languages do, we do have ideas about the "hidden gender" of words. Each student in the class should write privately for each of the following pairs which is masculine and which is feminine:

chicken soup and beef soup   pink and purple
chocolate and vanilla   knife and fork
salt and pepper   fork and spoon

Compare the choices of the class members. Was there a lot of consistency? Were there any differences in choices made by the males and the females? In each case why do you think most people made the choices they made?

     b) Make up a few pairs of words and try this "gender test" on some of your friends, using your own list.

from OTHELLO

～

W I L L I A M   S H A K E S P E A R E

Othello is a play about love and jealousy by Shakespeare that ends in tragedy. The play opens in Venice where Brabantio is told that his innocent young daughter has eloped with Othello, a Moor from North Africa who leads the armed forces of Venice.

ACT ONE, SCENE THREE

(*Enter a Messenger.*)

Messenger. The Ottomites, reverend and gracious,
  Steering with due course toward the isle of Rhodes,
  Have there injointed them with an after fleet.
First Senator. Ay, so I thought. How many, as you guess?
Messenger. Of thirty sail; and now they do restem
  Their backward course, bearing with frank appearance
  Their purposes toward Cyprus, . . .
Duke. 'Tis certain then for Cyprus . . .
First Senator. Here comes Brabantio and the valiant Moor.
  (*Enter Brabantio, Othello, Cassio, Iago, Roderigo, and Officers.*)
Duke. Valiant Othello, we must straight employ you
  Against the general enemy Ottoman.
  [*To Brabantio*] I did not see you. Welcome, gentle signior.
  We lacked your counsel and your help tonight.
Brabantio So did I yours. Good your grace, pardon me.
  Neither my place, nor aught I heard of business,
  Hath raised me from my bed; nor doth the general care
  Take hold on me; for my particular grief
  Is of so floodgate and o'erbearing nature
  That it engluts and swallows other sorrows,
  And it is still itself.
Duke. Why, what's the matter?
Brabantio. My daughter! O, my daughter!
Senators. Dead?
Brabantio. Ay, to me.
  She is abused, stol'n from me, and corrupted
  By spells and medicines bought of mountebanks;

CHARACTERS

MESSENGER

FIRST SENATOR

DUKE OF VENICE

BRABANTIO
(a Senator) father to Desdemona

OTHELLO
(the Moor) in the military service of Venice

CASSIO
a lieutenant

IAGO
(an ensign) a villain

RODERIGO
a gentleman

(OTHER) SENATORS

ATTENDANTS

DESDEMONA
(daughter to Brabantio) wife to Othello

For nature so prepost'rously to err,
Being not deficient, blind, or lame of sense,
Sans witchcraft could not.

Duke. Whoe'er he be that in this foul proceeding
Hath thus beguiled your daughter of herself,
And you of her, the bloody book of law
You shall yourself read in the bitter letter
After your own sense; yea, though our proper son
Stood in your action.

Brabantio. Humbly I thank your Grace.
Here is the man—this Moor, whom now, it seems,
Your special mandate for the state affairs
Hath hither brought.

All. We are very sorry for't.

Duke. [*To Othello*] What in your own part can you say to
this?

Brabantio. Nothing, but this is so.

Othello. Most potent, grave, and reverend signiors,
My very noble and approved good masters,
That I have ta'en away this old man's daughter,
It is most true; true I have married her.
The very head and front of my offending
Hath this extent, no more. Rude am I in my speech,

And little blessed with the soft phrase of peace,
For since these arms of mine had seven years' pith,
Till now some nine moons wasted, they have used
Their dearest action in the tented field;
And little of this great world can I speak
More than pertains to feats of broils and battle;
And therefore little shall I grace my cause
In speaking for myself. Yet, but your gracious patience,
I will a round unvarnished tale deliver
Of my whole course of love—what drugs, what charms,
What conjuration, and what mighty magic,
For such proceeding I am charged withal,
I won his daughter—

Brabantio. A maiden never bold,
Of spirit so still and quiet that her motion
Blushed at herself; and she, in spite of nature,
Of years, of country, credit, everything,
To fall in love with what she feared to look on!
It is a judgment maimed and most imperfect
That will confess perfection so could err
Against all rules of nature, and must be driven
To find out practices of cunning hell
Why this should be. I therefore vouch again
That with some mixtures pow'rful o'er the blood,
Or with some dram, conjured to this effect,
He wrought upon her.

Duke. To vouch this is no proof,
Without more wider and more overt test
Than these thin habits and poor likelihoods
Of modern seeming do prefer against him.

First Senator. But, Othello, speak.
Did you by indirect and forced courses
Subdue and poison this young maid's affections?
Or came it by request, and such fair question
As soul to soul affordeth?

Othello. I do beseech you,
Send for the lady to the Sagittary
And let her speak of me before her father.
If you do find me foul in her report,
The trust, the office, I do hold of you
Not only take away, but let your sentence
Even fall upon my life.

Duke. Fetch Desdemona hither.

Othello. Ancient, conduct them; you best know the place.
(*Exit Iago, with two or three Attendants.*)
And till she come, as truly as to heaven

I do confess the vices of my blood,
So justly to your grave ears I'll present
How did I thrive in this fair lady's love,
And she in mine.

Duke. Say it, Othello.

Othello. Her father loved me; oft invited me;
Still questioned me the story of my life
From year to year, the battle, sieges, fortune
That I have passed.
I ran it through, even from my boyish days
To th' very moment that he bade me tell it.
Wherein I spoke of my disastrous chances,
Of moving accidents by flood and field,
Of hairbreadth scapes i' th' imminent deadly breach,
Of being taken by the insolent foe
And sold to slavery, of my redemption thence
And portance in my travel's history,
Wherein of anters vast and deserts idle,
Rough quarries, rocks, and hills whose heads touch
heaven
It was my hint to speak. Such was my process.
And of the Cannibals that each other eat,
The Anthropophagi, and men whose heads
Grew beneath their shoulders. These things to hear
Would Desdemona seriously incline;
But still the house affairs would draw her thence;
Which ever as she could with haste dispatch,
She'd come again, and with a greedy ear
Devour up my discourse . . .
   . . . I did consent,
And often did beguile her of her tears
When I did speak of some distressful stroke
That my youth suffered. My story being done,
She gave me for my pains a world of kisses.
She swore in faith 'twas strange, 'twas passing strange;
'Twas pitiful, 'twas wondrous pitiful.
She wished she had not heard it; yet she wished
That heaven had made her such a man. She thanked
me,
And bade me, if I had a friend that loved her,
I should but teach him how to tell my story,
And that would woo her. Upon this hint I spake.
She loved me for the dangers I had passed,
And I loved her that she did pity them.
This only is the witchcraft I have used.
Here comes the lady. Let her witness it.

(*Enter Desdemona, Iago, Attendants.*)

Duke. I think this tale would win my daughter too.
Good Brabantio, take up this mangled matter at the best.
Men do their broken weapons rather use
Than their bare hands.

Brabantio. I pray you hear her speak.
If she confess that she was half the wooer,
Destruction on my head if my bad blame
Light on the man. Come hither, gentle mistress.
Do you perceive in all this noble company
Where most you owe obedience?

Desdemona. My noble father,
I do perceive here a divided duty.
To you I am bound for life and education;
My life and education both do learn me
How to respect you. You are the lord of duty,
I am hitherto your daughter. But here's my husband,
And so much duty as my mother showed
To you, preferring you before her father,
So much I challenge that I may profess
Due to the Moor my lord.

Brabantio. God be with you. I have done.
Please it your Grace, on to the state affairs.
I had rather to adopt a child than get it.
Come hither, Moor.
I here do give thee that with all my heart
Which, but thou has already, with all my heart
I would keep from thee. For your sake, jewel,
I am glad at soul I have no other child,
For thy escape would teach me tyranny,
To hang clogs on them. I have done, my lord . . . .

Duke. The Turk with a most mighty preparation makes
for Cyprus . . .
. . . Th' affair cries haste,
And speed must answer it.

First Senator. You must away tonight.

Othello. With all my heart . . . .

Duke. Let it be so.
Good night to every one. [*To Brabantio*] And, noble
signior,
If virtue no delighted beauty lack,
Your son-in-law is far more fair than black.

First Senator. Adieu, brave Moor. Use Desdemona well.

Brabantio. Look to her, Moor, if thou hast eyes to see:
She has deceived her father, and may thee.

A C T I V I T I E S

**Othello
pp. 55–59**

1. With a partner, discuss this section of *Othello* using the following questions as guides to understanding.
   a) At the beginning of the passage, what threat is facing Venice and how is Othello asked to help?
   b) What is Brabantio's charge against Othello?
   c) How does Othello say he won Desdemona for his wife?
   d) Which version of the elopement does Desdemona's story prove true?

2. The Duke of Venice must make a decision about the charge against Othello. Initially he promises to throw the "bloody book of law" at the man who has "beguiled" Brabantio's daughter. Later he defends Othello. In a small group, give a percentage value to each of the following reasons for his change of mind.
   a) The fact that he needs Othello to lead the Venetian army against the Turks;
   b) Othello's eloquent defense of himself;
   c) Desdemona's version of how their love developed.
Compare the figure your group gave to each reason with those of other groups. Be prepared to give reasons for your figures.

3. In your journal, discuss which relationship comes first— a son or daughter's love for and obedience to parents or a person's feelings for the one he or she loves.

4. At the end of this scene, Brabantio makes a prophecy about what the future holds for Othello and Desdemona. In Shakespeare's play both Othello and Desdemona are dead by the end of the play. Write your version of what happens between the scene that you've just read in this unit and their deaths. You may want to read the rest of the play or watch a theatrical or video production of it to see how your version corresponds with Shakespeare's.

5. Make up a modern version of this scene to perform for the class.

from SALT-WATER MOON

DAVID FRENCH

CHARACTERS

MARY SNOW

JACOB MERCER

THE PLACE:—The front porch and yard of the Dawes' summer house in Coley's Point, Newfoundland.

THE TIME:—An August night in 1926.

The front porch of a house that was built in the last half of the nineteenth century, probably by a ship's captain or local merchant. It has a solid feel about it, this porch. You just know that the interior of the house would consist of oak banisters and newel posts, wide halls and high ceilings. And that every timber was hand-chosen and pit-sawn and constructed by men who built houses the way they built boats—to last.

On stage right of the porch is a rocker.

There is not much of a yard, because they built their houses close to the sea in those days to make easy access to the waters where they made their living. In fact, the house stands quite close to a road that runs in front of it, a gravel road skirting the rocky embankment that holds back the sea. Some indication of this road should be on the set, though it need not be realistic.

It is a lovely night in August, 1926. A warm night in this tiny outport at the edge of the sea, a night lit by the full moon and a sky full of stars.

At rise: Mary Snow is alone on stage. She sits on the front step, training a telescope on the sky. Mary is seventeen, a slender, fine-boned, lovely girl with short black hair. She is wearing a short-sleeved yellow satin dress and black flat-heeled shoes. She wears no makeup except for a slight hint of red on her cheeks. The only jewellery she wears is her engagement ring.

Slight pause. Then Mary rises and crosses into the stage left part of the yard and again peers at the sky through the telescope.

A moment later Jacob Mercer's voice is heard offstage, singing faintly as though he were some distance down the road stage right. His voice carries so faintly, in fact, that Mary spins around and faces that direction, listening intently, not sure whether it is her imagination.

Jacob: (*to the tune of "Pretty Redwing"*)
Oh, the moon shines bright on Charlie Chaplin,
His boots are crackin' for the want of blackin',
And his baggy trousers they want mendin'
Before they send him, to the Dardanelles.

(Mary stands riveted to the spot, her eyes searching the shadow-pocketed road, almost afraid of what might walk into view, but still straining to listen . . . But the song has ended, and there is only silence. With an inward shrug, she assumes it is imagination—the ghost of last summer—and resumes her study of the stars.)

(At that moment Jacob Mercer appears on the road stage right. He is about six months older than Mary, a solidly-built, good-looking young man in a store-bought suit and brown fedora. In his right hand he holds a cardboard suitcase held together with a rope tied in a half-hitch knot. At first sight of Mary, he instinctively sets down the suitcase and removes his hat. He watches her so intently it is as though he is holding his breath . . . Finally, Jacob clears his throat, and Mary whirls around, startled. They stand motionless, staring at one another for a long moment)

Jacob: (*finally*) Hello, Mary. (*Then*) Aren't you even going to acknowledge me? (*Pause*) The least you could do is make a fist.
Mary: (*beat. Quietly*) It was you I heard . . .
Jacob: What? Just now?
Mary: I heard your voice on the road, and I said to myself, No, it couldn't be him . . .
Jacob: It is. (*Then*) Why? Who'd you t'ink it was, a spirit? The ghost of Bob Foote roaming the roads? Poor Uncle Bob in blackface out for a last howl at the moon?
Mary: That's not funny, Jacob.
Jacob: It wasn't meant to be.

Mary: Making fun of the poor old soul, and him tonight in a closed casket. It's not right.

(*Slight pause*)

Jacob: (*crosses slowly to the porch*) Don't tell me you still believes in spirits? I can hardly credit it, a young girl like you. (*Nods at the house*) The Right Honourable and Lady Emma must find it some odd. (*He sets down the suitcase*)

Mary: I don't see what's so odd about that, believing in spirits.

Jacob: Don't you?

Mary: No.

Jacob: What? Looking at the sky t'rough a spyglass and over your shoulder for ghostes? (*Pronounced 'ghostus'*) You don't find that odd?

Mary: No. Neither do Mr. and Mrs. Dawe.

Jacob: Then Jerome must, him being a schoolteacher. He must wonder who in the world he's become engaged to.

Mary: Just because I takes an interest in the stars, Jacob, don't mean I shuts my eyes to the wonder that's around me. Now do it?

Jacob: I suppose not.

Mary: The day Father died in the Great War, Mother saw him at the foot of the bed in Hickman's Harbour. He was killed at Beaumont Hamel, more than two t'ousand miles away, yet Mother woke up to find him standing side-on to the bed, and she stared at him, she said, till he faded into the light of morning.

Jacob: I knows. I've heard you tell it.

Mary: Well then. (*She turns away*)

(*Pause*)

Jacob: Oh, look, Mary, it's a shame to get off on the wrong foot after all this time. I'm sorry I said that. It just slipped out.

Mary: What?

Jacob: That crack about old Bob looking like a bootblack. I never meant to make light. That's just me.

Mary: No odds. I don't imagine Mr. Foote minds now.

(*Slight pause*)

Jacob: It's bad enough that he's dead at all, but to come home looking like the ace of spades . . . Must be tough on Mrs. Foote.

Mary: No mistake.

Jacob: I saw the wreath on the door as I was passing, so I went inside to pay my respects. There was a crowd in the parlour, the closed casket sitting on two wooden chairs. I figured it was Mrs. Foote inside, till she walked out of the kitchen with the Right Honourable and Lady Emma.

Figured old Bob was still on the Labrador along with Father and wouldn't be back till next month.

(*Slight pause*)

Mary: He was sitting in the bunkhouse, they said, and bent down to take off his boots. He died before he hit the floor.

(*Slight pause*)

Jacob: Is it true what I heard? Is it true Mrs. Foote went down to the wharf yesterday to meet the mailboat? Hoping to get a letter from Bob?
Mary: True.
Jacob: Instead there's a pine box on the deck with his body in it. And Bob in that box all packed in salt.
Mary: It's a sin.
Jacob: Takes t'ree weeks for the boat to get here. And him burnt black from that rock salt. Jesus.

(*Pause*)

Still, he couldn't have picked a nicer night for a wake, could he? It's some lovely.

(*Pause*)

It's that bright out I bet I can read the hands on my pocket watch. (*He removes his watch from his vest pocket*) Look at that. Ten to ten. I can pick out the maker's name, almost: Tisdall . . . (*Winds the stem for something to do*) . . . Yes, maid, it's some night. Not the best time to be studying the stars, though. Not with a full moon. (*Slight pause*) It's hard to see the stars with the naked eye on a night like this. (*Slight pause*) I suppose that's why you'm using the spyglass. (*Slight pause*) What kind is it?
Mary: Yes, you can't wait to hear the answer, can you? Standing there with your eyes afire, drooling to hear what make of telescope.
Jacob: Don't be foolish.
Mary: Well, as if you cares what make it is, Jacob Mercer. You're just spitting out the first words that pop in your mouth.
Jacob: I wouldn't have to, Mary, if I wasn't made to feel a stranger.
Mary: Well, you *are* a stranger.
Jacob: I wasn't once.
Mary: You are now.
Jacob: Suit yourself.

(*Pause*)

(*almost to himself*) Some welcome home this is.

Mary: What did you expect, a band? A band with me at the head, clapping my hands: 'Why, it's the Prodigal Son, boys! All the way back from Toronto! Strike up the drum!'

Jacob: Now who's making fun?

Mary: You're lucky I'm still speaking to you! Some wouldn't let you step foot in the yard! (*She sits on the step*)

(*Pause*)

Jacob: All I asked just now was a simple question. There's no call to be sarcastic.

Mary: Isn't there?

Jacob: No. It don't become you. A yellow dress becomes you, Mary, more than sarcasm . . . Not that you don't have every right to be cross. I don't blame you, I suppose.

Mary: So you shouldn't.

Jacob: No. You have every right to carry a grudge. Every right in the world. I'm the first to admit it. Besides . . .

Mary: Besides what?

Jacob: Besides, I already knows the make of spyglass. It's called a Black Beauty. We have one at the house. Father got it from a Sears-Roebuck catalogue back in 1902. Ours has a cracked lens.

Mary: Oh, you t'ink you're some smart, don't you. Well, you're not, Jacob Mercer. And you're not one bit funny, either.

Jacob: That's not what you used to say.

Mary: I'm learning all about the stars now. That's more than I ever learned with you. I can see the satellites of Jupiter with this telescope, and the mountains of the moon.

Jacob: Imagine that. Imagine that cold white eye up there with mountains in it.

Mary: The moon has more than mountains. The moon has valleys and seas and bays. All as dry as a biscuit, Jerome says. All with beautiful names.

Jacob: Such as?

Mary: Ocean of Storms, for one. Sea of Rains. Bay of Rainbows. Lake of Dreams.

Jacob: That's the only water Jerome McKenzie could sail without getting his socks wet, the Lake of Dreams.

Mary: Don't you start in on Jerome, either. He knows a lot more than you gives him credit for.

Jacob: A year ago you wouldn't have said that. A year ago you had your own notions about the moon. Remember that?

Mary: No.

Jacob: You don't recall saying the Man in the Moon was set there for not obeying the Sabbath? He wasn't good enough for Heaven, you said, so God set him betwixt Heaven and Earth. You don't recall saying that?

Mary: No.

Jacob: Sure you do. I had a toothache that night, and we walked to Clarke's Beach so's Billy Parsons could charm my tooth. 'Don't pay him,' Mother said. 'Mind now. And don't t'ank him, either, or the charm won't work.' Oh, that was some night.

Mary: I don't recall.

Jacob: You don't seem to recall very much, suddenly, and you with a memory on you like a camera.

Mary: (*rises*) Well, perhaps it suits me *not* to remember. As if you're any different. You remembers only what you wants to remember, Jacob, and the rest you forgets. (*Starts up the steps*)

Jacob: Like what?

Mary: Like what? (*Turns to face him*) Like running off last August, that's what! Or has that suddenly slipped your mind?

(*Jacob says nothing*)

Didn't have the courage to say goodbye, did you? Not so much as a card in the past year!

Jacob: I'm no good with cards . . .

Mary: You wrote your mother.

Jacob: Once.

Mary: Twice.

Jacob: Twice then.

Mary: I saw her at church that Sunday just before we went back to St. John's in the fall. She told me you was boarding with Sam and Lucy Boone on Oakwood Avenue. Working for the Fairbanks Block and Supplies.

Jacob: Yes. Making concrete blocks.

Mary: A whole year you've been gone, boy, and now you just walks in off the road. Steps off the nine o'clock train in Bay Roberts and expects me to recall some old night when Billy Parsons charmed your tooth. Are you forgetting I'm spoken for?

Jacob: I'm not forgetting.

Mary: Then you haven't changed one bit, have you? Still the same, in spite of your fancy hat! Still the schemer!

(*Pause*)

Jacob: It wasn't just some old night, and you knows it. A lot happened that night besides my toothache.

Mary: A lot's happened since.

Jacob: I suppose.

Mary: Too much.

Jacob: Perhaps.

Mary: Then don't keep dragging up what's best forgotten. Leave it buried.

Jacob: Can't be done, Mary. Nights like this brings it all back . . . The smell of honeysuckle on the road. The new moon that night like a smile over the Birch Hills. A smile that became a grin. Remember that?

Mary: Yes, a lot you noticed the moon.

Jacob: Indeed I did.

Mary: You hardly gave it a second glance. Stumbling along the road to Clarke's Beach, your hand tight to your jaw. Whimpering like an old woman.

Jacob: I don't recall.

Mary: No, you wouldn't.

Jacob: You wasn't much comfort, if it comes to that. Harping on spruce gum every inch of the way.

Mary: I mentioned it once.

Jacob: Once?

Mary: Once. 'Why don't we get some spruce gum?' I said. 'That'd kill the pain.'

ACTIVITIES

Salt-Water Moon
pp. 61–67

1. Because there are only two characters in the play, it is important that the movements of the characters, and the music/sound and lighting be as interesting as possible. Work with a partner and
a) block the movements (see the Student Handbook, page 207) of the two characters for the portion of the play presented here;
b) make notes on any sound effects or music for this scene;
c) describe the lighting for this scene.

2. Work with a partner and list examples of dialect. Discuss why the playwright might include dialect in a character's speech, and write a note on your discussion.

3. Research the references to the history and geography of Newfoundland that are mentioned by Mary and Jacob. Prepare a brief presentation to the others reading this selection, or make brief notes that could accompany the text of the play for other readers.

4. Prepare a taping of the part of the play presented here. This might be for a radio broadcast and could include some of the sound effects mentioned in activity #1.

5. Work with a partner who is going to read this play and predict what you think will happen between Jacob and Mary. Make point-form notes to refer to as you finish the play.

6. Choose two or three of the whole-book activities on page 204 of the Student Handbook to complete as you read the play or when you have finished reading it.

A C T I V I T I E S

**Developing Your Voice
End of Unit Activities**

1. Find a poem or a passage in a novel or story that you feel has something important to say about male/female relationships. Read it aloud to the class. Be prepared to explain what the passage means to you and why you chose it to read to the class.

2. Your class should be divided into five groups for this activity. Each group prepares a poster-collage using quotations and pictures that reveal male/female relationships at each of the following stages of life:
a) childhood   c) young adulthood   e) old age
b) adolescence   d) middle age

3. Working with two or three other students, brainstorm a list of problems connnected with relationships that concern people of your age. Divide the list among the members of the group and try to find a movie, television show, book, or magazine article dealing with each of the issues. Make a display or list of your findings to help other students find information.

4. Working with a partner, write a short one-act play that reveals the nature of a relationship between two characters in the play.

5. Stage a debate in which the resolution states that friends are more valuable than lovers. See page 187 of the Student Handbook for suggested debate procedures.

6. Make an anthology of love poetry. Your anthology should have a cover, a dedication page, a contents page, an introduction, graphics to illustrate the poems, and a one- or two-sentence comment on each poem.

7. Read one of the following novels and plays. Each focusses on a particular relationship. Choose one of the whole-book activities on page 204 of the Student Handbook to complete after you read the book.
a) *Ordinary People* by Judith Guest
b) *Flowers for Algernon* by Daniel Keyes
c) *On Golden Pond* by Ernest Thompson
d) *A Little Love* by Virginia Hamilton
e) *A Farewell to Arms* by Ernest Hemingway

C A R E E R S

People in these careers are usually interested in relating to people or communicating with, or about, them.

Health Administrator or Supervisor
A health administrator is responsible for the organization and management of health services, such as hospitals, chronic care institutions and health planning boards. With the assistance of professional staff, a health administrator directs, maintains and controls programs and services. She or he must have a broad knowledge of the social and economic aspects of health care and must keep informed on developments in the field of public health.

Training and Qualifications
Many colleges offer courses for jobs as hospital department supervisors.

Salary
Salaries for health care administrators and supervisors vary depending upon age, location, experience, and education. The estimated salary for health administrators was about $20 000 in 1984.

Other Careers:
- Social Service Worker
- Gerontologist
- Recreation Director/Leader
- Police Officer
- Personnel Clerk

R E S O U R C E S

Novels
A Solitary Blue—Cynthia Voigt (Fawcett Juniper, 1983)
The Great Computer Dating Caper—Ernesto T. Bethancourt (Crown, 1984)
Summer of My First Love—Isabelle Holland (Fawcett Juniper, 1966)

Films
Brighton Beach Memoir, Universal/Rastar 1986; 108 min
Children of a Lesser God, Paramount 1986; 110 min
Thanks for the Ride, NFB; 28 min
My American Cousin, Spectra Films 1986; 88 min
When, Jenny, When? (Paulist Communications) International Telefilm 1978; 25 min

Extra! Extra! Read All About It

VOICES

from
METAMORPHOSIS
DAVID SUZUKI

Distortion of news can come about in many ways. A severe restriction reporters must deal with is the limitation of space or time. A newspaper reporter who has to summarize an all-day meeting or a two-hour lecture in a six-inch column cannot possibly cover it all. And when television news items vary from fifteen to ninety *seconds*, the superficiality is even greater....

I have a special aversion for headlines. Writing up headlines is a very demanding art and is done by people who specialize in it. They don't write the articles. In 1971, Sandy Ross wrote an article about me in *Maclean's* magazine. In one part of the article, I was discussing the ramifications of genetic engineering. The whole article documented my concerns about the enormous power and danger of the technology. He correctly quoted me in this context as saying, "Make me a dictator with the power to say who mates with whom and I could give you a race of people you wouldn't recognize." I went on to warn of the hazards of this kind of thinking. The headliner wrote, "Make me a dictator, and in three generations I could give you a race of people you wouldn't recognize." All of the context of the remark was gone, and for years after, various people who hadn't read the article but remembered the headline would call me a fascist.

LETTERS: OUR POLICY

We like your letters.

Readers' letters help us as a newspaper to provide the widest possible forum for subjects of public interest.

We'd like to encourage your continued participation in letter-writing. And we'd like to set out some specific guidelines to make it easier to get your letters to the editor published.

1. All letters must bear the writer's signature for publication. It helps to include your phone number as well, in case we have to check back with the writer. In the past we have permitted the use of pseudonyms as long as we knew who the author was. But we've discontinued that. We believe if you want to say it, you should sign it.

2. Rare exceptions to this signature policy will be considered in cases where we could indicate in an Editor's Note a justifiable reason why the writer's name is being withheld.

3. Copies of letters to third parties will not necessarily be reproduced in full.

4. The newspaper reserves the right to edit all letters for length, libel, taste, or non-verifiable information put forth as fact.

5. Concise letters which get the point across clearly have the best chance of early publication.

We encourage you to write and share your views, feelings, ideas and comments with others.

The Telegraph–Journal
The Evening Times–Globe
Saint John, New Brunswick
April 13, 1988

LEILA HEATH, RADIO REPORTER

(talking about working for a newspaper before she became a radio reporter)

What was really interesting about that job was that I had to contact young people who were considered role models in Toronto's Black community, and the job allowed me to travel around the city. I would go out with a photographer and do an interview. The job taught me how to organize material, how to approach people, how to set up and conduct interviews, and prepare the story for the next issue of the paper.

OLYMPIC STORIES IRK READERS

ROD GOODMAN, Star Ombudsman

"Disgusting. Horrible. Dreadful. Unfair. Sexist."

They are not music to an ombudsman's ear, but on some days that's his diet of criticism from angry readers.

So it was this week after The Star, in its Olympics coverage, dusted off Brian Orser as a loser, Karen Percy as the blonde from Banff, and curlers in general as overweight and over the hill.

It started with a front-page story in last Saturday's editions under the byline of sportswriter Mary Ormsby, opening with:

"It took a 21-year-old blonde from Banff less than 90 seconds yesterday to do what the Canadian men had failed to do at the Olympics—win a medal."

The same byline appeared in the sports section over an expanded story of Karen Percy's skiing medal, this one omitting reference to the male skiers, but retaining the "blonde" classification.

The comparison with male athletes was inserted by the sports desk, which defended the "blonde" reference as factual and descriptive, but not sexist.

Some readers—and Star staffers—disagreed. "Classifying women by hair color surely is a sexist practice unless it's relevant to the story," a news editor (male) wrote.

The Star's style guide says: "Treatment of the sexes should be even-handed and free of stereotypes offensive to either sex." Some readers obviously found it offensive. I didn't view it as offensive to women, but I didn't find it relevant, either.

The waves of the *blonde* affair hadn't died down when Jim Proudfoot, who has covered the international skating scene for years, wrote that Brian Orser, Canada's second-place finisher in men's figure skating was "a loser."

*The Toronto Star
February 27, 1988*

A C T I V I T I E S

1. Form a group of four and assign each member one of the monologues to read aloud to the group. Take a moment to read the monologues over silently before reading them aloud to each other.

Voices
pp. 72—74

2. Hold a group discussion about the monologues, considering:
■ the most positive aspects of newspapers presented;
■ the details that reveal negative aspects of newspapers;
■ what it is like to write for a newspaper.

3. Make an entry in your journal, using one of the following to start:
■ The sections I always read in the newspaper are . . .
■ The sections I never read are . . .
■ I never/seldom read a newspaper because . . .

Lunar Module Lifts Off Moon

GEORGE BRIMMELL AND BOB COHEN

OUSTON—The Eagle has started to fly home to its mother ship after nearly twenty-two hours on the moon during which man's footprints were left in the lunar dust and in the history of mankind.

The two Apollo 11 astronauts blasted off from the moon shortly before 11 a.m. MST and within minutes reached the relative safety of lunar orbit—the first time anything had ever rocketed away from the moon.

It was the only aspect of the Apollo 11 mission that had never been tested—and it had to work, just right, just as it did—or commander Neil Armstrong and pilot Edwin Aldrin would almost certainly have been doomed. . . .

The successful lift-off means that Eagle is manoeuvering for its historic link-up with Collins and Columbia, and a safe ride home later this afternoon. . . .

And now, all the critical phases of the mission behind them, the moon men can prepare for a relatively easy coast back to earth, with splash-down in the Pacific late Thursday morning.

Just before take-off, the astronauts dumped out all their space "junk"—so they had as little weight as possible to lift.

Left behind, along with U.S. flag, the two-ton descent stage of the lunar module, scientific gear, are their overshoes, the porta-ble life support systems that enabled them to walk outside the spaceship, cameras, gloves, and old food containers.

As one scientist-astronaut put it: "The moon will look like a bad picnic."

It was 7:56 p.m. MST on Sunday when Armstrong achieved immortality as he set his left foot gingerly on the surface of the moon.

"That's one small step for man, one giant leap for mankind," were his first words as he stepped on the lunar surface less than seven hours after the Apollo 11 had made its epic landing.

When the lunar module lifted off this morning the Apollo crew had been on the moon for 21 hours, 36 minutes and 22 seconds.

It had taken roughly 10 minutes for Armstrong to get through the hatch of the lunar module, work his way from its "front porch" down the nine steps to the alien, eerie surface of the moon.

At last there he was—a ghostly figure, his movements like a movie in slow motion—his words crackling back a quarter million miles through the depths of space.

He said: "I'm going to step off the LM now . . . "

And, still holding the ladder with his right hand, moving cautiously in his bulky space suit, Armstrong touched the moon with his foot.

About 20 minutes later Aldrin became the

second earthling to plant his footprints on the moon.

And a little after 11 p.m. the two astronauts were back in Eagle, back with the most precious material ever known to man—samples of the lunar soil.

Their nuggets make the Hope Diamond pale in value. These chunks of the moon, to be transported back to earth for analysis, could hold the key to the solar system's history.

They may well tell the age of the moon . . . its origin . . . and explain some of the mysteries of interplanetary relationships . . .

Armstrong and Aldrin accomplished what men have dreamed of since time immemorial—and all mankind shared in the exhilaration of their discovery.

Earlier—before they had emerged from Eagle—Buzz Aldrin conveyed a moving message to the world. About three hours after the lunar touch-down, Aldrin asked "every person listening in . . . wherever they may be . . . to pause and contemplate the events

of the last few hours . . . and to give thanks in his or her own way." . . .

The astronauts raised the stars and stripes—and had a telephone call from the president of the United States . . .

The moon surface easily withstood the shock of the Eagle's landing. The four-legged machine sank only one or two inches into the dust—boding well for future moon landings.

With oxygen life packs strapped to their backs, the astronauts went about their work with the calmness of a Sunday afternoon gardener on earth. They set up on the moon instruments that will continue to give scientists on earth information for some time to come.

Through the magic of television, an estimated 500 000 000 people around the world had a ringside seat to man's greatest adventure.

There were memorable utterances during the day of high adventure.

There were Armstrong's words when Eagle separated from the command ship to start the dangerous descent: "The Eagle is flying."

There were Armstrong's—and man's—first words from the moon's surface after touch-down: "Houston . . . Tranquility Base here. The Eagle has landed." . . .

They unveiled a stainless steel plaque bearing these words:

"Here men from planet earth first set foot upon the moon, July, 1969, AD. We came in peace for all mankind."

They left on the moon a disc on which messages from the leaders of 76 nations including Canadian Prime Minister Trudeau had been recorded. They will return to earth with them the flags of 136 nations, including Russia. And they left behind mementos for three Americans and two Russians who died for the cause of space exploration.

Calgary Herald
July 21, 1969

Cape Breton Post

TURKS' PLIGHT MOVES PEOPLE OF QUEBEC

ST-EUSTACHE, Que. (CP)— When 125 Turks protesting their possible deportation arrived in this town at the end of the first day of a march on Ottawa, they didn't look like they had completed a 40-kilometre slog in just 5½ hours.

Although many wore thin jackets and cheap shoes and maintained a tough pace of better than seven kilometres an hour through the suburbs from Montreal's north end, nobody seemed the worse for wear when they arrived in front of the Roman Catholic church in this town west of Mirabel airport.

One of the marchers, Mustafa Doygun, 29, said, "Everything is OK. I'm not tired yet but tomorrow maybe."

And Richard Lanoux, who mans the switchboard for the town's police and fire departments, said, "Everybody appeared in pretty good shape when they got here. They weren't even hungry. They said they had eaten on the road."

A bus carried their food and luggage.

When they marched two abreast up to the church at about 7:30 p.m. EDT, they were welcomed by about 90 local residents including Rev. Andre Racine, the parish priest.

Seeing the trekkers had blankets but no sleeping bags, Racine arranged to get gym mats from a nearby Catholic school transferred to the parish hall for marchers to sleep on.

As the Turks bedded down, St-Eustache police stood by outside the parish hall to make sure they would have a quiet night.

It is not the first brush the church has had over principles with government authorities. Its walls still carry the scars of British army cannonballs fired at it during the 1837 rebellion by Lower-Canadian patriots.

But the Turks are not planning anything quite as violent.

"We aren't for confrontation, threats or blackmail," march organizer Atanas Katrapani said.

He said the group just wants to persuade Immigration Minister Barbara McDougall to cancel deportation orders against them or strike an understanding with Quebec that would give them a chance to stay in Canada.

The marchers are among 2000 Turks who came to Canada in 1986-87, apparently tricked by con artists into believing the country badly needed laborers. Many said they paid their way by selling all their possessions.

While about 400 have since returned to Turkey, the remaining 1600 thought they had a chance of staying here when Quebec and Ottawa reached a deal two weeks ago that suspended some deportations.

But the deal fell through over a disagreement on the number allowed to stay.

"You can say what you want from a legalistic point of view," said Katrapani, a junior college teacher who was born in Turkey of Greek parents.

"But from a humanitarian point of view, it is cruel to expel people who have lived here for a year and a half."

Cape Breton Post April 5, 1988

A C T I V I T I E S

1. Any news story should contain the most important facts about the event. The facts most often contain the "5 Ws" and the one "H" (who, what, why, when, where, and how). With a partner, read through one of these stories and identify which parts of the story correspond to the five "Ws" and to the one "H."

**Headline News Stories
pp. 76–78**

2. Imagine that you have been asked to interview one of the astronauts immediately following his return to earth or one of the Turkish refugees. With a partner make up five to ten questions you would ask. Role-play the interview with your partner using the questions you created. You may wish to do some additional research before you proceed with the role-playing.

A PICTURE IS WORTH 1000 WORDS

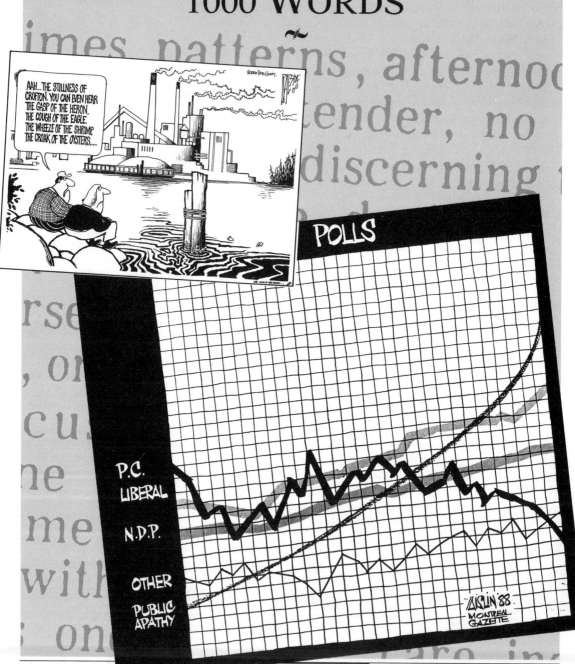

◄ Twenty-one people were injured and two dozen cars were smashed when ice-rink-size chunks of concrete roof collapsed into the Save-on-Food store in Burnaby, B.C. on Saturday, April 23, 1988.

▼ It was roundup time for $3^1/_2$ hours on sections of two of Canada's busiest highways as police officers and humane society staff tried to coax back 20 cattle that had escaped from an over-turned tractor-trailer. The truck carrying 93 cattle crashed on a Keele Street ramp at the Highway 400-Highway 401 intersection on Sunday, April 24, 1988 at 11 a.m.

Feature Photography Award, 1986 ▶

Gerry Bookhout has been taking pictures as long as he can remember. For this picture, he spotted a group of Mennonite children playing on a swing in a rural school yard but had to return several times before he got the cloud formation he wanted for a background.

Feature Photography Award, 1983 ▼

Bruno Schlumberger, 34, a freelance photographer for the Ottawa Citizen, won the feature photography award for this shot of a woman dragging her reluctant grandson to his first day at school.

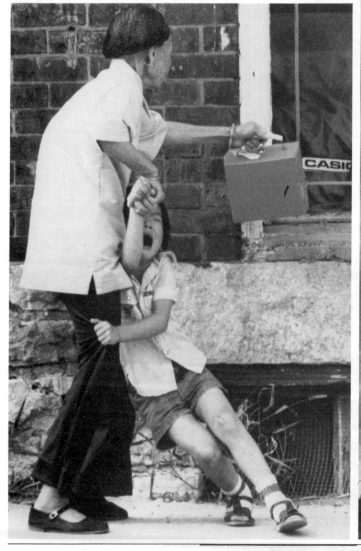

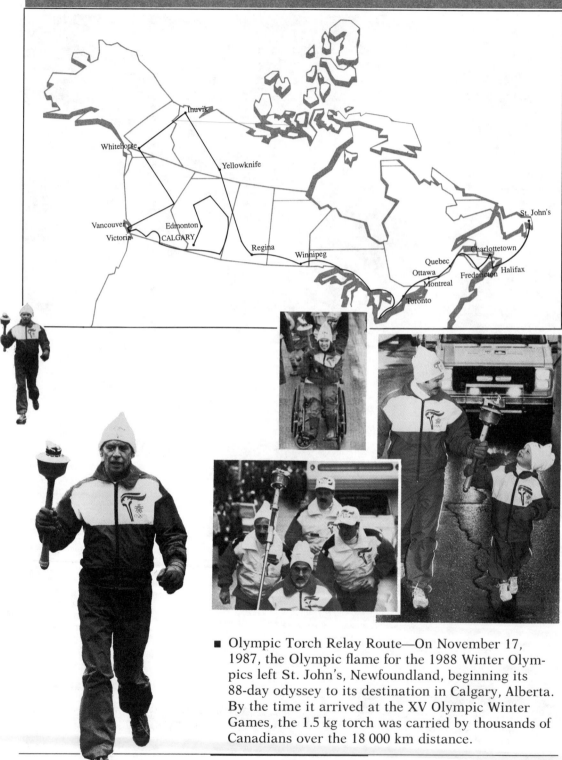

■ Olympic Torch Relay Route—On November 17, 1987, the Olympic flame for the 1988 Winter Olympics left St. John's, Newfoundland, beginning its 88-day odyssey to its destination in Calgary, Alberta. By the time it arrived at the XV Olympic Winter Games, the 1.5 kg torch was carried by thousands of Canadians over the 18 000 km distance.

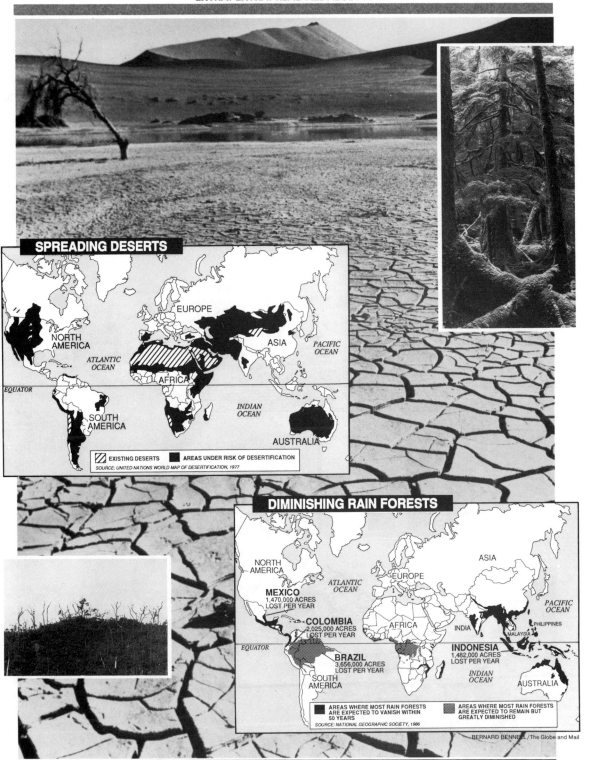

SPREADING DESERTS

EUROPE

NORTH
AMERICA

ASIA

*PACIFIC
OCEAN*

*ATLANTIC
OCEAN*

AFRICA

EQUATOR

SOUTH
AMERICA

*INDIAN
OCEAN*

AUSTRALIA

◪ EXISTING DESERTS ■ AREAS UNDER RISK OF DESERTIFICATION

SOURCE: UNITED NATIONS WORLD MAP OF DESERTIFICATION, 1977

DIMINISHING RAIN FORESTS

NORTH
AMERICA

ASIA

*ATLANTIC
OCEAN*

EUROPE

MEXICO
1,470,000 ACRES
LOST PER YEAR

*PACIFIC
OCEAN*

AFRICA

INDIA

PHILIPPINES

COLOMBIA
2,025,000 ACRES
LOST PER YEAR

MALAYSIA

EQUATOR

BRAZIL
3,656,000 ACRES
LOST PER YEAR

INDONESIA
1,482,000 ACRES
LOST PER YEAR

SOUTH
AMERICA

*INDIAN
OCEAN*

AUSTRALIA

■ AREAS WHERE MOST RAIN FORESTS
ARE EXPECTED TO VANISH WITHIN
50 YEARS

▦ AREAS WHERE MOST RAIN FORESTS
ARE EXPECTED TO REMAIN BUT
GREATLY DIMINISHED

SOURCE: NATIONAL GEOGRAPHIC SOCIETY, 1986

BERNARD BENNELL / The Globe and Mail

87

Focus on facts . . .

Let's get physical!

27% Active
44% Moderately active
29% Sedentary

Who's really active?

48% 15-24yrs
40% 25-44 yrs
12% 45-54 yrs

Of the 27% of Canadian adults who are physically active, 31% males and 23% females are active enough to anticipate additional years of life expectancy experts claim.

" Exercise which makes one breathe more heavily than normal"

ACTIVITIES

A Picture Is Worth 1000
Words
pp. 80—88

1. Editorial cartoons are created in response to current issues and news stories and are a pictorial statement of the cartoonist's opinion. With a partner, discuss the editorial cartoons on pages 80–88 and decide:
   a) whether they are on a local, national or international subject;
   b) whether the cartoonist has used symbols to get an idea across (A symbol is an object that represents another object or an idea. For example, the maple leaf and the beaver are often used to represent Canada.);
   c) the messages you think the cartoonists intend to convey.

2. Make a collection of different kinds of editorial cartoons; for example, you might select cartoons that present more than one side, use symbols, have no captions, and are on various subjects.

3. After reading a few captions under photographs in your local paper, write a caption for each photograph in this section.

4. With a partner, discuss the difference between a "feature photograph" (page 84) and a "spot news photograph" (page 82). Find an example of each in your local paper.

5. It is often said that a picture is worth a thousand words. This can also be true of maps and charts. Try to write the information included in one of the maps or chart (pages 86–87) in words. Discuss the following:
   a) Why do you think the editor of the paper chose to present the information graphically?
   b) Do you prefer maps and charts presenting information in newspapers to stories in words? Why?

6. Find a story in your local newspaper that you feel could have been more successfully presented through a map or chart. Put the information into the form of a map or chart and present it to the other students in your class to see which version they prefer.

REGINALD FEATHERSTONE

~

Four decades ago, the name Reginald Featherstone was legendary among merchant mariners and shipowners along these coasts, and rightly so.

Captain Featherstone was a marine salvor without equal, whose incisive mind and shove-ahead demeanour often spelled the difference between a ship which lived to see more time at sea or went to Davy Jones's Locker.

It was Captain Featherstone who, with a slew of Nova Scotians and Newfoundlanders, gave hope to vessels in distress. As the heroes of two exciting books about the sea and seadogs, he and his company came to life in 'The Grey Seas Under' and 'The Serpent's Coil' as the embodiment of salvors.

During peacetime and at war, the tugboats operating alone and far asea hauled in many thousands of tons of shipping that might otherwise have been lost to commerce and the war effort.

When he died this week at the age of 92, many years after his exploits were confined to the logbooks of shipping companies and the records of Lloyd's of London, Captain Featherstone was rightly remembered as being among the best of the salvors, the sturdy scavengers of the sea.

The Halifax Chronicle-Herald/The Mail Star
February 24, 1988

ARROGANT OFFICIALDOM

❧

T he immigration service, by its unreasonable conduct, encourages people to try to sneak into Canada or to circumvent the rules. People who try to follow the rules sometimes find that the government itself does not follow its own rules.

Winchell Alvero, who is still in the Philippines, and his sister, a Canadian citizen living in Winnipeg, followed the rules. The authorities delayed her correctly timed application to sponsor his move to Canada—and then rejected it for being too late. Judge Francis Muldoon of the Federal Court of Canada, who heard her appeal, found that the officials who handled the case had been negligent, lackadaisical and entirely wanting any reasonable sense of urgency. He ordered the government to allow Mr. Alvero into Canada as it should have done two years ago—and to pay his sister's $2000 in legal fees for arguing with the department.

The immigration authorities, however, are not only negligent, lackadaisical and lacking a sense of urgency. They are also slow to take a hint. They are now appealing Judge Muldoon's ruling, which will keep Mr. Alvero and his sister waiting further months.

That is what it can be like waiting in line to enter Canada by the supposedly well-ordered rules the country has established.

There is another way into Canada, which is to arrive at an airport or seaport and claim to be a refugee. Canadians are sometimes astonished by the large numbers of people wishing to enter Canada who make patently

false claims of persecution in order to get a foot in the door. Such people are said to be queue-jumpers abusing Canada's good nature. They are told they should go back and wait in line like other people—like Winchell Alvero, for instance.

Mr. Alvero would have achieved quicker results if he had shown up, claimed refugee status and waited for an amnesty. He would be settled here by now. An adviser familiar with the authorities' way of administering their own rules could not confidently urge Mr. Alvero to wait in line and deal honestly with the Canadian authorities because there is no assurance that the Canadian authorities will deal honestly with him.

The line-up at Canada's refugee wicket would get shorter if people could be sure of honest dealing, straight answers and fair treatment at the other wicket, the regular take-a-number-and-wait-your-turn wicket.

Winnipeg Free Press
February 24, 1988

The Toronto Star

PUT GOONS ON ICE

~

Seldom has a more blatant, intentional, and unprovoked attack been committed on a hockey rink. The television cameras caught it all for fans of the National Hockey League, including the young ones.

Philadelphia Flyers tough guy Dave Brown brutally cross-checked New York Rangers forward Tomas Sandstrom across the side of the head, after play had stopped during a game in New York Oct. 26. Sandstrom collapsed to the ice and spent the night in hospital with a slight concussion.

Okay, fans thought, here's the clear-cut case that will allow the NHL to demonstrate there is no room in its ranks for gladiators on blades. It was the perfect chance to show that the league was finally heeding the cries of political and community leaders, parents and countless commissions across Canada and the United States.

The league blew it. It meted out a 15-game suspension, during which Brown's absence will scarcely be noticed. Although the third most severe in NHL history, this punishment will not deter further attacks. After all, the five-game suspension slapped on Brown last March for hitting the same player with his stick didn't prevent this one. In the escalating competition for enforcement, the Flyers will blithely slot in their second best goon.

If Brown had attacked Sandstrom on a New York or Toronto street, he probably would be facing criminal charges and subject to a jail sentence. But this is the National Hockey League, and the law of the land isn't applied, as it should be, on the rink.

Brown should be facing a year off to think about his style of, uh, hockey. The owners of the Philadelphia Flyers, who hired Brown for his ability to intimidate players, should be facing a massive fine. The message would be clear.

The Toronto Star November 4, 1987

The Globe and Mail

A VICIOUS HOCKEY ACT, OR NOT?

~

WILLIAM HOUSTON

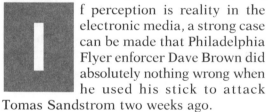

If perception is reality in the electronic media, a strong case can be made that Philadelphia Flyer enforcer Dave Brown did absolutely nothing wrong when he used his stick to attack Tomas Sandstrom two weeks ago.

Television viewers in Canada and the Eastern United States watched in amazement as Brown viciously cross-checked the New York Ranger forward in the face with his stick, after a goalmouth scramble in the third period during a Monday night game at Madison Square Garden.

Sandstrom fell to the ice and lay there with no discernible movement. Dazed, he was helped and then taken to the hospital where he stayed overnight. It was discovered he had a slight concussion.

The attack, which many said was the worst they had seen, was condemned by just about everyone. John Davidson, a former Hockey Night in Canada analyst who now does

Ranger cable telecasts, seemed to articulate the outrage at the time of the incident.

As it developed, Davidson said over the air, "There (Brown) he goes again. There's a cross-check to the face."

After a pause, he said, "You really wonder what makes this person tick.

"This is beyond belief. What a senseless, idiotic play, again by Brown. You tell me he deserves to play in this league? They (the Flyers) are out of their minds. Send him to another league some place.

"Get a doctor out to help this guy (Sandstrom). . . . This is a sick individual. They should put this guy in jail."

But the people on the Flyer cable telecast saw the whole thing differently. Sandstrom was to blame, they said, because he played possum.

Bobby Taylor, a former Flyer backup goalie who did some work for CTV's Friday night games a couple of years ago, was the Flyer analyst.

With him was play-by-play man Gene Hart, who is widely regarded as one of the biggest cheerleaders in the business, as well as a long-standing Flyer apologist.

Last winter, for example, Hart wrote a long article in the Flyer magazine explaining why the team's intimidation—fighting and stick work—is not goon hockey but instead an example of the honored Flyer tradition of supporting one another.

When the incident occurred, Taylor said, "Sandstrom is playing dead, because he doesn't want to get up and retaliate."

"He wants the Flyers to pick up another five-minute major, as he did in the game in Philadelphia last year," replied Hart.

"He (Sandstrom) took a slash at Hextall," Taylor said. "He's going to stay down there to make sure he doesn't get up, because he might have to answer to it. Acting school."

When the Flyer management heard about the remarks from Taylor and Hart, the two broadcasters were told to apologize, which they did during the next Flyer telecast.

But, arguably, Taylor and Hart were not the only media people in Philadelphia to miss, or perhaps more accurately, distort the story.

The thrust of the Philadelphia Daily News game report was the return of Hextall from his eight-game suspension—not Brown's assault.

In the body of the story, it was written, "Regular-season hockey doesn't get any better than this, even though the finger-waggers and moralists were heard claiming that the high stick in the third period had spoiled everything."

There were, indeed, plenty of "moralists and finger-waggers." In addition to the New York Times condemning the incident in an editorial, a New York Daily News hockey reporter wrote, "The NHL is nuts to be sleeping in the same bed with a thug who cashes a paycheque only because he (1) strikes fear into talented players (2) has memorized the Flyers' bully manual (3) obeys coach Mike Keenan."

On the flip side, there were those in the media who implied that Sandstrom got what he deserved. Actually, Hockey Night In Canada analyst Don Cherry did more than imply. He came right out and said, at a Toronto Maple Leaf luncheon, that "It couldn't have happened to a nicer guy."

A Southam News wire story reported that Sandstrom is a dirty player, uses his stick a lot, is hated around the league, and has the nickname "Endangered Species." Sandstrom, the report stated, is one of the league's more accomplished "sneaky-dirty" players.

Stan Fischler, a New York hockey writer, didn't think it was a big deal. He wrote, "Sorry, but the Brown-Sandstrom business was small potatoes compared with some of the brutality of yesteryear. I remember the night Gordie Howe, Mr. Hockey himself, nearly removed (Lou) Fontinato's ear with his stick. The Red Wings figured Louie got what he deserved."

The Globe and Mail   November 12, 1987

A C T I V I T I E S

1. With a partner, read the editorials and make notes for each of them on the following (you may wish to set up your notes in chart form):

**Editorials
pp. 90—94**

- the issue or question raised in the editorial;
- facts used;
- opinion statements;
- conclusion drawn;
- suggested course of action;
- phrases or images that appeal to the emotions;
- intended audience.

After your notes are complete, compare your findings with another group's.

2. Write an editorial on a topic about which you have a strong opinion. Discuss with a partner who your audience will be, and what emotions you want to arouse in them. Use facts, opinion statements, and images to create feelings in your audience.

3. Work with a partner and reread the editorial "Put Goons on Ice" and the column "A Vicious Hockey Act, or Not?"

- Discuss how the writer of the editorial tries to convince readers that Dave Brown and the NHL made poor decisions.
- Discuss how the media in Philadelphia presented the issue.
- Compose an editorial for a Philadelphia newspaper which has a bias different from the *Toronto Star's*.

IF WE ARE ALL ACCOUNTABLE TO THE MEDIA, TO WHOM ARE THE MEDIA ACCOUNTABLE?

~

BEVERLEY BURLOCK

When I was a student in journalism at an illustrious university, we were regaled by our professor of television with his exploits in obtaining a story. He had broken numerous laws and codes, etc., but he was enormously proud of his achievement. After all, he had got the story when the other major network had been unable to.

One of the young students said, "But sir, what about the ethics of what you did?"

"Ethics, my dear" (he was talking to a female student), he said, scorning her naivete, "has nothing to do with it."

This from the profession which is now declaring its constitutional right to inform us at all costs about the unethical behavior of everyone else. Maybe it is time to question the ethical behavior of the media. What are their conflicts of interest? What loans/gifts do they accept? What is behind their less than objective choice of nouns, adjectives, verbs and adverbs? What do they leave out of stories; what stories do they ignore altogether?

One of our more famous and honourable senators is reported to have warned the weekly media in the late 50s that the enemy to watch in the future would be themselves and their peers in other fields.

We now are informed by the policy of the truth at any cost, even if it's only half the truth, because the public has the right to know.

Nearly everything else is accountable to someone at some time. Just exactly to whom is the media accountable? If we have no answer to that, then they have unlimited power, and that is very dangerous, especially if we are still working under the mistaken belief that if it's in "print" it must be right. *The Kingston Whig Standard*
February 22, 1988

CYCLISTS TURN PATIENCE TO FURY

~⁓~

CHARLES FRANK

The following article prompted a reader's response. (See page 99 for the response)

Where I was, getting ready to slip the Red Baron out onto Elbow Drive.

I checked left. Then right. Just as I was about to step on the gas, my eye caught a blur in the rear-view mirror. Without thinking, I jammed on the brakes.

In that split second, a white-helmeted cyclist sped past me on a 10-speed. Without breaking cadence or pausing to check for oncoming vehicles, he darted directly into the late-morning traffic. As cars screeched to a halt and horns blared, the cyclist continued on his way—but not before turning ever so slightly in his seat, raising his hand and offering the fuming drivers behind a quick, single-digit salute.

To say it was an obscene gesture is an understatement.

The real obscenity, of course, is the way he—and the hundreds of other morons like him who take to the streets at the first sign of spring—endanger not only their own lives, but the lives of others.

And no, not all cyclists are morons— although at this time of year it certainly seems that way.

No quadrant of the city is safe.

Some days you can run across (that is not, I repeat not, a Freudian slip) these cyclists lurching in and out of rush-hour traffic on Macleod Trail, laughing wildly at the chaos their antics have caused and hurling invective at motorists who dare to complain.

Other times (when they deign to travel herd-like, on a group outing) they can be found on any major thoroughfare, stubbornly plugging an inside lane or two and seemingly oblivious to the anger and hostility building in their wake.

(Which of course raises the question: is it more correct to call a group of cyclists a herd, or an obstruction?)

On still other occasions, overdosing on the adrenalin rush one can only imagine flying through red lights on Memorial Drive must bring, certain cyclists have been known to veer onto city walking paths—terrorizing small animals, helpless children and frail pedestrians.

I have tried to be understanding.

These people are frustrated, I've told friends who had, in the aftermath of a personal assault by a renegade cyclist, begun talking seriously about buying vintage four-by-fours and cleaning up the streets.

They've probably been locked up in their basements all winter—riding those awful stationary bicycles, keeping little charts of their progress on the wall and watching reruns of the Dukes of Hazzard.

Is it any wonder they need a period of adjustment when they get back out to the real world?

Not only that, I'd say, but those of us who

still have most of our faculties have to be prepared to make some concessions to those less fortunate. Perhaps these maverick cyclists had their ability to make rational judgments and obey rules of the road impaired by years of inhaling automobile exhaust.

(Remember now, these are adults who by their own choice parade around in public wearing skin-tight pants, $75 sneakers and a plastic crash helmet.)

But even mild-mannered observers of the human condition like myself can only rationalize irrational behavior for so long, before we too are forced to take a stand.

Enough is enough. It's time something was done either to get these rude, dangerous people off our streets or to deny them the privilege of riding on public roads in the first place.

And make no mistake, it *is* a privilege.

We've all heard militant cyclists argue vehemently that they're entitled to ride on the city's roadways. And we've listened to their rationalizations that like motorists, there will always be those cyclists who obey the rules of the road and those who don't.

Maybe so.

But you can't drive a car without qualifying for a licence. A licence, incidentally, which allows motorists who operate their vehicles dangerously, maliciously or in contravention of the rules, to be identified and reported to the authorities.

Not only that, but those motorists caught breaking the rules by police can have their licences revoked and their vehicles impounded, and they are subject to some rather intimidating fines.

And yes, we all know that even with those deterrents, there's no shortage of motorists disposed towards behaving badly and breaking the law. But imagine our roads without licensing regulations, a motor vehicle code and enforcement officers.

It's a scary thought.

Almost as scary as allowing cyclists to continue to roam our streets without some form of regulation.

Calgary Herald
March 21, 1988

MOTORISTS, CYCLISTS BENEFIT FROM CO–OPERATION

J O H N   W I N T E R D Y K

R e "Cyclists turn patience to fury!" by Charles Frank, Herald, March 21.

Being born and raised in Holland, where cyclists outnumber motorists; spending the last few years living on the West Coast where cyclists are not viewed as an aberration; and probably putting nearly as many miles on my legs as Frank puts on his car, I felt compelled to write this short rebuttal.

As an avid cyclist, I am among the first to admit that there are those who, while having mastered the basic skill of staying on their bikes, have no right to be on the streets either because of poor cycling technique and/or lack of road etiquette. These people should be regulated like regular drivers if they want to use the roadways.

A second group I'd like to see regulated because of the negative image they bring to other cyclists, are the couriers who use their mountain bikes to move about the congested downtown area in order to meet the needs of some business executive who thinks if it gets there within the hour, it's already too late.

Frank, given his myopic view, has probably spent minimal time, if any, in exploring the local countryside by bike. If he did, he would probably have long since realized that it is the auto driver who is more dangerous than the cyclist. Since moving here last year, I have already had more close calls, despite the nice wide shoulders, than during my seven years of cycling on the coast. Drivers in Alberta seem to be of the mentality that cyclists are worth less than the wildlife they cautiously avoid with the cars.

Rather than berate one another, perhaps it would be more appropriate and constructive to educate one another. Frank should get off his high horse or out of his Red Baron, and exercise some of the more humanitarian and utilitarian sides of himself. A little effort and education all around would go a long way.

Calgary Herald
April 6, 1988

RECYCLING

MARTIN R. HAASE

To the Editor:

Sir,—Your editorial, Cashing in on Trash, aptly points out some of the good reasons for waste recycling. But there is much more at stake than stopping the littering or saving money. Non-renewable resources are being used at a profligate rate and excess paper use is denuding our forests, which maintain the water cycle and provide us with an equitable climate. Incineration of wastes pollutes the air, and landfills. Besides, using valuable land, can damage water supplies. Less waste means less pollution.

Government recycling programs deserve high priority, but even before they come into effect individuals can do much to recycle on their own: organic matter can be composted for excellent garden fertilizer; much paper can be reused; and plastic shopping bags, which are thrown away by the millions to pollute the air or foul the land, can be taken back when shopping to be used many times. These free bags are not "free," as they increase ultimate costs to consumers and impose a cost on the environment when thrown away.

The Halifax Chronicle-Herald/The Mail Star
April 8, 1988

ACTIVITIES

1. With a partner, discuss the point that the writer of one of these letters is making. Decide if you agree or disagree with the position. Try to find an article in a newspaper you are reading that could be used as evidence for the position you take.

2. Besides the letters-to-the-editor column, there are many other columns that invite readers to write to a newspaper. With a partner make a collage of readers' letters written to your local paper in the course of a week. On a separate piece of paper, summarize the purpose or point of view of each of the letters.

3. With a partner, write a letter to your local paper on an issue that concerns you or to ask advice from one of the columnists your paper carries.

**Readers Write
pp. 96–100**

MUSCLE MUSIC: TUNE IN AND STRESS OUT

~

T A N Y A   M I L L E R

Military troops marching along barren roads during the Second World War may not have understood why it felt good to sing, they just did it, perhaps to ease the tension or to lighten the load.

Indians also used the magic of music in haunting drum rhythms for ceremonial occasions and for communication.

Today, various forms of music are still used for celebration, motivation, and to reduce stress, whether in a fitness class, for physiotherapy, or to help elderly people reminisce.

It is also widely thought that people not only move better to music than without, but that music makes the workout—whatever it should be—more fun and inspiring.

Blois Brooks, winner of the 1986 Nova Scotia Body Building Championship and contender for the 1988 National Body Building Championship, knows how important certain types of music are for him in training and competing successfully.

"I can't work out without music," he says. "It's important, it psyches me up."

Brooks, like many other athletes, listens to music that's inspiring while training for upcoming competitions.

"I have to listen to songs with a fast beat and good rhythm. Most pop songs seem to get my adrenaline flowing."

Eric Miller, an exercise physiologist at Ohio State University, tested the effects of music on the performance of 10 joggers. He had them jog for 30 minutes while listening to music, then for 30 minutes without. He discovered after taking blood samples of the subjects that their endorphin levels were much lower when they jogged to music.

Since endorphins are released into the body as a result of the amount of stress placed on it, Miller concluded that the joggers who listened to music perceived less stress than when they jogged in silence. All the subjects said it was easier to jog with music.

"People come to exercise classes for many reasons, but the single most important component in each class is the music," says Helen Burns, director of physical education and fitness at the YMCA in Halifax.

"We've simply had people leave a class when they didn't like the music, or even a certain song on a tape."

Brooks agrees that the right type of music can keep eager exercisers motivated.

"If someone changes the tape at the gym and puts on a slow song, everyone complains. They need that high-energy boost."

At the YMCA, Burns says, it's very important for the fitness instructor to pick music with the perfect number of beats per minute.

In every fitness class, there's a warm-up aerobic component and a cool-down phase. The beats per minute for each phase are different and very important in considering maximum benefits for the class.

She believes that there are various factors

that make up the motivational components in music.

"The rhythm, the beats per minute, the familiarity and even the lyrics must be considered. It can take months to compile the right songs for a tape."

However, these aren't the only factors to consider when making a tape for a class.

"Even if you include all of the right components," says Burns, "you're not going to satisfy everyone all of the time. Everyone has their reasons for liking a certain song and disliking another.

"I once played a slow moving piece, at the end of a pre-natal class, by Zamfir. After the class, an oriental lady asked me to never play that song again because it reminded her of the music played at oriental funerals."

Heavy-metal and punk music create the most complaints.

"People just don't like it; it seems to go right through them."

Although little research has been conducted on the effects of music on body rhythms, some researchers think certain music does affect the way in which our muscles respond to it.

"There's a significant link between auditory stimulation and the reaction of the calf muscle to certain pieces of music," says Janet Miller, a physiotherapist working at the Dartmouth Stroke Centre.

"The brain reacts to music in cycles and the preferred cycle for calf muscle stimulation is 2.1 cycles per second. It's also been discovered the type of music that contains this cycle is Scottish highland and military marching music.

"Have you ever noticed that certain pieces of music make you feel like dancing, some to sit and listen, and others have you swaying back and forth. The type of music that makes you sway is emitting a different cycle from dancing or exercise music," she says.

George Turnbull, a professor of physiotherapy at Dalhousie University, also believes that music introduces a concept of rhythm, and is interested in understanding more about the use of music in treatment of certain stroke victims.

"Stroke victims, who have damaged the speech centers in their brains, can often sing after the stroke, but can't speak. I'm interested in learning whether or not they can also move better to music, than without. There's a lot of debate about this issue because no one is sure why this happens. It could be that the singing does something to help them remember or reminisce."

When Janet Miller teaches her exercise therapy classes in Dartmouth she emphasizes the importance of music with the body rhythms of people with different injuries.

"It's essential to choose the rhythm to the particular injury involved. The music I use to teach stroke victims is much different from the music I use for people with rheumatism."

During high intensity aerobic workouts, there is concern that some people may overreact to the stimulation created by various pieces of music, and injure themselves.

"A lot of times, especially during a twisting song, an exerciser will lose their muscle control and start moving to the momentum. This repeated movement can lead to injury if the movement isn't controlled," says Burns.

Eric Miller concluded in his study with 10 joggers that music may help to tune out the body's perception of stressful input—increased heart rate and muscle use—and that the exerciser may perceive the exercise as less stressful and go beyond their limit.

While no one has yet defined what it is exactly about music that constitutes so much motivation, or lack of it, one shouldn't feel it's absolutely necessary to plug in the headphones or crank up the stereo just to have a proper workout—it could be that humming a simple tune is enough.

The Halifax Chronicle-Herald/The Mail Star
January 27, 1988

The Ottawa Citizen

A DREAM COME TRUE

MARTIN CLEARY

A week before the start of the Winter Olympic Games, Elizabeth Manley woke in the middle of the night in a pool of sweat. She had just skated the performance of her life in her dream Olympics.

She was crying. Her mother, Joan, was crying in the stands. The crowd was going wild.

But the excitement was too much for her and she checked out before the judges could tell her the colour of her medal.

Manley learned Saturday at the Olympic Saddledome the real world can parallel the dream world and for her the colour was silver.

The Gloucester Skating Club athlete, who has become a well-trained and thinking fighter this year, placed a brilliant second in the Olympic women's figure skating competition behind the German Democratic Republic's Katarina Witt. Debbie Thomas of the United States was third.

Her result equals Karen Magnussen's effort in 1972.

Barbara Ann Scott, skating for the Minto Skating Club, had Canada's best women's Olympic result with a first in 1948.

Looking like a champion, Manley, 22 breezed through her four-minute freeskating program with ease and confidence to win the most important part of the competition.

Her perfect freeskating program, which is worth 50 per cent of the final mark, allowed her to climb into second overall from third.

When Manley's short and long program results were combined, which are worth 70 per cent, she was the freeskating champion.

"I saw my mom running down the stairs (in my dream)," Manley said. "I looked for her at the end tonight (Saturday), but I couldn't find her.

"I couldn't hear the last 20 seconds of my program. I was crying in my spin and calling for my mom. My first reaction was to look for my mom."

When Manley woke from her Olympic dream, she talked to her mom at 3 a.m.

"My mom had tears in her eyes when I told her about the dream. She was praying for that moment. There have been so many nights when I've had coffee with her and I spill my guts."

Before that point, Manley was having difficulty concentrating. She was too anxious. But after the dream, her concentration and her training improved.

Manley has had more than her share of low points—health and personal difficulties, defeats on the ice, changing coaches and cities.

But no matter the hurdle, Manley has used her determination and the careful guidance of coaches Peter and Sonya Dunfield since 1983 to pick her up and give her an encouraging push into the future.

The use of sport psychologists Peter Jensen of Toronto and Terry Orlick of Ottawa in the past four years also have played a significant role.

"Sports psychologists have become important to our sport," Peter Dunfield said.

"We use Peter Jensen at competitions, and seminars to enhance her ability to cope with pressure. That might have been the winning edge."

Manley figures the dream was triggered by her "visualization" (imagining herself doing her program), which she does every night for 45 minutes before going to bed.

The disappointment of the 1987 world championships in Cincinnati did have a silver lining for Manley. She learned to become tough.

Manley had an opportunity to win a medal in Cincinnati, but the great performance by and celebration for American Caryn Kadavy caused Manley to lose her concentration. She struggled through a difficult program.

"We've been fighting that image ever since," Dunfield said. "The press has jumped all over it and says she's inconsistent. Nobody could have coped with that situation.

"But we never lost faith in her. We let her know she could do it and do it when it counts."

Manley felt the same way. The negative press has made her more aggressive.

"It made me a little fighter. I wanted to prove them wrong.

The Ottawa Citizen
February 29, 1988

Cape Breton Post

POLICE, SCHOOLS PLAN ALCOHOL-FREE GRADUATIONS

AL CASAGRANDE

Members of the Glace Bay Town Police Department in conjunction with the staff and students of the two high schools, Morrison and Saint Michael, are currently planning their fourth consecutive alcohol and chemical free graduation parties. Working closely on the program are the department's youth officers, Constables Adrian McNamara and Ronnie Donovan; Evan Kennedy of Morrison High; and Malcolm Marsh of Saint Michael.

Meetings have already been held at the two schools, says McNamara, adding, a great deal of interest has been generated by the students and the support and assistance given by the principals as well as the staff has been fantastic.

The program proved successful since it was initiated and every effort will be made to have this year's just as successful, adds McNamara.

"Why not make every day a drug and alcohol free day," is the approach being taken this year, says the officer. In the past, he says, the department stressed alcohol and chemical free graduations but this has been broadened with the help of the staff at the two schools.

Quoting statistics, McNamara said that Nova Scotia had 14 alcohol related fatalities in 1984 involving persons under the age of 20 and in 1987, only eight, adding, "We are hopeful zero will be recorded this year."

McNamara says a total of 258 motorists in the 16-19 age group had their licence revoked last year because of drinking and driving convictions in the province.

Through the assistance of Dick James, coordinator of alcohol and driving countermeasures and safe graduation, the department has obtained video movies and material which will be presented to the grade 12 students, says McNamara.

General assemblies are planned at the two schools along with awareness sessions for parents, he says, also noting students themselves have arranged a number of activities to promote safe graduation.

Support on the part of the public played a great part in past years and many businesses, organizations, individuals, as well as parents of the students made financial contributions, says McNamara.

The program has also been given support by both Ring 73 and the Hub Athletic Club in their announcements to the effect they will not rent their facilities for graduation parties where alcohol will be served. Attitudes are changing towards alcohol and social functions, he says.

Graduations of 1986 were the first in more than a decade in the province to note all celebrating students returned home safely, says McNamara. Such was the case again the following year and hopefully it can be repeated again this year, he says.

Cape Breton Post   April 5, 1988

A C T I V I T I E S

1. Most newspapers have a "lifestyle" section which includes articles such as "Muscle Music: Tune In and Stress Out." Look through the newspaper section of your school or public library or through newspapers at home and list the headlines of ten "lifestyle" articles on different topics. Make a note too of other places music stories are found in newspapers.

2. As a result of reading "Muscle Music: Tune In and Stress Out" or "Police, Schools Plan Alcohol-Free Graduations," write a letter to your physical education teacher or your graduation planning committee outlining the advantages of using music in class or having an alcohol-free graduation. Use information from the articles plus other ideas you supply yourself.

3. The medal won by Elizabeth Manley at the 15th Olympic Winter Games in Calgary in February 1988 was only one of many won by athletes from around the world at those games. Search through the microfiche or computer data bank files or vertical files at your school or public library to find a story on your favourite Olympic sport from past Olympic Games. Write a four or five sentence summary of the story and share it with a partner. Discuss with your partner the competitive qualities your stories' athletes have in common with Elizabeth Manley.

4. "Cover" one of your school's sports events for your school newspaper. Watch the game, interview players or coaches, and write up your sports story.

or

Write a "lifestyle" story for your school or local newspaper.

Feature Articles
pp. 102–106

The Toronto Star

TEENS LIVE IN DANGEROUS DREAM WORLD

DORIS ANDERSON

I looked into 25 achingly young faces; the girls, shy and guarded, the boys sprawling macho children with a what-the-hell-can-you-tell-me? look in their eyes.

They were all drop-outs from the high school system, now back in an alternate school. The teacher wanted to give them a pep talk about the importance of finishing school and getting some kind of training. I felt like a witch doctor who had been brought in to shake my rattles, perform a dance and frighten them back into the system. I'd been here before.

I began by asking how many of them expected to work all their lives. All the boys and a few of the girls raised their hands. I then asked them how many expected to marry. All the girls raised their hands, but only three boys abashedly responded to smirks and jeers from their pals.

Then I told them the statistical facts of their lives. All of them will work all of their lives, unless they win a lottery or end up on welfare. Almost all of them, the jeerers too, will marry at least once and one in three who get divorced will probably marry again. At least three of the girls, about one in 10, will have a baby before she is 20.

I pointed out that marriage for the boys isn't something to be avoided as an awesome burden and responsibility because it isn't any more. Men can, and do, shuck off the responsibilities of marriage pretty quickly and easily if they want.

But for the girls, marriage is one of the most dangerous gambles she can undertake; particularly if she gets married too soon, before she has equipped herself with good job skills, and if she has children too soon. In fact, by marrying too young and becoming a mother too soon, she will almost certainly sentence herself and her children to a life of poverty.

At least I caught their attention momentarily. They looked mildly startled. But all the statistics and all the hard evidence they see for themselves in their own families with their not-made-in-heaven marriages never quite registers. Life is going to be different for them.

I could read it in their eyes. All the love songs, rock videos, teen movies, advertisements and romance novels had told them it could all be magically easy, if they only believed it to be so. Ah youth!

The girls, particularly, are living in a time warp that's at least 80 years out of date. In 1900, nine of 10 women married. Once married, a woman spent almost 20 years raising children. Widowed in her mid 50s, she could expect to live another 10 years, and die in her own bed before her last child left home. Only one in five women worked outside the home.

But today, women work to support themselves and their families for about 30 to 40

years. Almost all women marry; that's the easiest of all the things they are called on to do. Most of them will have one, or at the most, two children. One in five will raise the children completely alone.

A young woman today can expect to live to be almost 80, but she'll end her life by herself. Two out of three of them will be living below or close to the poverty line at that age.

The priority in a woman's life used to be to find a husband who would be a good provider, and she hopes, kind to her. Then she was expected to have children. Only if the man couldn't earn enough, or was a drunk or deserted her, did she work.

Today, the priorities are completely turned around. The most important thing a young woman must do is prepare herself for the work force, because that's what she's going to be doing for most of her life. Then she should look for a husband; not to look after her, but to be an equal partner financially, as well as in the home and raising the children. If she starts the search as an independent self-supporting person, she has a lot better chance of attracting the right kind of man. Finally, they may decide to have children.

But to get that message across to teenagers seems almost impossible. Each generation seems to have to experience it for themselves before they wake up, and often, especially for the girls, it's too late by that time to do much about it.

Thankfully, the National Film Board has come to the rescue. *No Way! Not Me* is the first film in a series called The Feminization of Poverty. . . . The film can be rented. I would like to see it become compulsory viewing in every high school in the country.

The Toronto Star April 21, 1988

NATIVE PEOPLE SUFFER FROM OUR BRIGHT IDEAS

SUZANNE ZWARUN

Canadians rightly condemned Nazi experiments on humans. But it occurs to me we have our own group of human guinea pigs that we've been experimenting upon for a century.

By the latest turn in thought, hundreds of native foster children are being repatriated to reserves. It would take the services of Solomon to settle the question of whether the children being snatched from their long-time white foster parents are going to be better or worse off growing up on reserves. But the current turn-around in thinking is typical of what we've been doing for decades.

First, the white powers that be come up with a theory. We move people around like chess pieces for awhile. Then we decide— as natives go on living in poverty and dying too soon—that this theory isn't going to work. So we embrace a new theory and start the moving around all over again.

Once upon a time, we held to the theory native youngsters would be better educated at boarding schools. We took them from their families, shipped them hither and yon, and set about brainwashing them to think white. What else would you call strapping unilingual children for speaking the only language they'd been taught? Eventually, we decided we weren't doing people any favour when we erased their religion and their culture.

We're still working on a new theory.

Once upon a time, we held to the theory that the tuberculosis threat in the north could be eased if Inuit were shipped like cattle to southern hospitals. Taken by boat to a medical expedition ship offshore, they'd be X-rayed and ordered to stay aboard if TB was detected. Healthy children of sick parents were shipped back to shore with whomever was going; sick people simply vanished— 200 lost permanent track of their families since no one bothered to keep records. By current theory—judging from the TB outbreak among the Lubicon—we leave them to die where they are.

Once upon a time, we stripped Indian

reserves of their foster children.

The Alberta Association of Social Workers says that a decade ago almost all Alberta foster children were native. That was "because some reserves didn't meet middle-class white standards," says president Margaret Dewhurst. "So kids were removed because they were not being kept in absolutely clean homes with showers."

Three years ago, we abandoned the theory that if we could raise native children in white, middle-class homes they'd become white and middle class. We realize now "they shouldn't have been taken away in the first place", says Dewhurst. And so we "are trying to undo what they did, very slowly, bit by bit, case by case."

You only have to look at the bureaucratic nightmare that has ensued since the enactment of Bill C-31 to see it's a whole lot easier to do things than to undo them. You only have to look at Indian women who married and divorced white men and found themselves homeless, to look at the Inuit who have never found their families, to see that people get hurt beyond repair when they are the victims of experiments in social thinking.

The white foster parents whose children are being taken from them are suffering now. We don't yet know whether the native children will suffer permanent damage from being involved in what we're calling a tug of love or whether being raised on a reserve will save them from the alcoholism, jail sentences and suicide plaguing so many of the previous generation.

Maybe we have to try to undo our mistakes, however many people we hurt in the process of changing theories. But how long will it be before we abandon this theory, embrace another on how native children should be raised? And what are the chances, do you think, of any other group but natives being used as such guinea pigs?

women of their status when they married a white man. I've never figured out the thinking behind that theory—maybe Indian Affairs figured to have fewer charges to finance if it banished child-bearers. In the ripeness of time, we abandoned that theory. But in the three years since the federal government enacted Bill C-31 which eliminated the discriminatory law, we've not managed to regain Indian status for the majority of the 100 000 women who've applied.

Time after time, as we look back 25 years, we're willing to admit to inadvertent mistakes and insensitive bureaucracy. We're doing it again as white foster parents take to the streets to protest the repatriation to

Calgary Herald
April 6, 1988

The Leader Post

REINER'S PRINCESS BRIDE THE PERFECT FAIRY TALE

WAYNE MORIARTY

It is difficult to say what exactly is most brilliant about The Princess Bride, a movie that delivers on the promise of fencing, fighting, torture, revenge, giants, monsters, chases, escapes, true love, and miracles.

■ The direction of Rob Reiner (This is Spinal Tap, The Sure Thing, Stand By Me) is impeccable. Meathead, as he lovingly became known in TV's All in the Family, is a perfect four for four in the movie-making business and is now, without question, the hottest of all American film-makers.

■ The screenplay by Academy Award winner William Goldman (Butch Cassidy and the Sundance Kid), based on a Goldman novel, is at once wildly funny, both as a slapstick and satire, and wildly adventurous.

■ Arguably there hasn't been a movie cast this well since Gone With the Wind. Not only are the principal players perfect, but there's a huge cast of bit players who enter, explode with humour, then vanish: Wallace Shawn as Vizzini, the ill-fated leader of a band of kidnappers; Billy Crystal as Miracle Max, the Jewish miracle maker; Carol Kane as Valerie, the nagging Mrs. Max; Peter Cook as the clergyman with the speech impediment (stolen gag, but still funny); and lastly, Mel Smith as the festering Albino who runs the Pit of Despair.

■ Finally, equal to the inspired casting is every performance. The actors' characterizations are outstanding and diverse.

The Princess Bride may well be the first movie ever made to truly live up to that dreadful hype: "For the kid in all of us."

There are actually several stories going on here at the same time. The movie opens with a flu-stricken young boy (Fred Savage) moaning at his mother's promise that

Grandfather will be coming by this afternoon to entertain him. Grandfather (Peter Falk) arrives and begins reading the book *The Princess Bride*. The grandson can't believe he's going to have to endure what starts out promising to be, at best, mushy and boring. How good could the story of a hero named Westley (Cary Elwes) and a heroine named Buttercup (Robin Wright) possibly be?

"This book," Grandfather promises, "has everything: fencing, fighting, torture, revenge, giants, monsters, escapes, true love, and miracles."

And indeed, it has.

The film then becomes the story The Princess Bride, occasionally flashing back to the grandfather reading his grandson the adventure.

The story in the story is centred around the power of enduring love, as Westley, who has been separated from the fair Buttercup, battles a band of kidnappers and then the evil and moral-less Prince Humperdinck, for the return of his beloved.

While the adventure itself is first rate, above all else, The Princess Bride is comedy. Highlighted by the hilarious sequences involving the kidnappers, Vizzini (Shawn), the friendly giant Fezzik (who else, but wrestler Andre the Giant) and Spaniard Indigo Montoya (Mandy Patinkin gives the best performance of many great performances here), the movie is unrelentingly funny.

The Princess Bride is one of those movies you almost regret seeing because you'll never again be able to enjoy the experience of seeing it for the first time.

The Regina Leader Post
October 24, 1987

The Edmonton Journal

TURNER'S ENERGY, VOICE CAPTIVATING

HELEN METELLA

I don't want Tina Turner's body and stamina when I'm her age. I want it now.

At 48, the self-described "girl in the band" hopped, high-kicked and waddled her aggressive knee-first strut for the first 40 minutes of her Thursday show, then leapt up a staircase three stairs at a time to shimmy with abandon alongside percussionist Steve Scales.

So incredibly focused is her physical energy that even a scintillating saxophone solo by Deric Dyer in Private Dancer couldn't deflect the eye from the slinky involvement Turner orchestrated downstage with a silk scarf.

In two form-fitting red mini-dresses that displayed a figure more svelte than she possessed during her 1985 tour, Turner enhanced the beauty and power of a parade of five-star songs—from Proud Mary to the Terry Britten tunes of her second solo LP, Break Every Rule—before more than 10 000 ecstatic fans.

But the show's resounding success was owed to more than her athletics.

What's Love Got To Do With It received a standing ovation after the frank, funny entertainer told a crowd of men whom she was encouraging to sing the title line, "You ought to be good at this: you've been saying it all your lives."

Also, her thirty-plus years in the business

have taught her about cagey staging.

A few tons of lights and several artfully designed screens created imaginative, iridescent visuals.

A hydraulic lift that suddenly shot Turner ten feet in the air during We Don't Need Another Hero eradicated all memory of the film from which it came and doubled the impact of her voice.

Ah, yes, The Voice.

It was soft as a sable brush on Two People; as firm and precise as skate blades cutting figures on Typical Male and even raunchier than usual on Addicted To Love.

And no one builds a burning, twitching climax with the deliberate control that Turner exhibited on Let's Stay Together.

Rumors are that this is her last tour, but with an exquisite instrument like hers, and the fun she had with her determinedly rock-and-roll band, I'd say she's still ready for a tour that would challenge Springsteen and The Rolling Stones with its might.

The Edmonton Journal October 9, 1987

ACTIVITIES

1. Since a columnist generally does not report news, discuss with a partner what the role of a columnist in a newspaper is. Try to write a job description of a columnist.

Opinions
pp. 108–114

2. a) In one or two sentences, summarize the point of view expressed by Doris Anderson and Suzanne Zwarun in their columns.

b) Collect three columns from your local paper and, in one or two sentences, summarize the point of view of each.

3. After reading the film review and the concert review in this unit, with a partner, list the topics the writer of each article has chosen to include. For example, Helen Metella first writes about her overall impressions of the Tina Turner concert including her impressions of Tina's energy and her clothing. Wayne Moriarty uses "bullets" to highlight some of his more important topics. With your partner discuss other topics you might include in a review of a movie or a concert.

4. Write a review of the best film or concert you have ever seen. Note that in the opening paragraph you will want to capture the attention of your readers and in the closing paragraph you will probably want to sum up your feelings about the concert. Exchange reviews with a partner and comment on the strengths and weaknesses of each other's work. See page 186 of the Student Handbook for revising and editing guidelines.

from BIKO

DONALD WOODS

Donald Woods, a South African newspaper editor, writes about his friend Steve Biko, and about his own role in exposing Biko's murder to the press.

It was a black bombshell who bullied me into my first meeting with Steve Biko. My secretary rang through to tell me that a Dr. Ramphele was in the office and wished to see me. I knew from the name that Dr. Ramphele was black, and pictured an elderly gray-haired medico with an Uncle Tom diffidence. No image could have been further from the actuality.

She burst through the door, a slight figure in blue jeans and a white sweater, and stood challengingly in front of my desk with her hands on her hips, declaiming in a near-shout, "Why do you give all the headlines to sell-outs like Buthelezi and Mantanzima? Why don't you get to know the real black leaders? When are you coming to talk to Steve Biko? You know he is banned and can't come to you, so why don't you go to him? What's the matter with you?"

This was really something. There are a few black doctors in South Africa, and very few black female doctors, and though I had met black women in Zambia, London, and elsewhere with the poise and confidence to stride into a journalist's office to deliver such a tirade, I had never thought such people existed in my own country. Black women in South Africa, in fact most blacks, male or female, were highly diffident in the presence of whites.

This was a new breed of black South African—the Black Consciousness breed—and I knew immediately that a movement that produced the sort of personality now confronting me had qualities that blacks had been needing in South Africa for three hundred years. It was an exciting moment— a moment of discovery in my own country that added a new element to the whole national equation.

Something of this realization must have shown in my face, and I seem to recall that my response to the tirade, after initial shock, was a broad grin of sheer delight, because this astonishing Dr. Ramphele calmed down immediately, drew up a chair, and began a patient and quite amiable explanation of black political reality and Black Consciousness philosophy with the confident (and quite correct) assumption that all my other appointments had suddenly paled into insignificance.

As previously explained, I had had up to then a negative attitude toward Black Consciousness. As one of a tiny band of white South African liberals, I was totally opposed to race as a factor in political thinking, and totally committed to nonracist policies and philosophies. From the little I knew at that time of Biko and the Black Consciousness philosophy and organizations he had founded, he and they represented a repudiation of the liberal position, a fact illustrated by the way in which this man Biko had led a breakaway from NUSAS to found the blacks-only South African Students Organization, arguing that black students could only develop political self-reliance by "doing their own thing" as blacks. His argument that black students had to develop their own black identity appeared to me to be racist reasoning, and I regarded the foundation of SASO as an act of betrayal of the white liberal commitment. And I felt the same way about the other Black Consciousness groups Biko had founded, such as the Black Community Programs and all-black sports bodies and trust funds for maintenance of families of political prisoners. They seemed to me to be inversions of the apartheid mentality—racism in reverse.

Dr. Ramphele heard me out patiently, then burst out in another near-shout, "You've got the whole thing wrong, man! We're not racist. We're just insisting on being ourselves. You must come and talk to Steve, he'll explain the whole thing."

The meeting was arranged, and on the day I drove from East London to King William's Town, an hour away by car, I reviewed in my mind what I had heard and read of Biko.

From what I knew he was an unusually intelligent and charismatic personality who had won a dedicated following at an early age. I had been intrigued by the attitude of white NUSAS leaders toward him. I was an honorary vice-president of NUSAS, and had expected the white NUSAS leaders to resent Biko's breakaway move with all its implications of repudiation of their ideals. But they were strangely noncritical of his stance, much though they regretted it. I had been somewhat impatient with their apparent condonation of it all, regarding it as a rather weak-kneed compliance borne of white liberal reluctance to criticize blacks generally. In fact, I had adopted a strongly critical attitude, attacking SASO bitterly in editorials and speeches and accusing them of being as racist in their way as the Afrikaner Nationalists were on the other side of the spectrum. I was impatient with all this talk of black pride and "black is beautiful," maintaining that black was no more beautiful, or ugly, than white, and that there was no more merit or demerit in being born black than there was merit or demerit in being born white. All solid, straight-down-the-line liberal stuff, and valid enough.

But, as I was to learn, you simply have to be black in South Africa to perceive comprehensively every single nuance of the fact of blackness, and it is impossible to understand the totality of this experience through academic or theoretical idealism. This was what Biko had managed to convey to the young white NUSAS leaders and, this fact, together with his personal charisma, was what had impressed them and made them so reluctant to condemn Black Consciousness.

I had looked up the basic details of Steve Biko's short and stormy career. Born in King William's Town on December 18, 1946, he had begun his schooling at Brownlee Primary for two years, continued at Charles Morgan Higher Primary for four years, then moved on to Lovedale Institute to prepare for his matriculation. He was at Lovedale for only three months when the school was closed down as a result of strikes by senior pupils. He then moved to Marianhill in Natal, a Catholic institute, where he did very well. In 1966 he enrolled as a student at the University of Natal to study medicine, but after initial academic success became so involved in politics that his grades suffered and he was barred from further study. By this time, however, he was an acknowledged leader in several bodies he had founded or had helped to found, including the South African Students Organization (SASO) and the Black Community Programs, and had become a full-time organizer for these bodies, spreading the creed of the Black Consciousness movement he had launched, which had been the motivating philosophy behind the formation of these associations. Shortly thereafter, he had been banned and restricted to the King William's Town area.

His father, Mzimkhayi Biko, had died when Steve Biko was four, and he had an elder brother and sister and a younger sister. In 1970 he had married Nontsikelelo (Ntsiki) Mashalaba of Umtata, and they had two small sons.

ACTIVITIES

1. In a group of three or four, discuss the meaning of the term *racism* and explain what you think some "non-racist policies" might be for a newspaper, for a school, and for a country.

Biko
pp. 116—118

2. Dr. Ramphele accuses Donald Woods of misrepresenting the black cause in his newspaper headlines.
   a) Discuss with a partner how this is possible.
   b) Create several headlines for the moonlanding story (page 76) or another news story in this unit that show different biases. For example, a headline for the moonlanding story might be: U.S. Wastes Millions and Risks Lives.

3. Work with a partner who is also planning to read the rest of *Biko*, and predict what you think will happen as the story develops. Make point-form notes so that you may compare your predictions with what actually does happen in the book.

4. View the film *Cry Freedom*, which is based on Donald Woods' book, and write a review of it. See the film review on page 112 of this unit and the film review format in the Student Handbook (page 191) for a model and some hints for effective film review writing.

5. Choose one of the whole-book activities on page 204 of the Student Handbook to complete as you read the book or when you have finished reading it.

ACTIVITIES

**Developing Your Voice
End of Unit Activities**

1. With the help of your school's Course Option Selection Form, find items in your local newspaper that relate to every subject studied in your school. Label the stories and make a bulletin board display of your findings.

2. With the help of a calculator, determine what percentage of your local paper is advertisements and what percentage is news and feature stories. Write a report on your findings. You might want to send the report to the editor of the paper.

3. With a partner, turn the front page of your local newspaper into a radio newscast. You will have to rewrite the stories to emphasize the important details in order to fit them into the time requirements of radio. Listen to a radio newscast and time the length of the stories to get an idea of how long each item should be. Tape-record your radio newscast and present it to your class.

4. Arrange to tour your local newspaper.
   a) Before you visit the paper, make a list of questions you would like answered. (For example, you might want to know what (CP) means at the start of a story, who actually writes the editorials, or how much of the paper's revenues come from subscribers and how much from advertisers.)
   b) As you take the tour, compile a list of the different jobs people do there. When you return to school write a journal entry explaining which job seemed the most appealing to you and why.

5. If your community is served by more than one newspaper, form groups that have the same number of students in them as there are newspapers. Each student in the group should bring to class a copy of a different paper published on an established date (e.g., Monday October 24).
   ■ Select one story that all of the papers have covered.
   ■ Choose a story that was covered only by one paper.
   ■ Select an advertisement that appears in only one of the papers.

■ Analyse the bias and intended audience of the papers on the basis of the examples you have selected.

6. As a class project, prepare a school newspaper that contains many of the sections you found in a local paper.

7. Write a feature article on activities and programs taking place in your school and submit it to your local or community paper for publication.

8. Newsmagazines, as well as newspapers, report the news, but on a weekly rather than a daily basis. In a small group,
   a) collect copies of newspapers for a week. Choose a Canadian and an American newsmagazine for the same week, and compare how three or four news stories for the week are covered in the magazines and the newspaper. Consider the following:
   ■ the space allotted to the story;
   ■ the choice of cover story;
   ■ points of view presented;
   ■ deletions and additions to the story in the newsmagazine presentations of the stories; and
   ■ major stories not covered in the magazines.
   b) make a report to the class on your findings.

C A R E E R S

These careers are all related to work at a newspaper.

Photographer
A photographer operates a still camera to take photographs and processes exposed film. She or he determines the requirements of a particular photographic assignment and chooses an appropriate camera, film and any needed artificial lighting accessories. The photographer transports and sets up the equipment at an assigned location, selects and arranges a suitable background, and positions the subject. The work includes mixing chemicals and processing film in the dark room to make the negatives and prints.

Training and Qualifications
One-year certificate and two- or three-year diploma programs in photographic arts are available at most colleges. Some colleges may require an interview and portfolio of the student's creative work.

Salary
The estimated starting salary for photographers was $11 000 to $16 000 in 1984. Generally beginning salaries are low, although an experienced photographer with managerial ability can make a substantially higher salary by setting up her or his own business.

Other Careers
- Artist
- Data Processor
- Electrician
- Machinist
- Press Operator
- Sales Person
- Writer

R E S O U R C E S

Books
The Front Page—Ben Hecht and Charles MacArthur (Samuel French, 1928)
Cry Freedom—John Briley (Berkley Books, N.Y., 1987)

Films
The Edit, Kinetic Film Enterprises 1984; 13 min
Broadcast News, 20th Century Fox 1987; 135 min
All the President's Men, Warner/Wildwood 1976; 138 min

WORLD ISSUES

VOICES

TEENAGERS SPEAK OUT

Gillian Matthews: "It's frightening to think that a couple of people in the world have all the control over all of our futures. It doesn't matter if we go to peace marches or protests or anything. The people are supposed to have the power in a democracy but no one is listening. Maybe [U.S. President] Reagan will leave and a new president will come in and that will be different. Maybe it will be someone who will be younger, who will realize how crazy this is. I mean, Reagan was a movie star, what does he know about this stuff?"

Vlado Semiga: "No one trusts anyone anymore. Yet there isn't anyone who wants nuclear war. We have enough arms to kill ourselves over and over again, and it keeps on going."

Rob Mobilio: "The threat of nuclear war affects everybody. It's really scary to think someone just has to push a button . . . . AIDS is a joke with kids our age. We don't take it seriously. We don't think its going to happen to us."

Dawn Stevens: "I suppose when someone's friend dies of AIDS we'll start taking the threat more seriously. Right now we don't think it will affect us."

Kecia Rust: "I find a lot of problems in the world happen because of lack of research — like the drought in Ethiopia, which really bothers me. My main ambition is to get rid of prejudice in the world."

Tim O'Dacre: "It sounds kind of silly, I guess, but the two things I want to do are stop urban sprawl and clean up the water. Right now I think people are going to destroy themselves and take everything else with them.

Michelle Tam: "I've always believed a woman should be able to do for herself without depending on anyone else. I think a couple should share responsibilities."

Euge Chun: "Censorship is still too tough especially towards teens. People should have the right to listen, read, and see what they want, no one should have the authority to make the decision for you."

A C T I V I T I E S

Voices
pp. 124—125

1. In a group of four, assign the passages from "Teenagers Speak Out" to be read aloud. Read the statements made by teenagers in 1986-7. Identify the issues, discuss whether they are still important ones, and make a list of other modern issues which you feel are as important as or more important than these.

2. With a partner find one statement with which you both agree and one with which you both disagree. Brainstorm your reasons and write brief notes to the students quoted telling them why you agree and disagree with their statements.

3. Take a survey of the teenagers in your class (or use another sample of students from your school) to determine the issues which they feel are of greatest significance to young people this year. Ask them to write statements similar to the ones in this part of the unit, expressing their views on some of the issues. With a partner, write an article for the school newspaper based on your research or prepare your report in the form of a radio broadcast.

4. In your journal write your views on an issue about which you have strong feelings. This will probably be one of the issues you listed with your group in activity 1. You may wish to share your entry with a classmate who wrote on the same issue.

ABUSE DEFINED

What constitutes "abuse" for the purpose of professional reporting? A child suffers "abuse" in any of the following circumstances:

The child has suffered physical harm, either inflicted by the person having charge of the child or caused by that person's failure to adequately:
- care and provide for the child, or
- supervise the child, or
- protect the child;

The child has been sexually molested or sexually exploited by the person having charge of the child, or by another person where the person having charge of the child:
- knows or should know of the possibility of sexual molestation or sexual exploitation, and
- fails to protect the child;

The child requires medical treatment to cure, prevent or alleviate physical harm or suffering, and the child's parents or the person having charge of the child:
- does not provide the treatment, or
- refuses to provide the treatment, or
- is unavailable to consent to treatment, or
- is unable to consent to the treatment;

The child has suffered emotional harm, demonstrated by:
- severe anxiety, or
- severe depression, or
- severe withdrawal, or
- severe self-destructive or aggressive behaviour,

and the child's parent or the person having charge of the child:
- does not provide services or treatment to remedy or alleviate the harm,
- refuses to provide such services or treatment
- is unavailable to consent to such services or treatment
- is unable to consent to such services or treatment;

The child suffers from a mental, emotional or developmental condition that, if not remedied, could seriously impair the child's development, and the child's parent or the person having charge of the child either:
- does not provide treatment to remedy or alleviate the condition,
- refuses to do so,
- is unavailable to consent to treatment, or
- is unable to consent to treatment.

(from Ontario Ministry of Community and Social Services, 1986)

LUKA

SUZANNE VEGA

My name is Luka. I live on the second floor.
I live upstairs from you. Yes, I think you've seen me before.
If you hear something late at night, some kind of trouble,
    some kind of fight, just don't ask me what it was,
    just don't ask me what it was.

       I think it's 'cause I'm clumsy. I try not to talk too loud.
       Maybe it's because I'm crazy. I try not to act too proud.
       They only hit 'til you cry. After that you don't ask why.
       You just don't argue anymore, you just don't argue anymore,
          you just don't argue anymore.

Yes, I think I'm okay. I walked into the door again.
If you ask, that's what I'll say. And it's not your business anyway.
I guess I'd like to be alone, with nothing broken,
    nothing thrown. Just don't ask me how I am.
Just don't ask me how I am.

       Just don't ask me what it was. And they only hit until you cry.
       After that you don't ask why. You just don't argue any more,
       You just don't argue any more, you just don't argue any more.

FEAR

~

S A L L I E   B I N G H A M

urning the knob so slowly it seemed to glide, greased, under her palm, Jean finally opened the baby's door. It was early morning, the pink lambs and blue horses on the curtains just becoming visible; the crib, under its canopy, was still a pit of shadows, and Jean saw the brown bear, the snake, and the cat lined up at the rail, on guard.

She took a step toward the crib and stopped. The baby's smell, made of milk and powder and the soap she used in the washing machine, stood in front of her like a screen. She drew several breaths, trying to believe that since he smelled the same, nothing could be wrong. There had been so much crying the evening before, so much panic and screaming that she thought her observations might have been crazed.

Hearing him stir, she bent down. His eyes were open; he lay on his back, his hands out, and looked up at her as though he had always expected her to be there. "Hello, little duck," she said and reached in to pick him up. His body felt changed to her, limp, yielding; fat as a sack, she thought. Holding him tightly in her arms, she remembered how he had clung to her neck after she had punished him. "I'm sorry, I'm so sorry," she had sobbed, and he had repeated, "Orry."

Then she put him down. As his feet touched the floor, he began to whimper. Turning, he tried to clutch her knees as his legs splayed out. She moved back and he slid to the floor where he sat, whimpering and looking up at her. "You can do it," she whispered cheerily, and picked him up and set him again on his feet. He gave a cry and leaned

"There had been so much crying the evening before, so much panic and screaming . . ."

129

against her hands. She tried to push him away but he clung, crumpling at the same time at the knees. They're not working, she thought. The legs are still not working. She picked him up and rocked him in her arms.

He stopped crying immediately. "Here's the little kitty," she said, taking the animal out of the crib. As the baby seized the toy, she closed her eyes and buried her mouth in his cheek. It seemed to her that she ought to put him down again, to make sure, but she knew she would not be able to bear his crying. That was what had caused it, in the beginning—his crying. He would start over something so trivial—the cat had been misplaced, in this case—and his crying would wind on and on, endlessly on and on, growing into small shrieks that pierced her head. She had looked frantically for the cat and then, giving up, she had walked the baby up and down, trying to console him. It seemed to her that the crying would never stop. She was trapped inside the sound; the hour of the day and the day of the week drifted away and she was trapped, helplessly, inside the sound of a baby's screams. She had picked him up once more to try to comfort him but instead she had plunged him down onto the floor, plunging him again and again until his cries turned into hysterical screams. Then she had sat beside him on the floor, dazed, gasping for breath, and gone at last to open a window.

Coming back, she had seen him trying to get up.

Now, as she held him in her arms, she knew she had never really hoped, not even in the night when she had felt quite calm, lying against her husband's back. She had never really hoped. As soon as she had seen him trying to get up, she had known that she had hurt him in some terrible way. Her life had shriveled as she watched him, wallowing. She had never loved anyone as she had loved him, since she had felt his first tentative flutter inside her womb. She had been guiltily aware that she loved him more than she could ever love her husband, who was critical at times, and never really hers. But she had never hurt her husband, except glancingly, she had never even scratched the surface of all the offensive strangers she had known, she had hardly ruffled her parents' composure although she had hated them for years, and she had allowed people to disturb and wound her without even frowning. It was the baby she had hurt.

Still carrying him in her arms, she walked into the kitchen. Maria, the housekeeper, was standing at the sink, filling the percolator with water. She glanced at Jean, her

> "They're not working, she thought. The legs are still not working."

eyes glassy and aglow. Jean stopped abruptly. The woman had no way of knowing, had been out of the apartment when it happened. Jean went to the high chair and propped the baby inside its arms; he was still as limp as string. She had to take his hands from her shoulder finger by finger, but this time he did not cry. He looked at her with his round flat eyes which she had never been able to penetrate; his happy eyes, like buttons. He had always been a happy baby and she had known it was at least partly because she mothered him well, flying to satisfy his demands, giving up her sleep and her freedom too willingly and gladly, as though they had never meant anything at all.

"Will you give him his breakfast, please, Maria? It's so early, I'm going back to bed."

In the hall, she thought, I will wake up John and tell him what happened, and he will tell me what to do. She opened the bedroom door and the cold breeze from the window lapped against her ankles. Her husband, darkly bundled, lay in the middle of the bed. She stood with the doorknob in her hand, squeezing and turning it. It seemed to her that he must hear the sound and wake up, but he did not stir. She could not see his face, and she wished he would turn over so that she could at least see his eyes, which were generally kind. But he did not move. She had looked at him the evening before, intending to tell him, even imagining a scene with some tears but final comfort; looking at him, she had felt something fearful and cringing rise up inside her, authoritative, too, as though it possessed the final wisdom: do not tell him. No, never tell him. It was as though she had taken a lover, a foul black passion, and must guard with all her strength against the relief of revelation. John had remarked that she was looking pale.

"No, never tell him."

She went out of the bedroom and closed the door. In the kitchen, Maria was talking to the baby. Jean listened to her soft, pattering voice. Borne along on the sound, she went to the front door and opened it. Maria will take care of him, she thought; he will be all right as long as he is with her. She rang the bell for the elevator. The morning paper was lying on the floor, crumpled, a fallen bird; she picked it up and laid it neatly on the bench.

In the elevator, she realized that she was not dressed and looked down at her short housecoat. It would pass; only her slippers gave her away. She took them off and put them in her pocket.

Outside, she felt the gritty pavement under her feet and was frightened. Dog filth and the litter from an overturned garbage pail lay along her way; smoking pyramids of dog filth, torn streamers of paper stained with hamburger blood. She placed each foot heavily, wondering how long it would be before she felt something wet. Crossing the street, she went into the park.

The smoky morning sky lay along the tops of the trees; looking up, she saw the sun burning a hole the size of a penny. The trampled grass, shaggy as an old dog's coat, was lifting a blade at a time. She remembered spreading the plaid wool shawl here for the baby and herding him in from the edges; his white shoes had been as clean when they went as they had been at the start. Walking a little farther, she reached a point where one path led into the interior. The path she always took with the baby stretched along the edge of the street. The other, inside path was rutted from tree roots, and the only bench she could see had lost one of its legs. She had never hesitated before: the choice had been made for her by the sight of the baby's white bonnet, nodding like a peony inside the carriage hood. Now she took the broken path.

"Awkwardly, she pushed herself up off the bench and followed."

It was very early; she had passed one man with a dog, but otherwise the park was empty. Empty, but edged with the sounds and odd half-animate rustlings; she saw a squirrel move down a tree trunk with small crippled feet. She stopped to look back, wondering what the animal expected. His tail was as thin as an old feather. His eyes, however, were shining, and she hurried on, remembering the crib animals at the rail. She thought she heard the squirrel coming after her, on light crippled feet, and turned to shout and wave him away. A small man, muffled in a coat, passed her quickly, his breeze fanning her cheek.

She was so startled she sat down on the broken bench. Above the tops of the trees, the apartment buildings raised their crenelated towers; she looked the other way and saw the little man, hurrying on his small feet, turn the corner and disappear. Awkwardly, she pushed herself up off the bench and followed.

She was out of her territory at once; the plaid shawl had never been spread on these grassy places. She was astonished by the thickness of growth—weeds, mosses, trees; the park, abandoned, had grown up like the back fields of a lost farm. Purple nettles, their heads as big as apples, stood at the edge of the path. The sidewalk, cracked and cracked again by shadows, ran in semicircles down

into a little valley where a dry fountain lay half full of leaves.

At the edge of the pool, she stopped. A marble cupid, its flesh green with mold, raised an amputated elbow toward her. Its eyes were marked in the center by straight slits, like a cat's. Jean stood still and waited. Under her feet, the warm sidewalk grew cool and she imagined the green mold starting there and spreading around her like a shallow pool. The sounds of the city, sifted through the leaves, were as remote as summer thunder. She stood until her thighs began to ache, and then she sat down quickly on the lip of the pool.

She knew that she was being watched from the trees, and she sat carefully, her short robe drawn over her knees. Staring into the leaf-filled pool, she showed the back of her neck, bare and white, between her hair and the edge of her collar. As he watched from the shadow, he would catch the glint of white skin. Waiting, she began slowly to freeze, until she knew that soon she would be unable to lift her hand. She moved her head slightly, adjusting it for the last time, and saw that the cupid had a chain of beer-can tops around his neck.

As she waited, a blade of sunlight stretched slowly across the pavement, approaching her feet. After a long time, its point touched her toes, and she saw that she was shod in filth; only her insteps were still white. Revolted, she stood up. She had always hated dirt, any form of dirt, but public dirt collected from the feet of other people was intolerable. As she started purposefully back, she saw the trees, coalesced against her, shrouding the small black hole where the path ran toward the street.

Suddenly, she was afraid. Wishing could make anything happen, might already have set the disaster on its course. She stood prepared to defend herself and examined the ranks of trees. If he was watching, he must see that she was ready, her bare neck hidden now, her fists gripped. She remembered that he had been very small and thought that her assurance alone might quell him. But the wish, the terrible self-fulfilling wish for pain and mutilation still hung in the air above her like a beacon. She knew that he would see it and understand that her defences were only temporary. Panting, she began to walk slowly toward the entrance. Sweat ran down the insides of her arms, thick as honey. Her own smell, rank as the weeds', tortured her with its implications; animals, in danger, give off a hot rich stench. Moving carefully, on lead feet, she

> "She knew that she was being watched from the trees, and she sat carefully . . ."

began to believe that if she could reach the trees, she would be safe. It occured to her to run, but remotely, dreamily. She kept repeating, doggedly, that she did not want anything to happen, although she knew that her doubt would flash through as her bare neck had flashed, inviting the blow.

Shadows fell over her as heavily; she had reached the trees. She panted. The trees were around her now and she could no longer feel the weight of his eyes. He would be moving closer, in order to keep her in view. Lifting her knees, she began at last to run, jogging clumsily, her breasts jerking. Her body inside the housecoat was loose and thick as jelly, and she imagined her stomach dropping to her knees. Perhaps if he saw that she had borne a child, he would spare her. At that she began to run more quickly.

Dashing, her flesh quickening, she left the shade of the trees. Below the embankment, a bus stopped and passed on. She could see the faces of the passengers at their windows, and she wanted to call and hold her hands out to them. Running down the slope, she nearly collided with a large woman leading a brace of hounds. The woman muttered and scowled as Jean stared at her. Jean crossed the street, skipping through a stream of cars, and heard their wild cries remotely. Her own building shone in a special patch of sun. She rushed in and flung herself into the open elevator.

As soon as she opened the door of the apartment, she knew that she was too late. The smell of frying bacon still hung in the air, but the baby's dishes were heaped in the sink and his bib was lying like a fallen flag on the floor. She went from room to room, looking carefully, but she knew they had already gone.

Sinking down on the kitchen floor, she fixed her eyes on the linoleum. The history of the apartment, replacing her life, streamed around her, and she wondered if anyone else out of the dozens who had lived there had ever crouched down on the kitchen floor. She remembered picking out the tiles, with much effort and indecision; she remembered her satisfaction as they were laid down. Now the bright blue was melting into the old tiles beneath it and the floor was turning mud-colored again. She had imagined when they had first moved in that she would make a life consciously chosen in every detail, and she had put her hand on her stomach to feel the baby's light kick, sure that this was the first great choice and that the rest would follow. There had been a clear connection between the

"As soon as she opened the door of the apartment, she knew she was too late."

135

daisies she had arranged and her passion for her husband, between the pablum she had prepared and the love for the baby that had gradually grown and engulfed all the rest.

I loved him too much, she thought, and that is why they have taken him away.

Time passed: she heard the big electric clock draw its hand through several numbers. She did not dare to raise her eyes from the floor, and the back of her neck and her knees began to ache. She thought that if they found her like that, kneeling, they might forgive her. When she heard the front door open, however, she sprang to her feet, and screamed because of the cramped pain in her knees.

"Jean?" her husband called.

"I loved him too much, she thought, and that is why they have taken him away."

She ran down the dark hall which lengthened in front of her, a tunnel with their faces at the end. The baby, wrapped in a blanket, lay in the crook of Maria's arm; when he saw his mother's face, he began to cry, reaching out for her with both hands. Still too far away to touch him, she held out her arms, and her husband took the child and placed him in her hands. She did not dare to move him closer; she held him out at the ends of her arms, which trembled under his weight.

John pressed the baby against her chest, and she saw Maria's face, dark, without any smile. She turned to look at her husband. His hands, at her back and the baby's back, held them clamped together, but he was looking away. "He's all right, isn't he?" she asked softly.

"It was just a bruise, wasn't it? Neither of them answered. "Then what was it?" she asked, her voice rising.

"The doctor couldn't find anything wrong," John said finally. "He examined him, but he couldn't find anything wrong."

"But he couldn't walk! This morning—" She stopped herself.

Maria lifted the baby out of her arms and set him on the floor. He stumbled forward, his hands stretched toward the gleaming doorknob.

Jean sobbed.

"It's all right now," John said, touching her arm.

"But what happened?"

John looked away. The gap of their silent understanding widened between them; Jean knew they would never speak of what she had done.

The baby reached the doorknob and was patting it with his hand.

A C T I V I T I E S

**Children at Risk
pp. 127–136**

1. In your journal write your reactions to one of the selections in this part of the unit or write your own views on the topic of child abuse.

2. a) In a small group read the definition of abuse from the Ontario Ministry of Community and Social Services pamphlet.

b) As a group decide which category describes the abuse suffered by the narrator of "Luka," and by the child in "Fear."

c) With the others in your group make up a Charter of Rights for Children based on the abuse definition and what you read in "Luka," and "Fear." (See the Glossary, page 208, for definition of Charter of Rights.)

3. Write a letter to the narrator of "Luka" giving advice on how to deal with present and future abuse. Discuss your ideas with a partner before you begin to write and have your partner help you revise your draft letter.

4. Discuss with a partner how you felt about the mother in "Fear" and how you felt about the "cover-up" of the abuse. With the same partner role-play an interview between the mother and a counsellor she has gone to for help in preventing a repetition of what happened.

5. Set up an interview with a police officer, social worker, or children's aid worker to find out about his or her experiences with child abuse. Write a report on your interview and present it to the class.

or

Invite one of the people mentioned above to come to your class to talk on the topic of child abuse in your community.

6. Have a debate on one of the following resolutions:
- Children are the responsibility of their parents to be disciplined as the parents see fit.
- Therapy for child abusers is a more effective way of dealing with the abuser than criminal prosecution.

See the Student Handbook, page 187, for suggested debate procedures.

ILLITERACY: THE HUMAN COSTS ARE STAGGERING

DAVID SUZUKI

Books are a constant source of joy and stimulation to me. As my children were growing up, I took it for granted that they too would learn how to read and write. I simply assumed that high levels of literacy and education are facts of life in Canadian society. I was amazed, then, to discover that, for a significant portion of our population, these assumptions don't hold true.

The statistics are shocking: nearly five million Canadian adults read below the Grade 9 level, and one million can neither read nor write at all. These numbers cannot be explained away geographically because 70 per cent of illiterate Canadian adults live in urban areas and, consequently, are near learning facilities. Nor does the high rate of illiteracy relate to immigration—70 per cent of our illiterate adults were born in Canada.

It might be thought that in our era of electronic telecommunications, the need for literacy and books is not as great as it once was. Does it really matter any more whether we can read or not? The answer is a resounding *yes*. As Ken Dryden, the famed goalie of the Montreal Canadiens who recently served as Ontario Youth Commissioner, points out, "Most employers are looking for two things: experience and education," he says. "Since employers don't have

the time to interview 10 different people for the same job, they take shortcuts in the screening and selection process; one of the easiest routes is to eliminate applicants who do not have adequate education or literacy levels." Small wonder then that 60 per cent of illiterate Canadians are chronically unemployed.

Alarmingly, many of them are young Canadians. Says Dryden: "I think the biggest shock I had as Ontario Youth Commissioner was finding out that fewer than 60 per cent of young people in the province graduate from Grade 12. When I was in high school, I imagined that as I moved from grade to grade so did everyone else. But, in fact, it wasn't true then, and it certainly isn't true now."

Illiteracy has a ripple effect in both business and society as a whole. Janet Turnbull, vice-president of Seal Books in Toronto, remembers receiving a telephone call from John O'Leary, the head of Frontier College, a couple of years ago. O'Leary, who was trying to raise funds for the literacy-promoting organization, filled Turnbull in on illiteracy in Canada; he then asked for a $500 donation. "I'll do more than that—this problem is really hurting my industry," the publisher responded. "I went to see John, and by the end of our three-hour conversation I realized that illiteracy was hurting

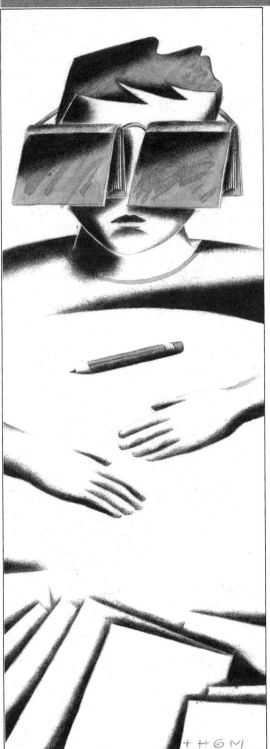

a lot more people than just those in my business." As a result, Janet Turnbull became the driving force behind forming the Canadian Business Task Force on Literacy and the Canadian Give the Gift of Literacy Foundation, two non-profit groups that are making us more aware of the extent and the consequences of illiteracy in Canada and that are actively doing something about the problem.

The cost of illiteracy to an individual is immense. We live in a society in which much of our communication is based on print. People who are illiterate cannot read a job application; if they hold jobs, they cannot read instructions, regulations or warnings. Even such matter-of-fact undertakings as looking up a number in a telephone directory or finding out what's on television are beyond the scope of the illiterate. "If we don't have the basic skills of reading and writing, we are rendered victims," says Dorothy Ungerleider, a California educational therapist and author of *Reading, Writing and Rage*. "Once when I was shopping in a market in Israel, I was unable to read any of the labels on the food packages. Suddenly I was seized with a sense of powerlessness. I felt I had lost control over my own destiny." Her momentary, foreign experience approximates what illiterate people go through every day.

Human beings are the greatest symbol users. The development of a written language for communication is one of the towering achievements of our species. It has enabled us to store vast amounts of information and knowledge and to pass it on to successive generations. With the advent of inexpensive, accessible print, all of recorded thought—our dreams, songs, poetry, history, philosophy and science—is accessible to everyone, *so long as one can read*. The real tragedy of illiteracy is being excluded from this wonderful, enriching and precious dimension of being human.

from

BLEAK HOUSE

~

CHARLES DICKENS

It must be a strange state to be like Jo. To shuffle through the streets, unfamiliar with the shapes, and in utter darkness as to the meaning, of those mysterious symbols, so abundant over the shops, and at the corners of streets, and on the doors, and in the windows! To see people read, and to see people write, and to see postmen deliver letters, and not to have the least idea of all that language—to be, to every scrap of it, stone blind and dumb! It must be very puzzling to see the good company going to church on Sundays, with their books in their hands and to think (for perhaps Jo *does* think at odd times) what does it all mean, and if it means anything to anybody, how comes it means nothing to me?

LEARNING TO READ AND WRITE

CINDY PRINCE

(Cindy is a student at Frontier College, Toronto)

Learning to read and write is not the end of the rope. It is one of the greatest things in life you can do for yourself.

Canada is a country which requires education. If you cannot read, you feel like a fish out of water. The best part is when you don't give up and you keep trying, because in this country everybody is so busy nobody has time to sit down and write for another.

I agree it is very embarrassing after reaching a certain age when you should be doing something else you have to learn to read and write. But once you get it in, no one can take it out. If you don't have it, someone will push you around.

I didn't get a chance to go to school the right way because I had to take care of my brothers and sisters.

I didn't realize how important education was until I got older, started travelling and meeting different kinds of people.

COMIC STRIPS TOO LITERATE FOR SOME

The whimsy of comic strips such as Herman and Hagar the Horrible seems to have lost its hold on adults who have trouble reading newspapers.

Once considered the main domain of readers who cannot or choose not to plow through editorials or stories about the shenanigans at city hall, the comic section is turned to considerably more often by richer and better educated adults.

More than half (51 per cent) of the respondents in the Southam Literacy Survey who are literate say they take a peek at strips like Doonesbury or try to figure out what's going on in the The Far Side or the even more bizarre Bizarro.

But only a little more than one-third (35 per cent) of illiterates who read the paper check out the increasingly sophisticated comic section.

And looking only at basic illiterates—those who have profound problems with reading and writing—30 per cent turn to the comics, even less than the 32 per cent of basic illiterates who say they read the editorial pages.

Overall, about three-quarters of newspaper readers say they regularly read about local, provincial, national and international events. At the low end of the scale, 19 per cent say they turn to the stock listings.

On average, literate adults who get the paper look at half of the 16 categories offered, one more than illiterates. Broken down by topic, literates read 13 subject areas more often.

Illiterates more often read about sports (54 to 50 per cent), horoscopes (51 to 49 per cent) and television listings (48 to 44 per cent).

Findings that show illiterates weekly watch an average of 19.2 hours compared to 15.5 hours for literates explain the difference in the search for what's on TV.

By Johnny Hart

B.C.

THE ABCs OF COURAGE

BOB GREENE

It is nearing dusk. The man has finished his day's labour; he is a plumber, and today he was working at a construction site, and his shift has ended.

Now he is sitting in the dining room of Mrs. Patricia Lord, in Cicero, Illinois. Mrs. Lord and the man are bending over a list of words.

"Can you try these now?" Mrs. Lord says.

"Yes," the man says.

He looks at the top word on the list. The word is *is*.

"Is," the man says.

"Yes," Mrs. Lord says.

The next word on the list is *brown*.

The man looks at it for a moment. Then he says: "Brown."

"Yes," Mrs. Lord says.

The next word is *the*.

"The," the man says, touching the word with his hand.

"Yes," Mrs. Lord says.

The next word is *sleep*.

The man hesitates. Seconds pass. He is having trouble with this one.

Finally he says: "Play?"

"No," Mrs. Lord says. "Look at it again."

The man stares. He says nothing. Then he says, "I don't know what it is."

"All right," Mrs. Lord says softly, "Skip it and come back to it later."

The man is fifty-five years old. He is trying to learn how to read. He is a large man, balding and wearing thick glasses; he bears a resemblance to the actor Ernest Borgnine. His plumber's work clothes—denim overalls, a flannel shirt—are still on. Today, as he does twice a week, he has driven straight from work to Mrs. Lord's house. His hands are dirty from his day's labour; as he points to the words on the spelling list you can see that he has not had time to stop and clean up. He has been coming to Mrs. Lord's house for just over a year.

The next word on the list is *down*.

"Down," the man says with confidence in his voice.

"That's right," Mrs. Lord says. "Very good."

The man—we will not name him here, because he has asked us not to—never learned to read as a child. His mother was sick and his father was an alcoholic; the boy did not do well in school, and at the age of twelve he dropped out and began to work. Sometimes his mother would try to teach him something; his father, if he had been drinking, would say, "What the hell are you bothering to teach him for? He don't know nothing.

The man went through most of his life hiding his secret. He learned to be a plumber; he married and started a family. He concealed his inability to read even from his wife and children; his wife did all the paper-work around the house, read all the mail, handled all the correspondence.

A year and a half ago, the man lost a job because he could not read. The company he was working for required each employee to take a written test about safety procedures. The man knew the rules, but could not read the questions. The company allowed him to take the test over, but he didn't have a chance. He couldn't admit the real problem.

Out of work, he felt panic. He heard that a local community college was offering a nighttime course in reading improvement. He enrolled. But as early as the first evening he realized that the course was meant for people who at least knew the basics of read-ing. After a few sessions he approached the teacher after class.

"I know you can't read," the teacher said to him. "If you'd like to keep coming just to see what you can pick up, it's all right."

Instead, the man went to a dime store and bought a book called *Reading Fun* for ninety-three cents. The book was designed for pre-school-aged children. On the pages of the book were simple, colorful pictures of ambulances and taxis and trucks, followed by the proper word for each picture. He looked at the pages and tried to teach him-self. He couldn't.

Finally, he sat down with his wife. "You know when I lost my job?" he said. And he told her he couldn't read.

Time went by. On television, he heard a public service announcement about private tutoring offered by the Literacy Volunteers of Chicago. He called up and explained about himself. The person on the other end of the line said that there were no suitable vol-unteers available at the moment. The man left his name.

Four months later, while he was out of the house, the literacy organization called. When the man arrived back at home, his wife said she had some news for him.

"There's a teacher for you," his wife said. "Her name is Pat."

Patricia Lord, fifty-nine, remembers the first time he showed up at her door.

"He was such a nice man," she said. "At first I didn't realize how deep his problem was. But it soon became clear—he didn't even know the alphabet."

So, twice a week, they started to work together. "He was so grateful," Mrs. Lord said. "I do this for free, but he kept saying that if I ever needed any plumbing done, even if it was an emergency in the middle of the night, he would do it for nothing."

She taught him the alphabet. She taught him how to print letters. She taught him the first words other than his own name that he had ever known how to read or write.

"We work with reading cards," she said. "He picks out the words that look interest-ing to him, and I'll teach him. One of the

far off in the future, though. I have a second-grade spelling puzzle book, and even that's way too advanced for him right now.

"But he's making progress. There's a list of about forty words that he knows now. When a lesson goes well, he is definitely elated. He'll smile at the end of the session, and he'll get more talkative than usual, and he'll just seem . . . lighter. I can tell that he's feeling good about it."

In the time since he started studying with Mrs. Lord, the man has found a new job. His employers do not know that he cannot read; he is deathly afraid that they will find out and that he will be fired again.

"I never liked to hear anyone called a dummy," he said. "Even when I was a kid, I didn't like it. In fact I once beat up another kid for calling a boy a dummy.

"Let's face it, though, when you work construction, the others would be embarrassed to work with you if they knew you couldn't read—wouldn't they? If they found out about me, I think they'd make it hard on me. Some people get their kicks like that."

He said it was losing the other job that convinced him he had to learn how to read. That, and something else.

"I've got a little granddaughter," he said, "I never want her to come up to me and say, 'Grandpa, read this,' and I can't do it. I already went through life not being able to read to my own children. I want to be able to read to my granddaughter."

He said he was proud of how far he had come in his life without knowing how to read. "I can take a blueprint and figure out how a whole building works," he said. "I built my own house. I think that's a pretty good accomplishment for a man who can't read. That, and going this far in my trade."

Still, he has always known how large the gap in his life was.

"All my life, I've wanted so badly to be able to read something," he said. "I've had to pretend, all my life. When I would go into

words he wanted to learn, for instance, was *chocolate*. He was fascinated by it because it was longer than most of the other words on the cards. So we learned it."

There are books scattered all over Mrs. Lord's home—*The Fate of the Earth*, by Jonathan Schell; *Findings*, by Leonard Bernstein; *Schindler's List*, by Thomas Keneally.

"I tried to explain to him about the pleasures of reading," she said. "It's something he's never known. I've always gotten so much information and so much joy from reading, but when I try to explain that to him, it's almost beyond what he can imagine. When I was young, I had a friend, and we'd go sit together in the park and just read for hours, and talk about what we were reading. The idea of something like that seems to intrigue him.

"I tell him that one of these days he'll be able to read a book," Mrs. Lord said. "That's a restaurant with people from the job. I would hold the menu up and pretend to be reading it. But I didn't understand a word. I'd always ask the waitress what the specials were, and when she'd say them I'd choose one of them. Or I'd order something that I knew every restaurant had.

"It was something I thought about all the time, but who could you go talk to? Many's the time that I wished I could read something. But I knew there couldn't be too many people willing to help a person like me, so I just did my best to keep it a secret."

"I've never written a letter in my life. When the holidays came, it was very hard for me to pick out a card for my wife. I'd look at the cards, but I'd have no idea what they said. So I'd buy her a flower instead."

Now that he is studying with Mrs. Lord, he said, he can at least hope that things will change.

"I dream that before long I can really read something," he said. "It doesn't have to be a lot, but just to be able to read something from start to finish would be enough. Mrs. Lord tells me that once you start to read, it comes easier all the time.

"It scares me that there's a possibility I can't do it. I'm fifty-five years old, after all. I get disgusted with myself if I have a bad day here and I miss a lot of words.

"But when there's been a good day I'll feel great at the end of our lesson. I'll go home and tell my wife, 'I learned this word.' Or I'll say, 'Teacher says I have good handwriting.' And then my wife and I will work on the spelling cards."

He said that, because he is working again, sometimes he will have to skip tutoring sessions. "It kills me when that happens," he said. "But the construction business is pretty good right now, and sometimes in the afternoon the boss will tell me that he needs me to work overtime. I can't tell him why I have to be here. So I'll go off to a pay phone and call Mrs. Lord and give her the bad news.

"I think about reading even when I'm at work, though. I'll be working, but I'll be reciting the alphabet in my head. I keep the spelling cards in my truck, and if it's time for a coffee break I'll go out there and work on my words."

He said that, before he started trying to learn to read, he never picked up a newspaper or a magazine. "Now I like to pick them up and look at them," he said. "I think to myself that maybe someday I can read them.

"And I'll go into a store now and pick up books. I'll pick up the ones that have covers that look interesting. And then I'll flip through them until I see some words that I know. Most of the pages are filled with words that I don't know. But then I'll see some words that Mrs. Lord taught me—*an* or *is* or *the*—and I'll stare at them. It feels so good to know them."

It is getting darker outside. The man has been up since before dawn. His truck is parked outside Mrs. Lord's house; motorists pass by on their way home.

At the dining room table, Mrs. Lord is helping him to write a sentence. "Let's try 'The cow is brown,'" she says. "First word *the*."

The man checks his list of words. Then, on a clean sheet of paper, he writes: *The*.

"Good," Mrs. Lord says. "Next word, *cow*."

He checks his list and writes the word.

"Very good," Mrs. Lord says. "Now *is*."

That word he knows easily. He writes it.

"Now *brown*," Mrs. Lord says.

He thinks for a second, then writes *brown* at the end of the sentence he has built.

"Right!" Mrs. Lord says. "End of sentence!"

The man looks up. There is something very close to pride in his eyes.

"I can't wait until I can write a letter." he says. "The first letter I write is going to be to my wife. I'm going to tell her how much I love her."

A C T I V I T I E S

1. In these selections, each author is writing about the topic of literacy. Work with a partner, and for each selection, discuss what point the writer is making about literacy and whether the point is made effectively.

Moving Toward Literacy
pp. 138–146

2. With a partner reread "The ABCs of Courage." Write a script for either a TV or a radio commercial that sells the idea of literacy classes to people who cannot read very well. Record your commercial and play it to another group. Ask the other group to evaluate its effectiveness.

3. In a journal entry, list ways that your daily life would be changed if you could not read or write. Compare your list with a partner's.

4. Be an investigative reporter. Research the statistics on illiteracy in your province (in particular, for the number of teenagers), and write a letter to the editor of your local newspaper. You might include the names of organizations in your community that assist people to learn to read and write.

AFTER THE SIRENS

HUGH HOOD

"This is an air-raid warning. We will be attacked in fifteen minutes."

hey heard the sirens first about four forty-five in the morning. It was still dark and cold outside and they were sound asleep. They heard the noise first in their dreams and, waking, understood it to be real.

"What is it?" she asked him sleepily, rolling over in their warm bed. "Is there a fire?"

"I don't know," he said. The sirens were very loud. "I've never heard anything like that before."

"It's some kind of siren," she said, "downtown. It woke me up."

"Go back to sleep!" he said. "It can't be anything."

"No," she said, "I'm frightened. I wonder what it is. I wonder if the baby has enough covers." The wailing was still going on. "It couldn't be an air-raid warning, could it?"

"Of course not," he said reassuringly, but she could hear the indecision in his voice.

"Why don't you turn on the radio," she said, "just to see? Just to make sure. I'll go and see if the baby's covered up." They walked down the hall in their pajamas. He went into the kitchen, turned on the radio and waited for it to warm up. There was nothing but static and hum.

"What's that station?" he called to her. "Conrad, or something like that."

"That's 640 on the dial," she said, from the baby's room. He twisted the dial and suddenly the radio screamed at him frightening him badly.

"This is not an exercise. This is not an exercise. This is not an exercise," the radio blared. *"This is an air-raid warning. This is an air-raid warning. We will be attacked in fifteen minutes. We will be attacked in fifteen minutes. This is not an exercise."* He recognized the voice of a local announcer who did an hour of breakfast music daily. He had never heard the man talk like that before. He ran into the baby's room while the radio shrieked behind him: *"We will be attacked in fifteen minutes. Correction. Correction. In four-*

teen minutes. In fourteen minutes. We will be attacked in fourteen minutes. This is not an exercise."

"Look," he said, "don't ask me any questions, please, just do exactly what I tell you and don't waste any time." She stared at him with her mouth open. "Listen," he said, "and do exactly as I say. They say this is an air-raid and we'd better believe them." She looked frightened nearly out of her wits. "I'll look after you," he said; "just get dressed as fast as you can. Put on as many layers of wool as you can. Got that?"

She nodded speechlessly.

"Put on your woollen topcoat and your fur coat over that. Get as many scarves as you can find. We'll wrap our faces and hands. When you're dressed, dress the baby the same way. We have a chance, if you do as I say without wasting time." She ran off up the hall to the coat closet and he could hear her pulling things about.

"This will be an attack with nuclear weapons. You have thirteen minutes to take cover," screamed the radio. He looked at his watch and hurried to the kitchen and pulled a cardboard carton from under the sink. He threw two can openers into it and all the canned goods he could see. There were three loaves of bread in the breadbox and he crammed them into the carton. He took everything that was wrapped and solid in the refrigerator and crushed it in. When the carton was full he took a bucket which usually held a garbage bag, rinsed it hastily, and filled it with water. There was a plastic bottle in the refrigerator. He poured the tomato juice out of it and rinsed it and filled it with water.

"This will be a nuclear attack." The disc jockey's voice was cracking with hysteria. *"You have nine minutes, nine minutes, to take cover. Nine minutes."* He ran into the dark hall and bumped into his wife who was swaddled like a bear.

"Go and dress the baby," he said. "We're going to make it, we've just got time. I'll go and get dressed." She was crying, but there was no time for comfort. In the bedroom he forced himself into his trousers, a second pair of trousers, two shirts and two sweaters. He put on the heaviest, loosest jacket he owned, a topcoat, and finally his overcoat. This took him just under five minutes. When he rejoined his wife in the living room, she had the baby swaddled in her arms, still asleep.

"Go to the back room in the cellar, where your steamer trunk is," he said," and take this." He gave her a flashlight

which they kept in their bedroom. When she hesitated he said roughly, "Go on, get going."

"Aren't you coming?"

"Of course I'm coming," he said, he turned the radio up as far as it would go and noted very carefully what the man said. *"This will be a nuclear attack. The target will probably be the aircraft company. You have three minutes to take cover."* He picked up the carton and balanced the bottle of water on it. With the other hand he carried the bucket. Leaving the kitchen door wide open, he went to the cellar, passed through the dark furnace room, and joined his wife.

"Put out the flashlight," he said." "We'll have to save it. We have a minute or two, so listen to me." They could hear the radio upstairs. *"Two minutes,"* it screamed.

"Lie down in the corner of the west and north walls," he said quickly. "The blast should come from the north if they hit the target and the house will blow down and fall to the south. Lie on top of the baby and I'll lie on top of you!"

"We're going to die right now . . ."

She cuddled the sleeping infant in her arms. "We're going to die right now," she said, as she held the baby closer to her.

"No, we aren't," he said, "we have a chance. Wrap the scarves around your face and the baby's, and lie down." She handed him a plaid wollen scarf and he tied it around his face so that only his eyes showed. He placed the water and food in a corner and then lay down on top of his wife, spreading his arms and legs as much as possible, to cover and protect her.

"Twenty seconds," shrieked the radio. *"Eighteen seconds. Fifteen."*

He looked at his watch as he fell. "Ten seconds," he said aloud. "It's five o'clock. They won't waste a megaton bomb on us. They'll save it for New York." They heard the radio crackle into silence and they hung onto each other, keeping their eyes closed tightly.

Instantaneously the cellar room lit up with a kind of glow they had never seen before, the earthen floor began to rock and heave, and the absolutely unearthly sound began. There was no way of telling how far off it was, the explosion. The sound seemed to be inside them, in their bowels; the very air itself was shattered and blown away in the dreadful sound that went on and on and on.

They held their heads down, hers pushed into the dirt, shielding the baby's scalp, his face crushed into her hair, nothing of their skin exposed to the glow, and the sound went on and on, pulsing curiously, louder than anything they had ever imagined, louder than deafening, quaking in their eardrums, louder and louder until it seemed that what had exploded was there in the room on top of them in a blend of smashed, torn air, cries of the instantly dead, fall of steel, timber, and brick, crash of masonry and glass— they couldn't sort any of it out—all were there, all imaginable noises of destruction synthesized. It was like absolutely nothing they had ever heard before and it so filled their skulls, pushing outward from the brainpan, that they could not divide it into its parts. All that they could understand, if they understood anything, was that this was the ultimate catastrophe, and that they were still recording it, expecting any second to be crushed into blackness, but as long as they were recording it they were still living. They felt, but did not think, this. They only understood it instinctively and held on tighter to each other, waiting for the smash, the crush, the black.

But it became lighter and lighter, the glow in the cellar room, waxing and intensifying itself. It had no colour that they recognized through their tightly-shut eyelids. It might have been called green, but it was not green, nor any neighbour of green. Like the noise, it was a dreadful compound of ultimately destructive fire, blast, terrible energy released from a bursting sun, like the birth of the solar system. Incandescence beyond an infinite number of lights swirled around them.

The worst was the nauseous rocking to and fro of the very earth beneath them, worse than an earthquake, which might have seemed reducible to human dimensions, those of some disaster witnessed in the movies or on television. But this was no gaping, opening seam in the earth, but a threatened total destruction of the earth itself, right to its core, a pulverization of the world. They tried like animals to scrabble closer and closer in under the north cellar wall even as they expected it to fall on them. They kept their heads down, waiting for death to take them as it had taken their friends, neighbours, fellow workers, policemen, firemen, soldiers; and the dreadful time passed and still they did not die in the catastrophe. And they began to sense obscurely that the longer they were left uncrushed, the better grew their chances of survival. And pitifully slowly their feelings began to resume their customary segmented play amongst themselves, while the event was still unfolding. They could not help doing the characteristic, the human

> **"But this was no gaping, opening seam in the earth, but a threatened total destruction of the earth itself . . ."**

thing, the beginning to think and to struggle to live.

Through their shut eyelids the light began to seem less incandescent, more recognizably a colour familiar to human beings and less terrifying because it might be called a hue of green instead of no-colour-at-all. It became green, still glowing and illuminating in the cellar like daylight, but anyway green, nameable as such and therefore familiar and less dreadful. The light grew more darkly green in an insane harmony with the rocking and the sound.

As the rocking slowed, as they huddled closer and closer in under the north foundation, a split in the cellar wall showed itself almost in front of their hidden faces, and yet the wall stood and did not come in on top of them. It held and, holding, gave them more chance for survival although they didn't know it. The earth's upheaval slowed

and sank back and no gaps appeared in the earth under them, no crevasse to swallow them up under the alteration of the earth's crust. And in time the rocking stopped and the floor of their world was still, but they would not move, afraid to move a limb for fear of being caught in the earth's mouth.

The noise continued, but began to distinguish itself in parts, and the worst basic element attenuated itself; that terrible crash apart of the atmosphere under the bomb had stopped by now, the atmosphere had parted to admit the ball of radioactivity, had been blown hundreds of miles in every direction and had rushed back to regain its place, disputing that place with the ball of radioactivity, so that there grew up a thousand-mile vortex of cyclonic winds around the hub of the displacement. The cyclone was almost comforting, sounding, whistling, in whatever stood upright, not trees certainly, but tangled steel beams and odd bits of masonry. The sound of these winds came to them in the cellar. Soon they were able to name sounds, and distinguish them from others which they heard, mainly sounds of fires—no sounds of the dying, no human cries at all, no sounds of life. Only the fires and cyclonic winds.

Now they could feel, and hear enough to shout to each other over the fire and wind.

The man tried to stir, to ease his wife's position. He could move his torso so far as the waist or perhaps the hips. Below that, although he was in no pain and not paralyzed, he was immobilized by a heavy weight. He could feel his legs and feet; they were sound and unhurt, but he could not move them. He waited, lying there trying to sort things out, until some sort of ordered thought and some communication was possible, when the noise should lessen sufficiently. He could hear his wife shouting something into the dirt in front of her face and he tried to make it out.

"She slept through it," he heard, "she slept through it," and he couldn't believe it, although it was true. The baby lived and recollected none of the horror.

"She slept through it," screamed the wife idiotically, "she's still asleep." It couldn't be true, he thought, it was impossible, but there was no way to check her statement until they could move about. The baby must have been three feet below the blast and the glow, shielded by a two-and-a-half-foot wall of flesh, his and his wife's, and the additional thickness of layers of woollen clothing. She should certainly have survived, if they had, but how could she have slept through the noise, the awful light, and the rocking? He listened and waited, keeping his head down and his face covered.

Supposing that they had survived the initial blast, as seemed to be the case; there was still the fallout to consider. The likelihood, he thought (he was beginning to be able to think) was that they were already being eaten up by radiation and would soon die of monstrous cancers, or plain, simple leukemia, or rottenness of the cortex. It was miraculous that they had lived through the first shock; they could hardly hope that their luck would hold through the later dangers. He thought that the baby might not have been infected so far, shielded as she was, as he began to wonder how she might be helped to evade death from radiation in the next few days. Let her live a week, he

". . . she slept through it, and he couldn't believe it . . ."

thought, and she may go on living into the next generation, if there is one.

Nothing would be the same in the next generation; there would be few people and fewer laws, the national boundaries would have perished—there would be a new world to invent. Somehow the child must be preserved for that, even if their own lives were to be forfeited immediately. He felt perfectly healthy so far, untouched by any creeping sickness as he lay there, forcing himself and the lives beneath him deeper into their burrow. He began to make plans; there was nothing else for him to do just then.

The noise of the winds had become regular now and the green glow had subsided; the earth was still and they were still together and in the same place, in their cellar, in their home. He thought of his books, his checkbook, his phonograph records, his wife's household appliances. They were gone of course, which didn't matter. What mattered was that the way they had lived was gone, the whole texture of their habits. The city would be totally uninhabitable. If they were to survive longer, they must get out of the city at once. They would have to decide immediately when they should try to leave the city, and they must keep themselves alive until that time.

"What mattered was that the way they had lived was gone . . ."

"What time is it?" gasped his wife from below him in a tone pitched in almost her normal voice. He was relieved to hear her speak in the commonplace, familiar tone; he had been afraid that hysteria and shock would destroy their personalities all at once. So far they had held together. Later on, when the loss of their whole world sank in, when they appreciated the full extent of their losses, they would run the risk of insanity or, at least, extreme neurotic disturbance. But right now they could converse, calculate, and wait for the threat of madness to appear days, or years, later.

He looked at his watch. "Eight-thirty," he said. Everything had ended in three-and-a-half hours. "Are you all right?" he asked.

"I think so," she said, "I don't feel any pain and the baby's fine. She's warm and she doesn't seem frightened."

He tried to move his legs and was relieved to see that they answered the nervous impulse. He lifted his head fearfully and twisted it around to see behind him. His legs were buried under a pile of loose brick and rubble which grew smaller toward his thighs; his torso was quite uncovered. "I'm all right," he said, beginning to work his legs free; they were undoubtedly badly bruised, but they didn't

seem to be crushed or broken; at the worst he might have torn muscles or a bad sprain. He had to be very careful, he reasoned, as he worked at his legs. He might dislodge something and bring the remnant of the house down around them. Very, very slowly he lifted his torso by doing a push-up with his arms. His wife slid out from underneath, pushing the baby in front of her. When she was free she laid the child gently to one side, whispering to her and promising her food. She crawled around to her husband's side and began to push the bricks off his legs.

"Be careful," he whispered. "Take them as they come. Don't be in too much of a hurry."

She nodded, picking out the bricks gingerly, but as fast as she could. Soon he was able to roll over on his back and sit up. By a quarter to ten he was free and they took time to eat and drink. The three of them sat together in a cramped, narrow space under the cellar beams, perhaps six feet high and six or seven feet square. They were getting air from somewhere although it might be deadly air, and there was no smell of gas. He had been afraid that they might be suffocated in their shelter.

"Do you suppose the food's contaminated?" she asked.

"What if it is? he said. "So are we, just as much as the food. There's nothing to do but risk it. Only be careful what you give the baby."

"How can I tell?"

"I don't know," he said. "Say a prayer and trust in God." He found the flashlight which had rolled into a corner, and tried it. It worked very well.

"What are we going to do? We can't stay here."

"I don't even know for sure that we can get out," he said, "but we'll try. There should be a window just above us that leads to a crawl-space under the patio. That's one of the reasons why I told you to come here. In any case we'd be wise to stay here for a few hours until the very worst of the fallout is down."

"What'll we do when we get out?"

"Try to get out of town. Get our outer clothes off, get them all off for that matter, and scrub ourselves with water. Maybe we can get to the river."

"Why don't you try the window right now so we can tell whether we can get out?"

"I will as soon as I've finished eating and had a rest. My legs are very sore."

He could hear her voice soften. "Take your time," she said.

When he felt rested, he stood up. He could almost stand erect and with the flashlight was able to find the window quickly. It was level with his face. He piled loose bricks against the wall below it and climbed up on them until the window was level with his chest. Knocking out the screen with the butt of the flashlight, he put his head through and then flashed the light around; there were no obstructions that he could see, and he couldn't smell anything noxious. The patio, being a flat level space, had evidently been swept clean by the blast without being flattened. They could crawl out of the cellar under the patio, he realized, and then kick a hole in the lath and stucco which skirted it.

He stepped down from the pile of brick and told his wife that they would be able to get out whenever they wished, that the crawl space was clear.

"What time is it?"

"Half-past twelve."

"Should we try it now?"

"I think so," he said. "At first I thought we ought to stay here for a day or two, but now I think we ought to try and get out from under the fallout. We may have to walk a couple of hundred miles."

"We can do it," she said and he felt glad. She had always been able to look unpleasant issues in the face.

He helped her through the cellar window and handed up the baby, who clucked and chuckled when he spoke to her. He pushed the carton of food and the bucket of water after them. Then he climbed up and they inched forward under the patio.

"I hear a motor," said his wife suddenly.

He listened and heard it too.

"Looking for survivors," he said eagerly. "Probably the Army or Civil Defense. Come on."

He swung himself around on his hips and back and kicked out with both feet at the lath and stucco. Three or four kicks did it. His wife went first, inching the baby through the hole. He crawled after her into the daylight; it looked like any other day except that the city was leveled. The sky and the light were the same; everything else was gone. They sat up, muddy, scratched, nervously exhausted, in a ruined flower bed. Not fifty feet away stood an olive-drab truck, the motor running loudly. Men shouted to them.

"Come on, you!" shouted the men in the truck. "Get going!" They stood and ran raggedly to the cab, she hold-

"Try to get out of town. Get our outer clothes off . . ."

ing the child and he their remaining food and water. In the cab was a canvas-sheeted, goggled driver, peering at them through huge eyes. "Get in the back," he ordered. "We've got to get out right away. Too hot." They climbed into the truck and it began to move instantly.

"Army Survival Unit," said a goggled and hooded man in the back of the truck. "Throw away that food and water; it's dangerous. Get your outer clothing off quick. Throw it out!" They obeyed him without thinking, stripping off their loose outer clothes and dropping them out of the truck.

"You're the only ones we've found in a hundred city blocks," said the soldier. "Did you know the war's over? There's a truce."

"Who won?"

"Over in half an hour," he said, "and nobody won."

"What are you going to do with us?"

"Drop you at a check-out point forty miles from here. Give you the scrub-down treatment, wash off the fallout. Medical check for radiation sickness. Clean clothes. Then we send you on your way to a refugee station."

"How many died?"

"Everybody in the area. Almost no exceptions. You're a statistic, that's what you are. Must have been a fluke of the blast."

"Will we live?"

"Sure you will. You're living now, aren't you?"

"I guess so," he said.

"Sure you'll live! Maybe not too long. But everybody else is dead! And you'll be taken care of." He fell silent.

They looked at each other, determined to live as long as they could. The wife cuddled the child close against her thin silk blouse. For a long time they jolted along over rocks and broken pavement without speaking. When the pavement smoothed out the husband knew that they must be out of the disaster area. In a few more minutes they were out of immediate danger; they had reached the checkout point. It was a quarter to three in the afternoon.

"Out you get," said the soldier. "We've got to go back." They climbed out of the truck and he handed down the baby. "You're all right now," he said. "Good luck."

"Good-bye," they said.

The truck turned about and drove away and they turned silently, hand in hand, and walked toward the medical tents. They were the seventh, eighth, and ninth living persons to be brought there after the sirens.

> "Sure you'll live! Maybe not too long. But everybody else is dead!"

HEY DIDDLE DIDDLE

~

PAUL DEHN

Hey diddle diddle,
The physicists fiddle,
    The Bleep jumped over the moon.
The little dog laughed to see such fun
    And died the following June.

LITTLE MISS MUFFET

~

PAUL DEHN

Little Miss Muffet
Crouched on a tuffet,
Collecting her shell-shocked wits.
    There dropped (from a glider)
    An H-bomb beside her—
Which frightened Miss Muffet to bits.

THE MONUMENTS OF HIROSHIMA

D. J. ENRIGHT

The roughly estimated ones, who do not sort well with our
  common phrases,
Who are by no means eating roots of dandelion, or pushing up
  the daisies.

The more or less anonymous, to whom no human idiom can
  apply,
Who neither passed away, or on,
  nor went before, nor vanished on a sigh.

Little of peace for them to rest in, less of them to rest in peace:
Dust to dust·a swift transition, ashes to ash with awful ease.

Their only monument will be of other's casting—
A Tower of Peace, a Hall of Peace, a Bridge of Peace
  —who might have wished for something lasting,
Like a wooden box.

DISARMING TEENS

~

SUSAN DELACOURT

Over hoots and catcalls from 500 jeering classmates, a 14-year-old Windsor high school student stands up and announces confidently: "No one would be stupid enough to start a nuclear war."

He may not realize it, but he has just explained the theory of nuclear deterrence and mutual assured destruction. Before the next hour passes, he and the others will also talk about weapons proliferation, radioactive waste and the military-industrial complex.

He also may not know that his sentiment is without exception, the first thing that is always said to four Montreal teen-agers who are touring the country talking about nuclear peril in presentations that will reach one in every 20 Canadian high-school students by May.

Though their goal is nuclear disarmament, it is their poise and grasp of the issues that has done most of the disarming in Canada to date.

No rag-tag band of radicals, they are the 1980s version of peaceniks—well-groomed, straight-A students who are tackling an idealistic mission in businesslike fashion.

In their wake, they are leaving hundreds of new anti-nuclear youth organizations and, maybe more importantly, a new image of the peace movement . . . .

The four who are presiding over these emotional discussions almost every day are Alison Carpenter, 17, Maxime Faille, 17, Desiree McGraw, 17, and Seth Klein, 18.

Though the group has only completed half the tour (the next three months will be spent in the West) the four have seen enough to know that nuclear concerns have grabbed the attention of Canadian teen-agers.

Their impressions appear to confirm what McMaster University professor Dr. K. Ross Parker found in a 1985 study: that 93.3 per cent of Canadian secondary-school students feel they have little or no influence in preventing nuclear war.

The same students say the threat of nuclear war is one of their top concerns, second only to the welfare of their parents.

Though these four teen-agers are not among the young Canadians convinced that nuclear war is unavoidable, they are worried enough to take a year off school, away from their families, to warn other students about what they see as dangerous international arms policies.

Inspired by smaller-scale school presentations carried out by their home organization in Montreal, the seven-hundred-member Students against Global Extermination, the four embarked on their journey confident that they could inspire others to the same depth of feeling about disarmament.

Their parents were also very encouraging. As Seth puts it, "all of us were raised to believe that if there's an issue that concerns us, we have the ability to address it."

The Montreal co-ordinator of the tour is, in fact, Alison's mother, Georgia Carpenter.

The teen-agers have squeaked by financially with seed money from, among others, the Canadian Institute for Peace and Security, the Canadian Auto Workers and continuing boosts from T-shirt sales and $125 honoraria at almost every school they visit.

During their presentations, they use vivid images, illustrating the cost of the arms race by describing piles of money 75 kilometres high.

They offer chilling facts that send shudders through their young audiences. One of their oft-quoted statistics is borrowed from Dr. Helen Caldicott, who reports in the film If You Love This Planet that there is a computer failure every half hour in the mechanisms that control missile-launching in the United States.

For a generation raised on technology, with computers in homes and classrooms, these four teen-agers display severe mistrust of the software that controls the superpowers' nuclear arsenals.

"We wouldn't trust it with our lives," Desiree said. . . .

A measure of the tour's success has been the extraordinary number of students who have formed anti-nuclear organizations of their own. According to the group's calculations, this has happened in 90 per cent of the 125 communities they have visited.

At Brennan High School in Windsor this week, about 50 students stayed almost two hours after school to talk about nuclear issues with Seth and Max.

The philosophy behind the group's approach to debate may explain at least part of its success with fellow teen-agers.

"We don't want to get into a debate that has to end with a winner and a loser," Alison tells a crowd of 500 Grade 9 and 10 students. That is the same kind of sentiment that breeds war, the group noted later.

Nor do they want to encourage political battles.

In one school they visited this week, a young girl told them: "If Ronald Reagan is crazy enough to send arms to Iran, he's crazy enough to push the button."

"We're not here to talk about the sanity of Ronald Reagan or [Soviet leader] Mikhail Gorbachev," Desiree told her.

The appeal for political balance is a deliberate effort to avoid earlier mistakes of the peace movement, sometimes accused of being too hard on the Americans and too easy on the Soviets.

"I think we've really learned from the peace movement's mistakes. . . . We're trying to create something that's going to appeal to a broad population."

Although all four may have believed they knew plenty before they headed out on the road, the tour has moderated all their views.

"I have definitely had opposition in the audience that has made me re-evaluate my own stand," Seth says, and the other three nod.

Just as their stand has been toned down, so has their outlook widened. None of them believe they would be content to be disarmament ambassadors forever, mentioning child abuse and battered women as other social issues that they would like to tackle in the future.

Next fall, Max and Desiree will resume their secondary studies in Montreal. Alison hopes to take journalism courses at Carleton University in Ottawa and Seth will be attending the University of Toronto.

They will be pleased if the tour results only in heightened awareness among young people—a goal not unlike their peacenik predecessors of the 1960s—but ever-practical, they are also keeping an eye on the tangible consequences of their coast-to-coast journey.

As they tell their audiences each day, many students in high schools today will be a large, new constituency in the next federal election.

"And if all of us are saying we want disarmament, the politicians will have to listen." they say.

ACTIVITIES

**Planet at Risk
pp. 148–163**

1. After reading "Disarming Teens," take a hardline position on the need for a strong defence system. With a partner, prepare a list of three or more questions you would ask the "Disarming Teens."

2. With a partner read the three poems in this section of the text. Discuss whether you feel the serious poem or the comic ones make their point more effectively. Do you think this topic is too serious for humour? Write a short poem of your own which states how you feel about the existence of nuclear weapons in your world.

3. With a partner discuss what the family in "After the Sirens" did to survive. Discuss what you would do if you heard such a report over the radio.

4. After reading "After the Sirens," make a journal entry indicating who you think will be better off after a nuclear war—the dead or the survivors.

5. Write a continuation of "After the Sirens" following the family as they struggle with conditions after World War III.

6. With a partner research and prepare a report to make to the class about one of the following questions:
a) What nations currently have nuclear weapons?
b) What films and books are available on this topic?
c) What position does each of Canada's political parties take on nuclear issues?
d) What lobby groups exist in Canada on nuclear issues and what are they saying?
e) What are the stages of a nuclear blast and its destructive power and what effect does each stage have on humans?
f) What is meant by M.A.D. in the context of nuclear weapons policy? Can there be a victor in a nuclear war?
See the Student Handbook (page 194) for tips on making oral presentations to the class.

A Future for Wild Life

Zoe Richmond-Watson

Forty-six different mammals and 101 birds are known to have become extinct since the seventeenth century. Today, nearly 2000 animal species are in danger of disappearing. Many are "protected" by CITES, the Convention on International Trade in Endangered Species. But poaching, pollution and loss of habitat continue to threaten their survival.

Whose responsibility? The African elephant is losing its natural habitat to farming and forestry. And demand for ivory has brought widespread poaching. A million or so elephants still survive in Africa, but between 1979 and 1983 at least 107 000 were killed for their tusks in the southern Sudan, Zaire, the Central African Republic, Zambia and Tanzania. Hong Kong and Japan are the main importers of ivory.

Poaching has also depleted the African rhino population: less than 2000 remain in Kenya, a mere 10 per cent of the 1970 population. Rhino horn is made into dagger handles in the Middle East, and in Asia is ground into a powder much prized for curing any ailment from flu to rheumatism.

Only 40 000 or so elephants survive in Asia as man cuts down tropical forests for timber and to make way for oil palm and other crops. And the number of Indian rhinos has fallen to around 1200.

Kangaroo meat and skins are also in demand, particularly in the United States. About 6 million kangaroos are killed in Australia each year and some species are now nearly extinct. Hunters claim that the animals deprive cattle and sheep of grazing. But critics contend that money is the prime motive for the slaughter.

Snakes, crocodiles and lizards are threatened, too. Snake meat is considered a delicacy in China. Crocodiles are exported from South America as pets. But they are mainly killed for their skins, which are made into fashionable bags and shoes.

Turtles are hunted for their shells and meat, which is made into soup. Commercial sand removal and increased pollution may also have contributed to their decline. The leathery turtle's eggs, a delicacy in the Far East, are sometimes stolen as they are laid.

Chimpanzees are also on the verge of extinction. Yet surveys show that beach photographers in the Canary Islands and on Spain's Mediterranean coast are using hundreds of chimps to boost their business. Critics maintain that for every chimp delivered alive, 6-10 others have died. And the survivors are doomed to misery and early death.

All these animals are threatened by man in his search for food, land, livelihood, or, more frivolous reasons such as fashion. Is it up to man to save them?

What future? The World Wildlife Fund, an international organization committed to conservation projects throughout the world, believes that conservation benefits all life on earth. But in the face of man's obvious indifference to nature, will conservationists succeed in saving endangered species? Or could elephants and rhinos and hundreds of other animals soon be as dead as the dodo?

THE PREDATOR

The little fox
was lying in a pool of blood,
having gnawed his way out to freedom.

Or the farmhand,
seeing his puny, unprofitable size
had slugged him after with a rifle butt

And he had crawled
to the country roadside
where I came upon him, his fur dust-covered

Hard to believe
a fox is ever dead, that he isn't
just lying there pretending with eyes shut.

His fame's against
him: one suspects him of anything,
even when there's blood oozing from the shut eyes.

His evident
self-enjoyment is against him also:
no creature so wild and gleeful can ever be done for.

But this fox was;
there's no place in the world any more
for free and gallant predators like him.

Eagle, lion
fox and falcon: their freedom is their death.
Man, animal tamed and tainted, wishes to forget.

He prefers bears
in cages: delights to see them pace
back and forth, swatting their bars despondently.

Yet hates himself,
knowing he's somehow contemptible
with knives and libraries the dirtiest predator of all.

Ghost of small fox,
hear me, if you're hovering close
and watching this slow red trickle of your blood

Man sets even
more terrible traps for his own kind.
Be at peace—your gnawed leg will be well-revenged.

LIFE OR DEATH

~

IAN HARVEY

I t's a question of life or death. Choose the rights of animals, and men, women and children will die. Choose humans and in Canada alone nearly 200 000 birds, rodents, cats, dogs, primates and other creatures will die in the space of a single year.

The use of animals in medical research, animal rights groups claim, is immoral and wrong and must be stopped—or at least severely curtailed.

Yet at what cost? Is a cure for cancer, AIDS or some other crippling and deadly disease being set back or blocked because of the political climate?

"There is no doubt some of the researchers here need to be watched," says Dr. David Mock, chairman of the University of Toronto's animal care committee. "We've stopped some projects and rejected others because of problems in the treatment of animals."

Once the animal rights movement fought to change conditions for animals in labs. Today it is engaged in a war to eliminate all animal research. Period.

Lifeforce Foundation's Peter Hamilton of Vancouver claims animals and humans have equal rights.

"It's a violation of those rights to take a healthy animal and introduce disease," he said, attacking all animal research as "unnecessary."

He and others see scientists involved in a conspiracy to milk governments and industrial grants to pursue meaningless research.

For every example of a benefit derived from animal research, Hamilton has a counter-argument: Scientists either lie or repeat work already done without animals.

Yet few crusaders—who have renounced meat and animal products in their vegetarian lifestyle—have opted to forego medical treatment or techniques developed through animal experiments.

"What some of these animal rights people need is a good dose of paralysis to give them some perspective," snorts quadriplegic Jocelyn Lovell, once a champion cyclist.

"We're against the aimless destruction of animals in aimless research," said Lovell, an activist in the Spinal Cord Society of Canada. "But we want a cure."

In Ottawa, Dr. Jack Delatorre uses cats in spinal research and is frustrated by a "conservative" mood.

"It's a depressing situation," he said. "There are so many stumbling blocks, I feel like I am blindfolded and have my hands tied behind my back."

His work has wide consequences: "One-fifth of Canadians will be aged 65 by 2001, and many will experience some kind of neurological disease—Alzheimer's, Parkinson's. . . ."

Head and spine injuries, most from motor

vehicle accidents, are the leading cause of death in children and young adults, he added. The cost of these diseases and injuries could bankrupt an overloaded health care system.

"We have to do the research now," he said. "I don't think what we are doing is wrong—you can't equate a cat's life with a baby's. And you can't stimulate biological systems like the spinal cord in a computer or use another animal like a fish—it has to be a mammal."

At Toronto Western Hospital Dr. Michael Fehling uses rats in his spinal cord research and muses he would consider using a larger animal if it were not for the "political climate."

He rejects claims that spinal cord patients, not animals, should be used in experiments.

"Some of these patients spend years learning to regain some functions," he said, noting spinal cord patients are a higher risk under anesthetic and any surgery could prompt further damage.

"The potential here involves everything, brain cells, limbs, eyesight and diseases like multiple sclerosis. It would be criminal to stop at this stage because a small group of individuals—however intelligent—share a different point of view."

At Princess Margaret Hospital, Rick Miller scribbles furiously on his chalkboard explaining genetics.

Miller began his career as a nuclear physicist, gazing outward and writing his thesis on stellar events. Today he casts his ice-blue eyes inward to the complexities of chromosomes and genetics.

"The work done here in the early 1960s with leukemia was all done with animals," the immunologist said. "Now juvenile leukemia which would kill in six months, and adult leukemia, can be cured."

Some 31 000 or more animals—almost all of them mice—are sacrificed in the quest to find the common denominator in the exploding field of immunology.

Connie Wilson doesn't mince words when it comes to choosing between her 16-year-old son Jaime and some lab rats.

"There's no choice," she said. "When it's your child you'd give anything—even the family pet if it would have made a difference."

Ten years ago juvenile leukemia brought a swift death. Now it's one of the most treatable forms of cancer. Twice in the past seven years Jaime beat it into remission with chemotherapy first developed in rats.

Far north of the city a 10-year-old boy dreams of his passage into adulthood and his driver's licence.

Stacey Jones, 10, is another medical success story who owes his life to biomedical research using animals.

He had liver disease and needed a transplant to live.

Dr. Rick Superina practised the delicate art of liver transplant surgery on small pigs at the U of T medical sciences building before he tackled the real thing.

He oversees the Hospital for Sick Children's 18-month-old liver transplant program and his office is dotted with Polaroid snapshots of his young patients.

But without transplants there would be no pictures and happy smiles, only sad memories.

"These are seriously ill children," he said. "They will certainly die without a transplant."

"If there's a benefit for humans then I'm all for animal research," said Stacey's father Denys, who spent an eternity wondering if his son would live.

And while tranplants are not always front page news any more, the quest continues for better techniques.

"I'm sure these animals suffered," Superina said. "But there's no other alternative. What should we do? Dry runs with human subjects?"

John McCardle of the New England Anti-

Vivisection Society thinks that's a good idea.

"The Jarvik-7 artificial heart was tested on five clinically dead patients," he argues. "The technology exists so what's the difference between someone donating specific organs or a whole body to medical science? They keep bodies alive now to preserve transplant organs."

There are 150 000 potential "neo-morts" every year who could replace animals in research, he said.

McCardle agrees medicine has much to thank animal research for but stresses technology must move forward.

While the plight of mice and rats may evoke outrage only in hardcore animal rights lobbyists, images of dogs, cats, rabbits and monkeys being used for research have a much wider impact.

Current legislation allows any registered research group to demand and receive unclaimed pets from shelters.

Opponents say it is cruel to take an animal that has known only companionship from humans and subject it to pain and suffering at the hands of scientists.

It should be noted that the domestic animals used are destined to be put down anyway because their irresponsible owners have failed to claim them.

At the U of T—where in 1985 2922 dogs and 964 cats were used in experiments—the practice is defended against allegations it is scientifically unsound and of dubious benefit.

At an average cost of $100 each, for quarantine, medical evaluation, treatment and housing, the pound dogs cost one-tenth of a specially bred animal.

Mock argues the majority of animals used in research never regain consciousness from the anesthetic.

"These animals are treated in almost the same manner that humans would be after surgery," stresses Dr. Greg Wilson, a researcher in heart pacemakers.

The pacemaker, a piece of bio-engineering so common-place today it is almost taken for granted, was developed in Toronto in the 1950s and research on it continues.

"We're aiming for a pacemaker that will last 10 years," said Wilson. "And while you can make some predictions about how a design will perform, until you get it in a living heart you just don't know."

One of the successes of such research is Dr. Andy McGee, 87, a retired radiologist whose morning rounds today are on the golf course.

"I like to keep moving," he said after his daily attempt to golf his age. "Too many people die in bed."

It is patients like McGee who Wilson sees as the beneficiaries of research—part of an aging population whose hearts need support but whose bodies cannot tolerate constant operations to replace worn-out batteries.

However, Wilson's efforts have been thwarted by the Toronto Humane Society, which last January secretly launched Project Rescue.

Workers posed as individuals to buy from Metro pounds more than 78 dogs that would have gone to research.

The program has cost the THS $3904 and eight dogs remain up for adoption. They have a 45% chance of euthanasia—higher than the average dog's chance for life if it came in off the street. And for every one of those dogs adopted, one other dog dies because it loses a chance for adoption.

David Nowland, the U of T's vice-president of research, said he's concerned the THS is "circumventing the spirit of the law" but adds there's nothing the university can do.

"Some people say we should use specifically bred dogs, despite the cost, because it's a fundamental principle," said Wilson. "But that would be even more of a waste. The pound animal will die and so will the purpose-bred animal."

from MAN KIND?
OUR INCREDIBLE
WAR ON WILDLIFE

❧

CLEVELAND AMORY

There is no better place to begin an examination of our treatment of our fellow creatures than with our language.

Take the word "animal." One of the dictionary definitions for "animal" is "a bestial person; a brute." On the other hand, one of the dictionary definitions of "beast" is "a brutal *person*"—italics ours.

Television is a particular offender. "He's an animal," says a character on one program. "He deserves to be killed." Meanwhile, on another program, a woman shouts to another, in utter contempt, "You're an animal!" Later in the same episode, when she learns she has misjudged that particular person, she apologizes, then points to someone else. "*He's* an animal," she says. And, as if this weren't enough, another program—an interview show—is promoted as follows: "A Tough Judge Says 'Don't Coddle Criminals, They're Punks, Vermin and Animals.'"

In real life the situation is, if anything, worse. One Illinois woman, Mrs. Florence Linzmeier, has made a habit of noting all unfavourable public uses of the word "animal." She observed that when a new U.S. attorney vowed war on Chicago's crime syndicate, he literally spat out, on TV news, the words "They're animals!" Mrs. Linzmeier wrote in protesting. "A few weeks later," she wrote me, "I was gratified to hear the district attorney refer to the hoodlum element as 'the scum of society.'"

In sports, the Boston Bruin hockey team, playing roughly, are known around the league as "The Animals." But so are tough teenagers, particularly motorcycle gangs. And even younger children get it. In fact, if your own act up at a party, what do you say to them? "Why," you say, "you behaved like wild animals." Wild, not in the sense of living in the wild but just *acting* wild.

On an individual basis, the situation is just as bad. We call each other names by animals—"You pig," "you swine," "you weasel," "you rat," "you skunk," "you baboon" or "you jackal." And we do it in the hope, of course, that as we do it we don't make too much of "a jackass," or perhaps just "an ass," out of ourselves. The second dictionary definition of "coyote" is "a contemptible sneak," of "bear," "a clumsy, ill-mannered *person*"—again, italics ours.

And how many of our similes are unfavourably animal-oriented? For every "brave as a lion," "busy as a beaver" or even "wise as an owl" or "cute as a bug," there are literally dozens of "cross as a bear," "mean as a snake," "sly as a fox," "dumb as an ox,"

"slippery as an eel," "stubborn as a mule," "silly as a goose," "crazy as a loon," "greedy as a pig" and so on. You may cry "crocodile tears," but if you're hurt, you'll squeal "like a stuck pig." You may be "hog tied," but it depends on "whose ox is being gored."

You "badger" someone; someone in turn "buffaloes" you. You're either "chicken" or "sheepish" or you're "toady" to someone, or you "go ape." You're "bull-headed" or a "dumb bunny" or "mousy." You have "bats in your belfry" or you're "batty" or you're up to "monkey business." If something is wrong, there's something "fishy." One animal, the lovable sloth, we have even named after one of the seven deadly sins.

A man is either a "wolf"—who will, of course, "turn"—or else he's an "old goat"; a woman can "look like a horse," or be "horse-faced," or, worse still, "a cow." She can also be a "shrew" or a "vixen." And, last but not least, we come to the animals closest to us of all—the cat and the dog. And we have words for them galore, all the way from our worst stocks—even stock-market officials refer to them as "cats and dogs"—to our lowest form of living—which would either be "in the doghouse" or, horror of horrors, the "cathouse."

And what are we when we are "catty?" Why, obviously, being mean. And if a woman is unattractive, what is she? Why, a "dog." Someone is "nervous as a cat" or "fraidy cat." Someone else "lets the cat out of the bag." Still a third person declares. "There are more ways than one to skin a cat."

We may "put on the dog," but more likely someone treats you "like a dog." You may "go to the dogs," or something may happen to you that "shouldn't happen to a dog." Our least important public office is all too clear in the expression "He couldn't get elected dog catcher." And, finally, if a woman can be a "bitch," surely our No. 1 epithet is someone who is the son of the same.

As for man, of course, he doesn't even consider himself an animal—which, considering the way he considers them, is probably, all things considered, the only considerate thing about him.

A C T I V I T I E S

Animal Rights
pp. 165–172

1. For one week, keep a record of the phrases people use that reflect either a positive or negative connotation of animals (for example, he is as blind as a bat.) Sources might be ads, TV and other media, classmates, and friends. Compare your list with another person's.

2. In a small group, discuss the meaning of the following quotations from the poem "The Predator":
"unprofitable size;" "His fame's against/him";
"Man, animal tamed and tainted, wishes to forget";
"Yet hates himself,/knowing he's somehow
  contemptible."

3. Work in a small group, and reread the two articles "Life or Death" and "A Future for Wildlife?"
- Make a note of which side of the argument each member of the group agrees with.
- Make a list of the techniques the writers used in order to interest the readers in their arguments.
- Have each member of the group prepare a 1-minute argument for the side he or she doesn't agree with.

4. Write a letter to an agency, institution, or company that might be able to influence an aspect of animal rights. For example, if you are concerned about the use of animals in scientific experiments, write to the science or medical faculty of a university in your province, giving your views on this issue. Your librarian or teacher will be able to help you figure out whom you could write to about your concern.

or

Read several articles on the use of animals for dissection in our schools. With a partner prepare questions to ask a science teacher, the department head of science, and students who have dissected animals. Interview several people, collate your findings, and report back to the class. Invite some of the people you interviewed to hear your presentation or prepare a brief written report and give the report to those people.

5. Stage a debate on another issue of animal rights: furs as clothing, exotic pets, using animals for cosmetics testing, or the use of traps. See the Student Handbook, page 187, for suggested debate procedures.

from THE THIRD WAVE

ALVIN TOFFLER

A new civilization is emerging in our lives, and blind men everywhere are trying to suppress it. This new civilization brings with it new family styles; changed ways of working, loving, and living; a new economy; new political conflicts; and beyond all this an altered consciousness as well. Pieces of this new civilization exist today. Millions are already attuning their lives to the rhythms of tomorrow. Others, terrified of the future, are engaged in a desperate, futile flight into the past and are trying to restore the dying world that gave them birth.

The dawn of this new civilization is the single most explosive fact of our lifetimes.

It is the central event—the key to understanding the years immediately ahead. It is an event as profound as that First Wave of change unleashed ten thousand years ago by the invention of agriculture, or the earthshaking Second Wave of change touched off by the industrial revolution. We are the children of the next transformation, the Third Wave.

We grope for words to describe the full power and reach of this extraordinary change. Some speak of a looming Space Age, Information Age, Electronic Era, or Global Village. Zbigniew Brzezinski has told us we face a "technetronic age." Sociologist Daniel Bell describes the coming of a "post-industrial society." Soviet futurists speak of the S.T.R.—the "scientific-technological revolution." I myself have written extensively about the arrival of a "super-industrial society." Yet none of these terms, including my own, is adequate.

Some of these phrases, by focusing on a single factor, narrow rather than expand our understanding. Others are static, implying that a new society can come into our lives smoothly, without conflict or stress. None of these terms even begins to convey the full force, scope and dynamism of the changes rushing toward us or of the pressures and conflicts they trigger.

Humanity faces a quantum leap forward. It faces the deepest social upheaval and creative restructuring of all time. Without clearly recognizing it, we are engaged in building a remarkable new civilization from the ground up. This is the meaning of the Third Wave.

Until now the human race has undergone two great waves of change, each one largely obliterating earlier cultures or civilizations and replacing them with ways of life inconceivable to those who came before. The First Wave of change—the agricultural revolution—took thousands of years to play itself out. The Second Wave—the rise of industrial civilization—took a mere three hundred years. Today history is even more accelerative, and it is likely that the Third Wave will sweep across history and complete itself in a few decades. We, who happen to share the planet at this explosive moment, will therefore feel the full impact of the Third Wave in our own lifetimes.

Tearing our families apart, rocking our economy, paralysing our political systems, shattering our values, the Third Wave affects everyone. It challenges all the old power relationships, the privileges and prerogatives of the endangered elites of today, and provides the backdrop against which the key power struggles of tomorrow will be fought.

Much in this emerging civilization contradicts the old traditional industrial civilization. It is, at one and the same time, highly technological and anti-industrial.

The Third wave brings with it a genuinely new way of life based on diversified, renewable energy sources; on methods of production that make most factory assembly lines obsolete; on new, non-nuclear families; on a novel institution that might be called the "electronic cottage"; and on radically changed schools and corporations of the future. The emergent civilization writes a new code of behaviour for us and carries us beyond standardization, synchronization, and centralization, beyond the concentration of energy, money, and power.

This new civilization, as it challenges the old, will topple bureaucracies, reduce the role of the nation-state, and give rise to semi-autonomous economies in a postimperialist world. It requires governments that are simpler, more effective, yet more democratic than any we know today. It is a civilization with its own distinctive world outlook, its own ways of dealing with time, space, logic, and causality.

Above all, as we shall see, Third Wave civilization begins to heal the historic breach between producer and consumer, giving rise to the "prosumer" economics of tomorrow. For this reason, among many, it could—with some intelligent help from us—turn out to be the first truly humane civilization in recorded history.

Two apparently contrasting images of the future grip the popular imagination today. Most people—to the extent that they bother to think about the future at all—assume the world they know will last indefinitely. They find it difficult to imagine a truly different way of life for themselves, let alone a totally new civilization. Of course they recognize that things are changing. But they assume today's changes will somehow pass them by and that nothing will shake the familiar economic framework and political structure. They confidently expect the future to continue to the present.

This straight-line thinking comes in various packages. At one level it appears as an unexamined assumption lying behind the decisions of businessmen, teachers, parents, and politicians. At a more sophisticated level it comes dressed up in statistics, computerized data, and forecasters' jargon. Either way it adds up to a vision of a future world that is essentially "more of the same"—Second Wave industrialism writ even larger and spread over more of this planet.

Recent events have severely shaken this confident image of the future. As crisis after crisis has crackled across the headlines, as Iran erupted, as Mao was de-deified, as oil prices skyrocketed and inflation ran wild, as terrorism spread and governments seemed helpless to stop it, a bleaker vision has become increasingly popular. Thus, large numbers of people—fed on a steady diet of bad news, disaster movies, apocalyptic Bible stories, and nightmare scenarios issued by prestigious think tanks—have apparently concluded that today's society cannot be projected into the future because there is no future. For them, Armageddon is only minutes away. The earth is racing toward its final cataclysmic shudder.

On the surface these two visions of the future seem very different. Yet both produce similar psychological and political effects. For both lead to the paralysis of imagination and will.

If tomorrow's society is simply an enlarged, Cinerama version of the present, there is little we *need* do to prepare for it. If, on the other hand, society is inevitably destined to self-destruct within our lifetime, there is nothing we *can* do about it. In short, both these ways of looking at the future generate privatism and passivity. Both freeze us into inaction.

Yet, in trying to understand what is happening to us, we are not limited to this simpleminded choice between Armageddon and More-of-the-Same. There are many more clarifying and constructive ways to think about tomorrow—ways that prepare us for the future and, more important, help us to change the present.

This book is based on what I call the "revolutionary premise." It assumes that, even though the decades immediately ahead are likely to be filled with upheavals, turbulence, perhaps even widespread violence, we will not totally destroy ourselves. It assumes that the jolting changes we are now experiencing are not chaotic or random but that, in fact, they form a sharp, clearly discernible pattern. It assumes, moreover, that these changes are cumulative—that they add up to a giant transformation in the way we live, work, play, and think, and that a sane and desirable future is possible. In short, what follows begins with the premise that what is happening now is nothing less than a global revolution, a quantum jump in history.

Put differently, this book flows from the assumption that we are the final generation of an old civilization and the first generation of a new one, and that much of our personal confusion, anguish, and disorientation can be traced directly to the conflict within us, and within our political institutions, between the dying Second Wave civilization and the emergent Third Wave civilization that is thundering in to take its place.

When we finally understand this, many seemingly senseless events become suddenly comprehensible. The broad patterns of change begin to emerge clearly. Action for survival becomes possible and plausible again. In short, the revolutionary premise liberates our intellect and our will.

To say the changes we face will be revolutionary, however, is not enough. Before we can control or channel them we need a fresh way to identify and analyze them. Without this we are hopelessly lost.

One powerful new approach might be called social "wave-front" analysis. It looks at history as a succession of rolling waves of change and asks where the leading edge of each wave is carrying us. It focusses our attention not so much on the continuities of history (important as they are) as on the discontinuities—the innovations and breakpoints. It identifies key change patterns as they emerge, so that we can influence them.

Beginning with the very simple idea that the rise of agriculture was the first turning point in human social development, and that the industrial revolution was the second great breakthrough, it views each of these not as a discrete, one-time event but as a wave of change moving at a certain velocity.

Before the First Wave of change, most humans lived in small, often migratory groups and fed themselves by foraging, fishing, hunting, or herding. At some point, roughly ten millennia ago, the agricultural revolution began, and it crept slowly across the planet spreading villages, settlements, cultivated land, and a new way of life.

This First Wave of change had not yet exhausted itself by the end of the seventeenth century, when the industrial revolution broke over Europe and unleashed the second great wave of planetary change. This new process—industrialization—began moving much more rapidly across nations and continents. Thus two separate and distinct change processes were rolling across the earth simultaneously, at different speeds.

Today the First Wave has virtually subsided. Only a few tiny tribal populations, in South America or Papua New Guinea, for example, remain to be reached by agriculture. But the force of this great First Wave has basically been spent.

Meanwhile, the Second Wave, having revolutionized life in Europe, North America, and some other parts of the globe in a few short centuries, continues to spread, as many countries, until now basically agricultural, scramble to build steel mills, auto plants, textile factories, railroads, and food processing plants. The momentum of industrialization is still felt.

The Second Wave has not entirely spent in force.

But even as this process continues, another, even more important, has begun. For as the tide of industrialism peaked in the decades after World War II, a little-understood Third Wave began to surge across the earth, transforming everything it touched.

Many countries, therefore, are feeling the simultaneous impact of two, even three, quite different waves of change, all moving at different rates of speed and with different degrees of force behind them.

For the purposes of this book we shall consider the First Wave era to have begun sometime around 8000 B.C. and to have dominated the earth unchallenged until sometime around A.D. 1650-1750. From this moment on, the First Wave lost momentum as the Second Wave picked up steam. Industrial civilization, the product of this Second Wave, then dominated the planet in its turn until it, too, crested. This latest historical turning point arrived in the United States during the decade beginning about 1955—the decade that saw white-collar and service workers outnumber blue-collar workers for the first time. This was the same decade that saw the widespread introduction of the computer, commercial jet travel, the birth control pill, and many other high-impact innovations. It was precisely during this decade that the Third Wave began to gather its force in the United States. Since then it has arrived—at slightly different dates— in most of the other industrial nations, including Britain, France, Sweden, Germany, the Soviet Union, and Japan. Today all the high-technology nations are reeling from the collision between the Third Wave and the obsolete, encrusted economies and institutions of the Second.

Understanding this is the secret to making sense of much of the political and social conflict we see around us.

WAVES OF THE FUTURE

Whenever a single wave of change predominates in any given society, the pattern of future development is relatively easy to discern. Writers, artists, journalists, and others discover the "wave of the future." Thus in nineteenth-century Europe many thinkers, business leaders, politicians, and ordinary people held a clear, basically correct image of the future. They sensed that history was moving toward the ultimate triumph of industrialism over premechanized agriculture, and they foresaw with considerable accuracy many of the changes that the Second Wave would bring with it: more powerful technologies, bigger cities, faster transport, mass education, and the like.

This clarity of vision had direct political effects. Parties and political movements were able to triangulate with respect to the future. Pre-industrial agricultural interests organized a rearguard action against encroaching industrialism, against "big business," against "union bosses," against "sinful cities." Labour and management grappled for control of the main levers of the emergent industrial society. Ethnic and racial minorities defining their rights in terms of an improved role in the industrial world, demanded access to jobs, corporate positions, urban housing, better wages, mass public education, and so forth.

This industrial vision of the future had important psychological effects as well. People might disagree; they might engage in sharp, occasionally even bloody, conflict. Depressions and boom times might disrupt their lives. Nevertheless, in general, the shared image of an industrial future tended to define options, to give individuals a sense not merely of who or what they were, but of what they were likely to become. It provided a degree of stability and a sense of self, even in the midst of extreme social change.

In contrast, when a society is struck by two or more giant waves of change, and none is yet clearly dominant, the image of the future is fractured. It becomes extremely difficult to sort out the meaning of the changes and conflicts that arise. The collision of wave fronts creates a raging ocean, full of clashing currents, eddies, and maelstroms which conceal the deeper, more important historic tides.

In the United States today—as in many other countries—the collision of Second and Third Waves creates social tensions, dangerous conflicts, and strange new political wave fronts that cut across the usual divisions of class, race, sex, or party. This collision makes a shambles of traditional political vocabularies and makes it very difficult to separate the progressives from the reactionaries, friends from enemies. All the old polarizations and coalitions break up. Unions and employers, despite their differences, join to fight environmentalists. Blacks and Jews, once united in the battle against discrimination, become adversaries.

In many nations, labour which has traditionally favoured "progressive" policies such as income redistribution, now often holds "reactionary" positions with respect to women's rights, family codes, immigration, tariffs, or regionalism. The traditional "left" is often pro-centralization, highly nationalistic, and anti-environmentalist.

At the same time we see politicians, from Valéry Giscard d'Estaing to Jimmy Carter or Jerry Brown, espousing "conservative" attitudes toward economics and "liberal" attitudes toward art, sexual morality, women's rights, or ecological controls. No wonder people are confused and give up trying to make sense of their world.

The media, meanwhile, report a seemingly endless succession of innovations, reversals, bizarre events, assassinations, kidnappings, space shots, governmental breakdown, commando raids, and scandals, all seemingly unrelated.

The apparent incoherence of political life is mirrored in personality disintegration. Psychotherapists and gurus do a land-office business; people wander aimlessly amid competing therapies, from primal scream to *est*. They slip into cults and covens or, alternatively, into pathological privatism, convinced that reality is absurd, insane, or meaningless. Life may indeed be absurd in some large, cosmic sense. But this hardly proves that there is no pattern in today's events. In fact, there is a distinct, hidden order that becomes detectable as soon as we learn to distinguish Third Wave changes from those associated with the diminishing Second Wave.

An understanding of the conflicts produced by these colliding wave fronts gives us not only a clearer image of alternative futures by an X-ray of the political and social forces acting on us. It also offers insight into our own private roles in history. For each of us, no matter how seemingly unimportant, is a living piece of history.

The crosscurrents created by these waves of change are reflected in our work, our family life, our sexual attitudes and personal morality. They show up in our life-styles and voting behaviour. For in our personal lives and in our political acts whether we know it or not, most of us in the rich countries are essentially either Second Wave people committed to maintaining the dying order, Third Wave people constructing a radically different tomorrow, or a confused, self-canceling mixture of the two.

The conflict between Second and Third Wave groupings is, in fact, the central political tension cutting through our society today. Despite what today's parties and candidates may preach, the infighting among them amounts to little more than a dispute over who will squeeze the most advantage from what remains of the declining industrial system. Put differently, they are engaged in a squabble for the proverbial deck chairs on a sinking *Titanic*.

The more basic political question, as we shall see, is not who controls the last days of industrial society but who shapes the new civilization rapidly rising to replace it. While short-range political skirmishes exhaust our energy and attention, a far more profound battle is already taking place beneath the surface. On one side are the partisans of the industrial past; on the other, growing millions who recognize that the most urgent problems of the world—food, energy, arms control, population, poverty, resources, ecology, climate, the problems of the aged, the breakdown of urban community, the need for productive, rewarding work—can no longer be resolved within the framework of the industrial order.

This conflict is the "super-struggle" for tomorrow.

This confrontation between the vested interests of the Second Wave and the people of the Third Wave already runs like an electric current through the political life of every nation. Even in the non-industrial countries of the world, all the old battle lines have been forcibly redrawn by the arrival of the Third Wave. The old war of agricultural, often feudal, interests against industrializing elites, either capitalist or socialist, takes on a new dimension in light of the coming obsolescence of industrialism. Now that Third Wave civilization is making its appearance, does rapid industrialization imply liberation from neocolonialism and poverty—or does it, in fact, guarantee permanent dependency?

It is only against this wide-screen background that we can begin to make sense of the headlines, to sort out our priorities, to frame sensible strategies for the control of change in our lives.

As I write this, the front pages report hysteria and hostages in Iran, assassinations in South Korea, runaway speculation in gold, friction between Blacks and Jews in the U.S., big increases in West German military spending, cross burnings on Long Island, a giant oil spill in the Gulf of Mexico, the biggest antinuclear rally in history, and a battle between the rich nations and the poor over the control of radio frequencies. Waves of religious revivalism crash through Libya, Syria, and the U.S.; neofascist fanatics claim "credit" for a political assassination in Paris. And General Motors reports a breakthrough into technology needed for electric automobiles. Such disconnected news-clips cry out for integration or synthesis.

Once we realize that a bitter struggle is now raging between those who seek to preserve industrialism and those who seek to supplant it, we have a powerful new key to understanding the world. More important—whether we are setting policies for a nation, strategies for a corporation, or goals for one's own personal life—we have a new tool for changing that world.

To use this tool, however, we must be able to distinguish clearly those changes that extend the old industrial civilization from those which facilitate the arrival of the new. We must, in short, understand both the old and the new, the Second Wave industrial system into which so many of us were born and the Third Wave civilization that we and our children will inhabit.

A C T I V I T I E S

**The Third Wave
pp. 174–181**

1. In a group of four, make a chart of the history of the world according to Toffler's wave theory. In your chart identify the time period of each wave, its main characteristics, the lifestyle of the people, and identify a place in the world where each wave exists today. In your chart you might include a pre-history period for the time before the first wave.

2. Make a journal entry in which you explain which historical period described by Toffler you feel would provide you with the greatest opportunity for happiness. Be sure to make clear what aspects of the period make it appealing to you.

3. Work with a partner who is also going to read the rest of this book, and make up five or six questions which you hope will be answered in the remaining chapters. Keep your questions handy to see how many of them have been answered by the time you finish reading the book.

4. Choose two or three whole-book activities on page 204 of the Student Handbook to complete as you read the book or when you have finished reading it.

A C T I V I T I E S

1. Choose an issue which is of interest to you and, over the course of several weeks, follow the coverage of your issue on television and in local newspapers.
   a) Keep a log of television coverage of the issue. Each entry in your log should contain at least the following information: date, channel, summary of what was reported, accompanying visuals, and the bias of the reporter, if any.
   b) Keep a scrapbook containing newspaper articles on your issue. For each article note the date and time of the newspaper and highlight the main ideas of the article.
   c) Compare and contrast the points of view of two or more reports and the thoroughness of the coverage.

2. Design a unit on a world issue of your choice for use in another grade 12 class. You may want to work with a partner or in a small group to find a short story, a poem, or song, and a piece of non-fiction to include in your unit. Decide what your objectives will be in having students read and discuss the pieces you have selected and present these objectives along with brief summaries of the selections to your teacher in the form of a proposal.

3. Song writers often use lyrics and music to express their views on issues. Write a song or poem about an issue which is extremely important to you.
or
Write a play about an issue which is important to you for presentation to a class of younger students. Before performing your play for this class, design and produce a flyer to advertise it and to highlight the issue.

4. Hold a debate or a series of debates on an issue in which the whole class is interested. See the Student Handbook (page 187) for suggested debate procedures.

CAREERS

These careers are related to the world issues raised in this unit.

Animal Health Technician
An animal health technician generally works under the direction of a veterinarian in a private clinic. She or he does laboratory tests on animals, operates the radio-graph, takes X-rays, assists in surgery and is able to anesthetize animals. She or he also acts as a liaison between the veterinarian and the public. Animal health care workers also do research in industries, government and hospitals and universities which are directly or indirectly involved in animal health.

Training and Qualifications
There are two-and three-year programs at various colleges in animal health and animal care technology.

Salary
In 1984, an average starting salary was $13 700 but the pay is gradually increasing.

Other Careers:
- Law Clerk
- Custom Inspector
- Activist
- Veterinarian's Assistant
- Police Officer

RESOURCES

Novels
Dibs: In Search of Self — Virginia M. Axline (Ballantine, 1964)
The War between the Classes — Gloria Mikowitz (Delacorte, 1985)
Brother in the Land — Robert Swindells (Puffin Plus, 1984)
Never Cry Wolf — Farley Mowat (Bantam Seal, 1963)
A Whale for the Killing — Farley Mowat (Bantam Seal, 1981)
Films
If you Love This Planet, NFB; 25 min
The Best Kept Secret, NFB; 10 min
Yes, You Can Say No, Canadian Learning Company; 19 min
Acid Rain: Requiem or Recovery, NFB; 26 min
Testament, Paramount Films 1983; 90 min
When the Wind Blows, (animated), New World Video 1988; 84 min

STUDENT HANDBOOK

CHECKLISTS

ABOUT THE CHECKLIST FOR REVISING

The checklist below provides some questions that you and your partners should consider when you look over your rough drafts.

CHECKLIST FOR REVISING

Have I said what I wanted to say in the way I wanted to say it?

- Did I discuss my ideas with partners before I began to write?
- Did I begin my piece of writing in a way that gets the reader's attention?
- Do the details I have written about come in the best order?
- Are some of my points repetitive or unnecessary?
- Have I used the same words too often?
- Have I used vivid and interesting words to describe actions, objects, and people?
- Do I have a strong and appropriate ending?
- Do my partners clearly understand what I am trying to say?
- Are my paragraphs too long? Are they long enough to make my point?
- Did I keep my audience in mind as I was choosing my words?

When you revise or edit, you rework your rough draft to make your writing as clear and as interesting as possible.

ABOUT THE CHECKLIST FOR PROOFREADING

The checklist below is designed to help you catch problems in punctuation, spelling, and sentence structure. Proofreading is the final clean-up of a piece of writing before you place it in the Polished Writing File.

CHECKLIST FOR PROOFREADING

Have I checked my writing for surface errors?

- Did I double-check the spelling of all words I was unsure about?
- Did I leave wide margins so that my work is uncrowded and easy to read?
- Did I indent each new paragraph?
- Did the punctuation I used make my meaning clear?

- Did I capitalize names and titles and the first word of each sentence?
- Did I use a variety of sentence types?
- Did I use complete sentences where necessary?

When you proofread, you try to find and correct mistakes in surface details, such as punctuation, grammar, usage, spelling, and handwriting.

DEBATING

There are many possible debate formats. The one that follows is easy to use, fair, and a favourite of students. You can modify the time guidelines to suit your needs.

Debate Procedure

1. The chair introduces the topic, introduces the speakers, explains any time limits, and announces the judges' decision.

2. The first speaker for the *affirmative* should
   a) give a brief introduction to the topic;
   b) define any necessary terms;
   c) note any points agreed on by all debaters;
   d) note any issues to be excluded;
   e) state clearly and *briefly* all the affirmative points;
   f) prove the point he or she has chosen to deal with. (5 min)

3. The first speaker for the *negative* should
   a) state the agreements or disagreements with the interpretation of the first speaker;
   b) state the arguments of the negative side;
   c) indicate who will prove the arguments;
   d) refute *briefly* the arguments of the first speaker;
   e) present his or her arguments. (5 min)

4. The second speaker for the affirmative should
   a) refute the first speaker's arguments for the negative;
   b) state his or her own arguments and proof. (3 min)

5. The second speaker for the negative should
   a) refute the arguments of the second speaker for the affirmative;
   b) state his or her own arguments and proof. (3 min)

6. The third speaker for the affirmative should
   a) refute the arguments for the second speaker for the negative;
   b) state his or her own arguments and proof. (3 min)

7. The third speaker for the negative should
   a) refute any arguments for the positive as yet unanswered;
   b) state his or her own arguments and proof;
   c) sum up the arguments for the negative. (4 min)

8. The first speaker for the affirmative, in the final statement, should
   a) *not* introduce fresh evidence;
   b) only refute arguments already made;
   c) sum up the affirmative arguments. (1 min)

Definition
refute—to prove a statement or argument to be wrong or false

HOLDING CONFERENCES

Holding a conference is a way of reviewing, with other people's assistance, what you have written. When you sit down with a partner or your teacher to have a conference, you have an opportunity to talk about your ideas to someone who wants to listen.

What does having a conference involve? Your partner will ask you questions about your work, and in answering them, you will come to understand your work better. You can hold a conference with your partner to see how your ideas are forming as you begin to write, and you can also hold a conference to discuss the various stages of your work as it moves from first draft to a final, polished effort.

No two conferences will be exactly alike, but in every case, you will be working co-operatively with one or more partners to explore and shape your ideas.

Here are some questions that you and your partner may want to ask during a conference.

Why Am I Writing or Saying This?
Am I trying to
- organize facts;
- convince someone about something;

- record my feelings;
- share an idea;
- tell a story;
- explain a situation;
- do any or all of the above?

Who Is My Intended Audience?
Am I writing or speaking to
- myself;
- a friend;
- a relative;
- someone I dislike;
- an unknown audience?

What Am I Writing or Talking About?
What am I trying to say? What information do I already have? What information, if any, do I still need?

How Am I Organizing My Ideas?
What form will I use for what I have to say? Will I use
- a letter;
- an explanation accompanied by an illustration;
- a chart;
- a brief note;
- a script;
- a biographical sketch;
- an audio-visual presentation;
- an oral report?

   As you revise, edit, and proofread your writing, you may find spelling, punctuation, and grammatical errors. When you have a conference with your partners or your teachers, they too may find parts of your work that need rewording.

INTERVIEWING TECHNIQUES

Before you interview someone, you must prepare carefully. Here is a step-by-step checklist to help you prepare for and conduct a successful interview. For sample interviews, listen to news and other broadcasts on radio and television and check *Maclean's* magazine, which contains an interview each week.
- Decide what it is you want to find out, and formulate questions that will lead you to the information you are seeking.

- When you are making up your questions, start with "basic fact" questions—*who?, what?, when?, where?, why?,* and *how?*

  Try to ask very few questions that will produce only a yes/no answer. Your interview will be very boring if you restrict yourself to this type of question! Try to get your interviewee to tell you his or her personal stories.

  Your questions should be **specific** when you want specific information (e.g., Why did you make that decision?). Use **open-ended** questions when you want the interviewee to explore an idea or reflect on some aspect of his or her life (e.g., If you had to make the choice again, would you do it? Why?).

  Adapt and change your written questions as the interview proceeds. You may hear a piece of information or an idea that you didn't take into account when you were making up your questions. Make one up on the spot to explore these new leads! You can always return to the safety of your original questions when you want to!

- Set up your interview either by phoning or by writing to the person you wish to interview. Always be polite, speak clearly, and agree to meet at a place and time that is convenient for him or her.

- Take your questions, a pen or a pencil (and a back-up tool), and a notebook to the interview. You may also wish to take along a tape recorder to record the interview. It it common practice to ask the permission of the interviewee before recording the conversation.

- Thank your interviewee when the interview is over, and follow up with a brief thank-you note a few days later to show your appreciation.

KEEPING A JOURNAL

Keeping a journal lets you explore new understandings and connect them with what you already know. A journal is a place where you can write freely without worrying about whether your writing is good enough to show other people. Mainly, you are recording your own reflections and, through that process, perhaps coming to conclusions, or starting points for new awareness. You can always use the notes you have in your journal as the seed of some writing for a special audience, such as your classmates, your teacher, or some person or group outside school.

You may wish to use your journal (or your private disc, if you are using a computer) to record

- events or experiences that are important to you in some way;
- interesting conversations or discussions you have had;
- your emotions—maybe some occurrence has you feeling excited, angry, happy, sad, frightened, or curious;
- a thought or comment about an issue you have encountered while speaking with someone, reading a book or magazine, listening to the radio, or watching television, videos, or a movie;
- a list of things you want to accomplish, or goals you have set for yourself;
- advice that has been given to you about a specific problem you are facing.

If you're trying to figure out something and you find you're stuck, use your journal to write down everything you know about the problem and then look things over carefully. Sometimes you already have a solution—you just need a chance to see your thoughts on paper.

MEDIA REVIEW: FILM

Title of Film: _____

Production company: _____

Year: _____

Country of origin: _____

Actors: _____

Type of film (comedy, horror, drama, etc.): _____

Intended audience: _____

Plot summary: _____

_____

Were you interested in the story? Why?

_____

_____

Did you identify with any of the characters? Why?

_____

_____

Noteworthy, technical aspects (camera shots or angles, setting, lighting, special effects, etc.) that created a strong impression about character or mood:

_____

_____

Why do you think the film was made?

_____

_____

Was the film a box-office success?

_____

_____

Do you think the film is successful? Explain.

_____

_____

_____

MEDIA REVIEW: TELEVISION

Title of program: _____

Date of broadcast: _____

Time of broadcast: _____

Length: _____

Actors: _____

Type of program (sitcom, soap opera, etc.): _____

Intended audience: _____

_____

Plot summary: _____

_____

Were you interested in the story? Why?

_____

_____

Did you identify with any of the characters? Why?

_____

_____

Noteworthy technical aspects (costumes, music, special effects, etc.):

_____

_____

Is the program popular? Why?

_____

_____

Do you think the program is successful? Explain.

_____

_____

What values are presented in the program?

_____

_____

Advertisements
What products are advertised during the program?

_____

_____

Number of advertisements: _____

_____

What lifestyle is promoted by the products advertised?

_____

_____

_____

_____

_____

_____

_____

Oral Presentation Skills

SPEAK LOUDLY!

An oral presentation must be heard! It is therefore *extremely* important that you project your voice so that everyone in the group or in the class can hear you without straining.

PRESENT WITH ENERGY AND ENTHUSIASM

If you present your work as if it is boring, you will lose the interest of your audience. Remember, you have spent a long time preparing this material, you know it well, and you are eager to share what you have learned. Be confident! The nervous feelings will soon disappear.

INVOLVE YOUR AUDIENCE

Why should you be the only person to suffer through this experience? Get your audience involved by asking them questions ("Hands up if you've seen a certain movie . . .") or by asking them to fill out a brief questionnaire or survey. Brainstorm other ways of getting them involved in your presentation.

USE VISUALS!

People enjoy not only hearing about other people's experiences and ideas, but also seeing what they are talking about. A poster/collage of photographs, an information poster, a videotape, a pamphlet or booklet, a factsheet, an outline, an agenda, an overhead projection, sample items, a chart—any one of these things could make your presentation more effective. Audiotapes of interviews and music are also useful things to keep in mind when you are putting your presentations together.

TELL YOUR STORY!

Remember, in any sort of report or presentation, you are telling the story of how you gathered the information or ideas and of what you learned. You might want to introduce your topic with an anecdote and then continue with your story. It may be helpful to use point-form notes to jog your memory.

THE PERSONAL USAGE SHEET

Whenever you correct problems, you can record the process on a Personal Usage Sheet. First, state the problem that you had, and then record your corrected version. An example of a completed Personal Usage Sheet is provided below.

PERSONAL USAGE SHEET

NAME _____

Date	My Writing Partners	Title of My Written Work	Correct Usage of Word or Words
Sept. 18	Christopher	"Shopping"	*Problem* The use of "it's" and "its." *Corrections* "It's too hard to decide," I said. "Each guitar has its own sound."

PLANNING AND ORGANIZING OUTLINE

Choose from your research sheets and your own ideas the information to include in each of the sections of the outline.

Ideas/quotations for the opening paragraph or introduction
(Give the reader a clear idea of what your paper or presentation is about—the overall picture.)

Ideas/details/proofs for the main part (body) of your work
(Prove to your reader that what you said in the introduction is true. Back up your ideas—show the details of the picture. Each argument should be put into a separate paragraph.)

Ideas/quotes for the concluding paragraph or statement
(Summarize the points you have made. Draw some conclusions that refer back to your opening statements—go back to the full picture.)

_____

_____

RECORD OF INDIVIDUAL PARTICIPATION IN A GROUP AND SELF-EVALUATION FORM

We are often asked to describe our strengths and weaknesses in life. Applications for college admission, for a job, or for a promotion are examples. It is important for us to be able to evaluate ourselves honestly (after all, other records are available for verification) and positively (you want the position).

This form can help you develop the skill of positive and honest self-evaluation. Fill it in as if you are applying for a job that requires team work and leadership skills, as well as evidence of an ability to work and do a good job.

Title of Project:
Description of Project:
Name of Participant:
Names of Others in the Group:
Attendance (indicate number of sessions attended and held):

A) Assigning the Mark
On a scale of 1 (minimum) to 10 (maximum), I would rate my own contribution to the group process and the final product as follows: (circle one)

_____

	1	2	3	4	5	6	7	8	9	10
commitment to task										
focus on topic										
contribution of ideas										
encouragement of other group members' ideas										
leadership										

Overall, I would evaluate my work as: A   B   C   D   F

B) Rationale for the Mark: Contributions to the Project

1. How I helped in the planning stages (thinking of ideas, gathering information, drawing ideas together, etc.)

_____

_____

2. How I helped to keep the group together (encouraging others, relieving tension, finding solutions to problems, offering leadership when needed, etc.)

_____

_____

3. Tasks I did for the project (writing, typing, organizing material, designing format, doing artwork, etc.)

_____

_____

4. How I would change my contribution in future group projects to be more effective

_____

_____

5. **Confirmation**: We, the undersigned, have read what _____ has written and agree with what we have read.

   1. _____   4. _____

   2. _____   5. _____

   3. _____   6. _____

Research Skills: Notemaking Format

Topic: **Due Date:**

Source Information
Title:
Author:
Page numbers:
Publisher:
Publication date:
City of publication:

Information (in your own words)

_____

_____

Quotations (include page numbers)

1. _____

_____

2. _____

_____

Note: If your source of information is a film or a television program, you may want to use the review forms on pp. 191 and 192.

Ideas/details/proofs for the main part (body) of your work
(Prove to your reader that what you said in the introduction is true. Back up your ideas—show the details of the picture. Each argument should be put into a separate paragraph.)

_____

_____

Ideas/quotes for the concluding paragraph or statement
(Summarize the points you have made. Draw some conclusions that refer back to your opening statements—go back to the full picture.)

_____

_____

USING LANGUAGE TO LEARN

People speak and write not only to be understood, but also to understand. Every time you come across a new concept, you naturally try to fit it into what you already know, and by talking through an idea or jotting down what you think about it, you get closer to understanding it. When you express your ideas, either in a conversation or in some kind of writing, you get a chance to check out your own thinking.

Talking with others about what you're learning will help you with all your subjects. It is just as important to talk to partners about how to plan a geography assignment, solve a problem in math, devise a good menu in food shop, or construct something in wood shop, as it is to discuss the meaning of the poem or story you're reading in English class.

Through your discussion you will come to an awareness of what you really think about what you've read. Also, your response will be influenced by the viewpoints others have expressed. At the learning stage, you are still letting ideas roam around in your head, and you are not yet ready to make a final, polished statement.

When you share ideas, feelings, opinions, and beliefs with others, whether in conversation or through your writing, you extend your view to see things you might not have seen by yourself. After you and your partners communicate your thoughts to each other and compare them, you will usually be ready to make a clear statement about what you have learned.

VOCABULARY

Many writing selections in this book present challenging words. Some of them may look familiar to you, although you may not know them well enough to use them accurately. In elementary school, your teacher often decided which words you should learn to spell and define. At this stage in your school career, and for the rest of your life, *you* should be the one to decide which words you need to know to understand the material you are reading. You don't have to look up every word you are unfamiliar with, but as an independent learner, you should be responsible for what you think and how you express yourself.

What are the advantages of knowing more words than you do now? You will be better able to understand the messages of others and to put your thoughts into words. Reading will be easier, not only in this class, but in all your subjects. Your written and oral work will benefit. The benefits will carry on into your working life. Employers value people who have well-developed skills of reading and writing, and who are good listeners and clear speakers. Most importantly, you'll feel better about yourself because you'll be able to make others understand your point of view.

VOICES

Each unit begins with a section called Voices. Voices is an assortment of writing that introduces you to the topic of the unit. Reading these short selections aloud to one another in small groups allows you to practise oral reading and to increase your vocabulary. Listening to others read stimulates your imagination and encourages active listening skills.

WORD PROCESSORS

A word processor is a computer program especially for people who write. If you had in front of you many pens, pencils, and sheets of paper, a pair of scissors, a bottle of glue, an eraser, a filing cabinet, a typewriter, and a photocopier, you might be able to do all of the things a word processor can do. Word processors take the drudgery out of writing. You can make notes, expand them into an outline, rearrange sentences, and move whole paragraphs, all without having to recopy your work each time you make a change.

Anything you write—letters, reviews, memoirs, stories, scripts—can be written on a word processor. It can also help you to make lists, charts, and reports neatly. You can use it as an aid to thinking by saving your ideas in point form or in an outline in the computer.

During the revising process, the word processor makes

it easy for you to change and expand your outlines and drafts into completed pieces of writing. After you proofread, you can make your adjustments on screen and then print out a final copy that doesn't have mistakes or messy corrections.

Using a word processor makes writing and editing fun, but it is still up to you to do the thinking that is behind every piece of good writing. You are the one who must decide which ideas you are going to put into the computer and how they should be arranged and developed.

WORKING IN GROUPS

It takes time to develop reading and writing skills. In the same way, discussion and group-work skills must be developed through experience and evaluation. The following lists of "Helpful Roles" and "Hindering Roles" will help you to become aware of the ways people work in groups. You can also use the lists to evaluate your own success as a team player.

Helpful Roles

1. *Organizing*
   - identifying goals
   - defining tasks

2. *Self-starting*
   - suggesting new ideas
   - volunteering to tackle a task

3. *Information-seeking*
   - asking questions
   - seeking facts
   - requesting clarification

4. *Information-providing*
   - offering ideas and their sources

Hindering Roles

1. *Fragmenting*
   - going off topic
   - introducing irrelevant information

2. *Resisting*
   - seeing problems where none exist
   - failing to exercise initiative

3. *Withdrawing*
   - appearing shy and insecure
   - daydreaming
   - fearing to say the wrong thing

4. *Information-withholding*
   - avoiding involvement in discussion

5. *Encouraging*
   - responding enthusi-
     astically to others
     and their ideas
   - inviting everyone's
     participation

6. *Summarizing*
   - summarizing
     points of discussion
   - simplifying compli-
     cated ideas

7. *Co-ordinating*
   - keeping discussion
     on topic
   - trying to involve
     everybody

8. *Challenging*
   - stimulating discus-
     sion by presenting
     different
     viewpoints
   - confronting weak
     ideas

9. *Mediating*
   - working to resolve
     differences
   - looking for alterna-
     tive solutions

10. *Tension-relieving*
    - expressing points
      with humour
    - making people
      feel good about
      themselves

5. *Belittling*
   - undercutting the
     suggestions of
     others
   - discouraging
     participation

6. *Smooth-talking*
   - pretending superior
     knowledge
   - oversimplifying
     problems

7. *Monopolizing*
   - hogging the
     discussion
   - interrupting others

8. *Arguing*
   - indulging in
     disagreement
   - disregarding the
     ideas of others

9. *Fence-sitting*
   - side-stepping the
     making of decisions

10. *Clowning*
    - disrupting progress
    - fooling around

THE WRITING FOLDER

The writing folder is a way of organizing your work and keeping a record of what you've done. It can be a large manila envelope, a binder, or a computer disc that holds these files:

1. Work in Progress File
2. Private Writing File
3. Polished Writing File

POLISHED WRITING FILE
revised, polished, proofread work that is ready for evaluation

PRIVATE WRITING FILE
journal writing and other personal writing

WORK IN PROGRESS FILE
contains notes and rough drafts

WRITING FOLDER

WHOLE-BOOK ACTIVITIES

1. Script a scene from the book. Choose an incident or event in the story that is mentioned but not written about in detail. With a partner, discuss what happened and what was said in the scene. Write the script and read the scene for a group of students who have read the book.

2. After reading the book, make up a game (perhaps like *Trivial Pursuit* or *Jeopardy*) based on information from the story. Work in a group, and play your game with another group of students who have also read the book.

3. Design a cover or a magazine/newspaper advertisement for the book. Remember that the purpose of both the cover jacket and the ad is to make the book appealing enough for the intended audience to buy it. Start by deciding who you want the book jacket or ad to appeal to. Find some samples and examine them before you begin. Work on your own or with a partner.

4. Create a radio/television advertisement for the book. Start by deciding who you want the ad to appeal to. After it is written, record or videotape the ad and play it back for a group of students. Ask those who have read the book if they think your ad is effective. Ask those who have not read the book if the ad prompts them to do so.

5. Write a poem, a rap, or a song, or do a recitation based on the book. Find an effective way to present your work. If you write a poem, you might want to print it on poster paper and illustrate it, or, if you're proficient at word processing, make a print-out of your poem including some graphic design elements. If you write a song or rap, you may want to record or videotape it. If you choose to do a recitation, choose a part of the book that you think is particularly moving, funny, or interesting. Perform it for a small group or the class after you have practised.

6. Take your friends on a tour of the book. In the form of an oral presentation, introduce a few of your classmates to the characters in the book, the story-line, the settings, and any other aspects of the book that you find interesting. Choose two or three short passages to read to them; these may be passages that are especially funny, touching, beautiful, or scary. You may work on your own or with a partner.

7. Conduct a panel discussion with the characters in your book.

■ In a group of five or six, decide who the panelists will be (choose the three most interesting characters) and who will role-play each of them.

■ The remaining group members will be the questioners. The two or three questioners should make up several questions about what happens to the characters in the book (including their feelings about certain events, why they made the choices they did, etc.—the questions should go beyond factual information).

■ Direct the questions at specific panelists who should respond in role as the character would.

■ After a couple of practice questions, you may wish to present your panel discussion to another group or the whole class. When you run out of prepared questions, try to keep the role-play going with spontaneous questions!

8. Draw a map or an illustration, or make a model of the setting of your book. If you decide on a map, think about the places where the action in the story takes place, and show where they might be located in relation to each other. Be sure to label or code your map to show what took place where. If you prefer to draw an illustration, choose two or three of the most important settings of the book and make notes on the side or back of the drawing indicating what took place in these settings and why it was important to the story. If you choose to make a model, select a setting that particularly appeals to you, build the model, and explain why you chose it. Work on your own for this activity.

9. Make a comic strip version of a section of your book. Choose a part of the book that you especially like, and turn it into a comic strip. Before you print the dialogue in the word balloons, have someone proofread it for you. Staple the pages together to make a book and read it to a small group, showing them the pictures as you read.

10. Retell a part of the book from the point of view of a different character than who narrates the story (or, if there isn't a narrator in the book, from the point of view of any of the characters). You may either tell or write the new version of the story. Work on your own or with a partner.

11. Imagine what happened to the characters before the book began or after it ended. Write a story in the same style as the book telling about the events of the years previous to the years in the book, or telling about what happened to the characters in the years following the years of the book. Discuss the possibilities with a partner, and working on a word processor, if one is available, take turns composing the story. If a word processor isn't available, take turns writing the story and revising it as you would on the word processor. Alternatively, it might be interesting for one of you to write what happened before the book began and the other to write what happened after it ended. Read your work to your partner, to a small group, or to the class.

12. Write the diary of one of the characters in the book. It is best to choose a character who is not the narrator since the story is already based on his or her perceptions. Make up a series of entries covering events that occur throughout the book, and read your entries to a small group. You may work on your own or with a partner.

GLOSSARY

ANALYSIS

An analysis of a piece of writing or an idea involves breaking it down into its component parts and then evaluating the parts to check for their validity or effectiveness.

ADVERTISEMENT

An advertisement is a paid announcement. Newspapers use graphic and print ads; radio uses oral language, music, and other audio effects; television uses audio effects, graphics, and print.

ANTHOLOGY OF LITERATURE

An anthology of literature is a collection of literary pieces such as poetry, short stores, and plays.

ARGUMENT

An argument is a statement, or series of statements, supporting either side (pro or con) of an issue.

BIBLIOGRAPHY

A bibliography is a list of books and articles on a topic with enough information provided so that anyone can find the original source (book, newspaper, or magazine) easily. The bibliography is usually found at the end of a book or essay. It also indicates the materials that the author consulted while researching the topic. The order of information in a typical bibliographical entry is the author (last name first), the title (underlined), the place of publication, the publisher, and the date of publication. A typical bibliographical entry looks like the following:

Mowat, Farley, *Never Cry Wolf*. Toronto: Bantam Seal, 1963.

An *annotated* bibliography includes a brief description of the contents of the book or article and can include some indication of the value of the item to a researcher.

BLOCKING

Blocking is a term in theatre for the planned movements of the actors as they act out a scene.

BRAINSTORM

Brainstorming is a way of collecting many ideas in a short time. To brainstorm, find a comfortable place to talk and write notes. Decide how much time you are going to spend brainstorming. Group members, one at a time, should tell their ideas about the topic or question at hand. One person, chosen before the brainstorming starts, should jot down all the ideas. Don't make comments until all the ideas are recorded and/or the time for brainstorming is over. After brainstorming you can talk about the ideas and choose which ones you want to take further.

CAPTION

A caption is a sentence or two that explains what is happening in a drawing or photograph. It tells the who, what, where, when, and why of the scene. A picture of a girl seated at a computer might have this caption: "After school, Carmella sits at the library computer to do research for her assignment." Captions that accompany cartoons have a different purpose; they are meant to amuse the reader.

CHARTER OF RIGHTS

A charter of rights is a written document that outlines the rights and privileges of a person or group.

COLLAGE

A collage is a pictorial design made from photographs and scraps of cloth, paper, string, and the like, all of which are arranged and glued on a background. The photographs often are clipped from newspapers and magazines. A collage can be used to make a statement about a topic or idea.

COMMERCIAL

A commercial is an advertisement on radio or television. It is usually constructed to be entertaining as well as to sell a product or service.

DEDICATION PAGE

Often, the author of a book or an anthology will dedicate the book to someone special. The dedication page is found at the beginning of the book and can be as simple as "For Mom", or include more detail about the reason for the dedication.

DIALOGUE

A dialogue is a conversation between two people. When you write a dialogue you must be careful to follow certain rules of punctuation so the reader knows which character is speaking the lines. Here are some lines of dialogue from *"Homecoming"*:

"I fell asleep," Dicey said. "What time is it?"

"I dunno." James said. "You've been asleep a long time. I'm hungry."

"Where's Momma?"

"I dunno, I'm hungry."

DIARY

A diary is a person's private record of his or her feelings and experiences. Here is a sample diary entry.

June 10, 1985

Arvinder woke me up early to tell me that lightning had struck the oak tree on our front lawn. I went to the window and I couldn't believe what I saw. The oak used to be 25 metres tall, but it wasn't half that size anymore. The top of the tree had fallen over into the driveway. There were wood chips and branches everywhere, as if the tree had exploded. Part of the tree trunk was black from the heat of the lightning. Finally I noticed my bike, or what was left of it. Arvinder thought it looked funny, all bent up, but I didn't see anything to laugh about.

EDITORIAL

An editorial is an article written by the editor of a newspaper; it presents one or both sides of an argument and often ends with a suggested action. See page 90 of *"Extra! Extra! Read All About It"* for a sample editorial.

FLYER

A flyer is a one-page summary of ideas on a given topic put together for the purpose of advertising an event, a service, or a product, or for the purpose of giving information on the topic.

IMAGES

Images are word pictures. They convey vivid and concrete sensual pictures in words to the reader. Images are most frequently found in poetry, but appear in all types of writing.

JOB DESCRIPTION

A job description is the written outline of the duties and responsibilities of an employee.

LIGHTING

Lighting in a dramatic production refers to all use of lights on stage. It involves the use of coloured lights, spotlights, and blackouts. Frequently the lighting of the scene enhances the dramatic impact of the text of the play for the audience.

LETTERS

Business Letter

A business letter is written for the purpose of conducting business with the person or organization to whom the letter is written. The following format should be adhered to:

heading: Your address and the date appear in the upper right-hand corner.

inside address: The name, title, and address of the person or organization to whom you are writing appear at the left-hand margin.

salutation: It is common to use *Dear Sir or Madam:* or *To Whom It May Concern:* if you do not know the name of the individual.

body: The body should be clear and concise.

closing: Yours truly, Very truly yours, and *Sincerely yours*, are all appropriate closings.

signature: Sign below the closing and type your name below your signature. (Use both your first and second names.)

Remember to type business letters and to proofread carefully for errors.

Friendly Letter

A friendly letter is less formal than a business letter. As you might expect, it is an informal letter written from one friend to another. The following format is followed:

heading: Your address and the date appear in the upper right-hand corner.

greeting: Dear Doug, or *Natalie*, are suitable greetings.

body: The language is informal and the expression much more personal.

closing: The most common closing is *Love,* _____

signature: You usually use only your first name and there is no need to type it under the signature.

Many friendly letters are handwritten although it is not inappropriate for them to be typed or written on a word processor.

Letter of Application

A letter of application is similar to a business letter. The differences lie in the *body* of the letter. Be sure to include reference to the position for which you are applying and a summary of the qualifications and personal qualities you possess which make you a good candidate for the job. You will also want to state briefly why you want the job and any other pertinent details requested in the advertisement for the job. It is wise to enclose a résumé with your letter of application.

Letter to the Editor

A letter to the editor, as its name implies, is a letter written to the editor of a newspaper in response to an article, a news story, an advertisement, etc. which has appeared in the newspaper. It is a vehicle for the expression of the writer's opinion. Some television news programs also receive and broadcast letters to the producers which are very similar to letters to the editor. See page 96 of *"Extra! Extra! Read All About It"* for samples of letters to the editor.

NOTE

A note is a very short version of a friendly letter. There is no address, just a *date, greeting*, brief message forming the *body* of the note, and a *closing*. In addition to conveying pieces of information, notes have the purpose of expressing sympathy over a death, congratulating someone for an achievement, etc. See also *"Point-form Notes"* for a different definition.

PHOTOGRAPHS

A *feature* photograph is one that is short to accompany a particular article or story and may be posed.
A *spot news* photograph is a dramatic depiction at a news event caught by an on-the-spot photographer.

POINT-FORM NOTES

Point-form notes are a brief listing of main ideas for future reference.

POINT OF VIEW

A point of view is your personal way of seeing an issue, an event, or another person.

POSTER

A poster is a graphic depiction of a product or idea with the intention usually of drawing it to the attention of others. Posters are often used in advertising to sell a book or a play; in education, posters are often used to present an idea like how to write an essay or that smoking is harmful to your health.

PRESS RELEASE

A press release is a short news story issued by an organization which gives information on an event sponsored by that organization or on a noteworthy accomplishment of someone in the organization. The organization issuing the press release hopes that it will motivate the media to publicize the news.

PROFILE

A profile is a short character sketch or description of some aspect of a person. A profile may give a brief summary of someone's life, or it may tell what is special about a person.

PROPOSAL

A proposal is a description or outline of a plan of action put forward for the consideration of the person for whom it has been prepared.

QUESTIONNAIRE/SURVEY

A questionnaire/survey is a research tool designed to gather information on people's views on a particular topic or issue. The questionnaire/survey is composed of a number of questions to which there may be yes/no answers or longer answers. Once the questions are formulated and the questionnaire/survey is given to a number of people, the answers are analysed and conclusions are drawn.

RADIO BROADCAST

A radio broadcast is a program using words and sound effects to communicate information or to entertain.

RÉSUMÉ

A résumé is a summary of information about a job applicant's personal, educational, and work experience. There are many formats to choose from, but all require a neat, well-organized, and easy-to-read presentation of factual information.

REVIEW

A review describes a book, film, record, television show, concert, or some other performance or work of art. The reviewer gives personal opinions of the strengths and weaknesses of what he or she saw or heard. Here is a brief movie review as an example:

Gung Ho

One step forward, two steps back. Director Ron Howard's new comedy is sure no Cocoon. Nor is it a Splash. And even Night Shift, with its erratic plot and juvenile, sniggering sense of humour, had more charm and energy. It's not that Gung Ho is a bad film. It just isn't a particularly good one. And that's disappointment. The premise—the culture clash that arises when a Japanese automaker sets up shop in Smalltown America—makes a better 60 Minutes segment than it does a big-screen comedy. And star Michael Keaton doesn't possess the charisma to overcome his badly conceived character, a self-serving assembly-line foreman who becomes the liaison between the Japanese management and the hometown working stiffs.

ROLE-PLAY

To role-play is to pretend that you are another person. If you were role-playing Sandra, for example (see *"Breath of God"*), you would try to think, act, speak, and react exactly the way she would.

SCRAPBOOK

A scrapbook is a blank book into which newspaper clippings, photos, or pictures are pasted for a permanent record.

SCRIPT

A script is the format for writing a play, whether it is to be presented on stage, on radio or television, or as a movie. The characters' names are followed by what they say (their dialogue). In addition to the dialogue, there are stage directions, which describe what the stage should look like, what special effects should be used, and how the actors should speak and move.

SYNOPSIS

A synopsis is a short summary of the important ideas in an argument or the main points in a story.

SUMMARY

A summary is a brief outline of the main ideas of a paragraph or a longer piece of writing.

TABLEAU

A tableau is a dramatic representation, usually of a historical event, depicted by silent and motionless persons or wax figures suitably posed. A tableau can be compared to snapshots of action and may be combined in a series of four or five to depict key moments.

PARENTING

VOICES

ACADEMIC MASQUERADE

BILL COSBY

Most fathers are such good people that they don't even mind having their wardrobes looted by the daughters they love, a point that brings us back to the subject of clothes. A few months ago, one of my sweaters disappeared; and then, two weeks later, another sweater disappeared, soon followed by a third. Were it not for my fourteen-year-old daughter's allergy to makeup, I would still be wondering what happened to those sweaters, or perhaps to my mind.

One day during that crime wave, my wife and I were summoned to school by the nurse because our daughter's face had suddenly swollen. Had she come down with the mumps in geometry? Or had she been attacked by killer bees? No, she had been attacked by the makeup she was putting on at her locker, the lipstick and eyeliner and blusher that she was secretly wearing at school to become a person I wouldn't have recognized. The other part of this disguise was a choice of my sweaters: her locker contained three of them, and one of my sports jackets too.

And so, I learned that part of my daughter's schedule at school was a fashion elective: every day she shed the drab clothes her mother had chosen and became Miss Supercool, with clothes that belonged to me and makeup I unwittingly had paid for when I'd thought I was giving her money for magazines.

On certain girls, this makeup looks like something out of a police lineup: funky stuff that complements pants rolled high above her socks, half-laced sneakers with holes artfully punched in them, and one of your sweaters with a shirttail showing below. She had to steal three of your sweaters, of course, because she certainly couldn't be seen wearing the same one two days in a row. But she still looks better in your clothes than you ever did, and you can't wait to kiss that grease-painted cheek.

Letter to Sylvia

My dearest Sylvia,

When I heard you on the phone, I collapsed! Such sweet sorrow, I have never known. They told me when I gave you up that I would forget. Time would heal the memory, erase the scars. I would have others. I was one of the lucky ones. Well, as you saw, I had four more. Each loved. But not a one that could replace you, the first. And no. I never did forget.

I have spent my whole life crying myself to sleep. You will never know the agony of giving away your child. Taking that last glimpse of your newborn. Holding your baby one last time. Imprinting the delicate features in your mind. Dwelling on the dainty mouth pursed in smile. The faint strands of hair. The pudgy fingers, curled in a fist. . . .

Perhaps I should have simply looked the other way. Turned my cheek. Pretended you were not there. It had all been a bad dream. Perhaps that would have eased the pain. Then you were gone. As quickly as you came. Me, alone in my room, without a husband to share my grief. To hold me. My arms empty, devoid of life.

Sylvia, we can never have those years back. I have a new life, and you yours. I'm sorry things didn't work out. I thought I had made the best decision. That's what they told me. If it's any consolation, they were wrong. So very wrong. Things didn't work out, for either of us.

As you requested, I have enclosed all the information on your background. I'm sorry about your little boy. That came from my side.

You will always be welcome in my house. Welcomed as a daughter. I will always be your natural mother. But not your parent. Not the one who wiped your runny nose, tied your shoelaces, or comforted you in sickness. No, not even the one who held your trembling hands on your wedding day, or beamed with pride as you walked down the aisle.

If only things had been different. . .

Trusting we will meet again.

Love,
Mother

LETTER TO TERI

Dear Teri,

It is difficult to grow up. It is very difficult to leave your home. It is not only hard on you, but on your family.

Perhaps, from your perspective, your feelings are justified. Let me tell you my feelings.

Children are a mixed blessing. They are a tremendous source of work, time spent, money invested, pain, joy, sadness, pride, closeness. You often wonder if they understand—or care—about the things you give them while you do without—the nights you bake all night to give them happy memories—the fears you have for them because they *do refuse* to understand that life is not really going to be a 'take' situation when they get out in it—as it is *now* while they are safe in the growing years.

I believe growing-up-years of safety are vital to a child. (Maybe I'm wrong) . . . Some parents protect their children long past the time when they are ready to make their own way in the world—to work as well as play. This makes children dependent and soft and makes parents feel strong and important. It makes me feel disgusted and sick because it is a manipulative thing to do. Some parents never protect their children and throw them into life's challenges very young without much preparation. If the child survives this it will be strong but it may know little about love and supportive feelings and attitudes—sharing and caring.

Remember the saying I used to keep on the refrigerator? "A mother is not a person to lean on but a person to make leaning unnecessary."

When the day comes for your child to leave home, you want them to be able to say, "Mom, I'm ready! I can do it, Mom! I'm going to fly on my own." It hurts when your child says,

"You don't love me. You don't want me or understand me. I'm getting out of here. I'm leaving you!"

You *are* ready to go, Teri. I assure you you *can* fly. It is time for you to do it. I don't think it was wrong for you to leave. I only wish you had chosen another way to do it. But, that was your decision. (Remember, it is as disgusting to be a manipulative *child* as it is to be a manipulative *parent*.)

You have mountains to climb—without me. I don't even know your world, I don't know your mountains.

You have my love. You have my support and my encouragement. (I cheer good.) You have me believing you can do what you *want* to do—whatever it is. That's all I can give you now. I've done the best I could do as your mother. I know I've failed you sometimes, it is unavoidable in raising a human being—especially when you are only a human being yourself, and you are still climbing your own mountains.

The best thing you can do is believe in yourself. Don't be afraid to try. Don't be afraid to fail. Just try again. Just dust yourself off and try again. (Remember the guy—Billy Joe Armstrong—who told me 'Don't bother to dust yourself off—just get up and *go!*')

The last and most important thing to remember is:

Philippians 4:13, 'I can do all things through Christ who strengthens me.'

My love and thoughts go with you. My first child. My daughter.

Love,
MOM

A CHILD CALLED NOAH

JOSH GREENFIELD

July 1, 1966

I'm a father. I'm drunk. I have another son. His name is Noah Jiro. He was born this evening a few minutes after seven and weighed seven pounds, ten ounces. And whereas Karl seemed to look like me at birth, Noah is luckier. He looks like his Japanese mother, Foumi.

I saw Noah Jiro as he passed on the way to the maternity ward. And next I saw Foumi. She was not very sleepy. Though induced at full term, it was supposed to be a natural childbirth, so I guess she had had only a pinch of anesthesia when it came time to sew her up. I followed the caravan. And soon I was standing at the nursery window, noting proudly to the stranger next to me how much hair Noah had.

I think of my dead father now. I think of the living Noah I already love. He seems like the son of my father to me, just as Karl is the son of my mother, I do not know why, but that is so. Of course, they are both the sons of Foumi too. But then nothing so important is ever that simple.

Anyway, I am happier than I ever thought I would be. I wanted a daughter. I know. But I rejoice in having a second son. Noah Jiro—the name is a breath of hope.

July 2, 1966

I am not such a good daddy. I am not used to the fulltime chore of baby-tending. I was a bit careless. I left Karl alone for a moment this afternoon when I went downstairs to put the laundry in the washing machine. I returned to find a broken glass on the floor, its shards splintered in many directions. Luckily Karl was not hurt.

I saw Noah in the hospital today. He seemed to look just the way Karl had looked during his first days of life. Suddenly, in a small but overwhelming way time stood still.

A C T I V I T I E S

Voices
pp. 216–220

1. Assign each member of your group of four one of the letters or monologues to prepare for reading aloud. Once you have practised, read your letter or monologue for the others in the group. After you have read it, comment briefly on how it affected you and ask the others for their reactions.

2. In your group discuss what you think are the qualities of a good parent and make a list to be posted in the classroom along with those of other groups working on this activity. How would you rate the men and women in the letters and monologues as parents, given the limited information available?

3. In your journal write about how well your parent(s) or guardian(s) have parented you or about how you might do as a parent. Read your entry to someone in your group, if you like.

4. Read the letter or monologue you find most interesting to one of your parents or guardians and ask him or her about the pleasures and difficulties of parenting.

CHILDHOOD THROUGH THE AGES

~

ELIN MCCOY

 gentleman-in-waiting and the nurse of little Comte de Marle often amused themselves tossing the swaddled infant back and forth across the sill of an open window. One day one of them failed to catch him, and the infant landed on a stone step and died.

The surgeon of the newborn Louis XIII cut the "fiber" under his tongue a few days after he was born, believing that if it remained uncut, Louis would be unable to suck properly and would eventually stutter. . . .

Throughout history, parents' treatment of infants and very small children has been characterized by psychological coldness and physical brutality that horrify most of us today. But this behavior becomes at least comprehensible when we realize some of the conditions of people's lives. The physical realities of life were oppressive. And there were severe parental limitations as well in addition to being influenced by unscientific medical knowledge and religious views about the nature of man, most adults had to concentrate so much of their energy on mere survival that they had little time to care for or worry about infants and small children.

Abusive and violent behavior was common among adults and, therefore, not looked on with disapproval when it appeared in the treatment of children.

In view of the following facts, consider what your experience as a parent and your child's experience as an infant would have been if you had lived prior to the eighteenth century.

Your child probably wouldn't have been wanted. Lack of birth control meant that having children was not a choice. For poverty-stricken peasants, an infant meant another mouth to feed—and food was precious—as well as interference with the mother's role as a worker whose contribution was necessary to the family's ability to survive. In all classes, the high risk of maternal mortality made the birth of a child a traumatic event. Even in the relatively healthy conditions enjoyed by the inhabitants of Plymouth Colony, 20 per cent of women died from causes related to childbirth (compared with under 1 per cent today), and in seventeenth-century England and France, the rates were much higher. It's no wonder that most children were probably unwanted.

Your infant would have had a good chance

of dying before his or her first birthday. In medieval England and seventeenth-century France, for example, between 20 and 50 per cent of all infants died within the first year after birth. Complications of childbirth, prematurity, diseases such as smallpox and the plague, and generally unsanitary living conditions, as well as such customs as baptism in icy water in freezing churches, took a heavy toll among vulnerable newborns.

The likelihood that one's infants would die discouraged parents from investing much affection or interest in them and from regarding them as special, unique individuals until it appeared more certain that they might live to adulthood.

Illegitimate infants and infants of poverty-stricken parents (and parents who felt they already had enough children) were often the victims of infanticide through deliberate murder, abandonment, or neglect. In ancient Greece, for example, infants, who seemed sickly or didn't have a perfect shape or cried too much or too little were "exposed," or abandoned to die, a decision that was made by the father shortly after birth. In mid-eighteenth-century England, so many babies—both legitimate and illegitimate—were abandoned to die in the streets of cities and towns that the first foundling home established in London received several thousand babies a year. In early America, infanticide seems to have affected only illegitimate children.

If you were well-off, your baby probably would have been breast-fed by someone else. In spite of the fact that all medical advice since Roman times had stressed that babies breast-fed by their own mothers had a better chance of survival, for eighteen centuries any woman who could afford it sent her infant to a wet nurse.

Recuperation from a difficult childbirth prevented some women from breast-feeding, but many others thought it too demanding, especially since it was customary for infants to breast-feed for as long as two years. Also, many husbands would not allow their wives to breast-feed, partly because medical opinion held that women who were breast-feeding should not engage in sexual intercourse.

Underlying these reasons may have been parents' desire to distance themselves emotionally from their infants.

In Renaissance Italy, middle-class infants were delivered to the *bália*, or wet nurse, immediately after baptism—two or three days after birth—and, if they survived, remained there for two years. Rarely did mothers visit their infants, and thus a baby was returned home at the end of that time to a stranger. . . .

The first groups of middle class women to change this 1800-year-old pattern on a large scale were the Puritans in the seventeenth century. Eventually, in the eighteenth century, there was a widespread cult of maternal breast-feeding in both America and England. Scholars have suggested that this shift may have contributed substantially to the shift in parental feelings for infants that began in the eighteenth century; certainly it reduced infant mortality.

Your infant would have spent little time with you. In the past, parents spent much less time with their children than even working parents do today and clearly did not feel the need to arrange supervision for them. Peasant women commonly left their infants and toddlers alone all day at home while they worked elsewhere. In one area of England during the thirteenth century, for example, half the infant deaths involved infants in cradles being burned while no one was home. Unsupervised toddlers frequently wandered off and drowned. In the middle and upper class, parental neglect took the form of turning toddlers over to the servants to raise.

Your infant would have been swaddled in tightly bound cloths from birth to as old as eight months. Emotional distancing, economic necessity, and faulty medical knowledge are also evident in another common practice—swaddling. . . .

Kept in tightly bound bandages, swaddled infants were totally isolated from their surroundings for the first four months or so. After that, only their legs were bound. They couldn't turn their heads, suck their own thumbs for comfort, or crawl. Swaddling that was too tight occasionally caused suffocation. Although doctors advocated changing the infant two or three times a day, this apparently was uncommon, and even Louis XIII developed severe rashes because of his swaddling bands.

Medical reasons for the practice included the beliefs that if free, the infant might tear off his ears or scratch out his eyes, that swaddling was necessary to keep infants warm in cold, draughty cottages, houses, and castles, and that it ensured that the infant's pliable limbs would grow straight so he would be able to stand erect. Even when the swaddling bands were removed from their legs, children were not allowed to crawl "like an animal," but were forced to stand with the help of bizarre contraptions. Convenience was another reason for swaddling: it caused infants to sleep more and cry less, so they could be left for long periods of time while mothers worked. Also, swaddled infants were easier to carry and could even be hung on a peg on the wall out of the way.

Your infant or child would probably have received harsh beatings regularly—from you or a servant—even for such "normal" behaviour as crying or wanting to play. For many centuries, discipline and teaching of the infant and young child concentrated on "breaking the child's will," which meant crushing all assertiveness and instilling complete obedience. This was accomplished through physical and psychological maltreatment that today we would consider "child abuse". . . .

These child-rearing practices as well as the difficult realities of life in the past, had important psychological effects on children's development. According to Professor Stone, (director of Princeton University's Shelby Cullom Davis Centre for Historical Studies) the isolation, sensory deprivation, and lack of physical closeness that resulted from swaddling; the absence of a mother because of death in childbirth or the practice of wet-nursing, the common experience for small children of losing parents and siblings, and the suppression of self-assertion through whipping and other fear-producing techniques all resulted in an "adult world of emotional cripples."

WHY TV IS KILLING THE IDEA OF CHILDHOOD

~

NEIL POSTMAN

Television is causing the rapid decline of our concept of childhood. . . .

If this pronouncement, on first hearing, seems implausible, let me hasten to tell you that the idea of childhood is not very old. In fact, in the Western world the idea of childhood hardly existed prior to the 16th century. Up until that time children as young as 6 and 7 were not regarded as fundamentally different from adults. As far as historians can tell, the languages of children, their dress, their games, their labor, and their legal rights were the same as those of adults.

It was recognized, of course, that children tended to be smaller than adults, but this fact did not confer upon them any special status. . . .

If you have ever seen 13th- or 14th-century paintings of children, you will have noticed that they are always depicted as small adults. Except for size, they are devoid of any of the physical characteristics we associate with childhood; and they are never shown on canvas alone—that is, isolated from adults. Such paintings are entirely accurate representations of the psychological and social perceptions of children prior to the 16th century. Here is how the historian J.H. Plumb puts it:

There was no separate world of childhood. Children shared the same games with adults, the same toys, the same fairy stories. They lived their lives together, never apart. . . .

Barbara Tuchman, in her marvelous book about the 14th century titled *A Distant Mirror*, puts it more succinctly: "If children survived to age 7, their recognized life began, more or less as miniature adults. Childhood was already over."

Now the reasons for this are fairly complicated. For one thing, most children did *not* survive; their mortality rate was extraordinarily high, and it is not until the late 14th century that children are even mentioned in wills and testaments—an indication that adults did not expect them to be around very long. In fact, probably because of this, in some parts of Europe children were treated as neuter genders. In 14th century Italy, for example, the sex of a child who had died was never recorded.

Certainly, adults did not have the emotional commitment to children that we accept as normal. Phillipe Aries, in his great book titled *Centuries of Childhood*, remarks that the prevailing view was to have several children in order to keep a few; people could not allow themselves to become too attached to something that was regarded as a probable loss.

We must also not forget that in a feudal society children were often regarded as mere economic utilities, adults being less interested in the character and intelligence of children than in their capacity for work. But I think the most powerful reason for the

absence of the idea of childhood is to be found in the communication environment in the Dark and Middle Ages. Since most people did not know how to read, or did not *need* to know how to read, a child became an adult—a fully participating adult—when he or she learned how to speak.

Since all important social transactions involved face-to-face oral communication, full competence to speak and hear—which is usually achieved by age 7—was the dividing line between infancy and adulthood. There was no intervening stage, because none was needed—until the middle of the 15th century.

At that point an extraordinary event occurred that not only changed the religious, economic, and political face of Europe but also created our modern idea of childhood. I am referring, of course, to the invention of the printing press. . . .

Less than a hundred years after Gutenberg's invention, European culture became a reading culture; i.e., adulthood was redefined. One could not become an adult unless he or she knew how to read. In order to experience God, one had to be able, obviously, to read the Bible, which is why Luther himself translated the Bible into German.

The importance of books of etiquette should not be overlooked. As Norman Elias shows in his book titled *The Civilizing Process*, the sudden emergence in the 16th century of etiquette books signifies that one could no longer assume that children knew everything adults knew—in other words, the separation of childhood from adulthood was underway.

Alongside of all this, Europeans rediscovered what Plato had known about learning to read: namely, that it is best done at an early age. . . .

What this came to mean in the 16th century is that the young had to be separated from the rest of the community to be taught how to read—that is, to be taught how to function as an adult. This meant that they had to go to school. And going to school was the essential event in creating childhood. The printing press, in other words, created the idea of school. In fact, school classes originated to separate students according to their capacities as readers, not to separate them according to age.

For the past 350 years we have been developing and refining our concept of childhood, this with particular intensity in the 18th, 19th and 20th centuries. We have been developing and refining institutions for the nurturing of children; and we have conferred upon children a preferred status, reflected in the special ways we expect them to think, talk, dress, play, and learn.

All of this, I believe, is now coming to an end. And it is coming to an end because our communication environment has been radically altered once again—this time by electronic media, especially television. . . .

It is my contention that, with the assistance of other media such as radio, film, and records, television has the power to lead us to childhood's end.

Here is how the transformation is happening. To begin with, television presents information mostly in visual images. Although human speech is heard on TV and sometimes assumes importance, people mostly *watch* television. What they watch are rapidly changing visual images—as many as 1200 different shots every hour. This requires very little conceptual thinking of analytic decoding. TV watching is almost wholly a matter of pattern recognition.

The *symbolic form* of television does not require any special instruction or learning. In America, TV viewing begins at about the age of 18 months; by 30 months, according to studies by Daniel Anderson of the University of Massachusetts, children begin to understand and respond to TV imagery. Thus there is no need for any preparation or prerequisite training for watching TV.

Unlike books, which may be scaled according to the ability of the reader, TV presents information in a form that is undifferentiated in its accessibility. And that is why adults and children tend to watch the same programs. . . .

To summarize: TV eases the dividing line between childhood and adulthood for two reasons: first, because it requires no instruc-

tion to grasp its form; second, because it does not segregate its audience. It communicates the same information to everyone simultaneously, regardless of age, sex, race, or level of education.

But it erases the dividing line in other ways as well. One might say that the main difference between an adult and a child is that the adult knows about certain facets of life—its mysteries, its contradictions, its violence, its tragedies—that are not considered suitable for children to know. As children move toward adulthood we reveal these secrets to them in what we believe to be a psychological assimilable way.

But television makes this arrangement quite impossible. Because television operates virtually around the clock—it would not be economically feasible for it to do otherwise—it requires a constant supply of novel and interesting information. This means that all adult secrets—social, sexual, physical, and the like—must be revealed.

And yet, as TV begins to render invisible the traditional concept of childhood, it would not be quite accurate to say that it immerses us in an adult world. Rather, it uses the material of the adult world as the basis for projecting a new kind of person altogether. We might call this person the adult-child.

For reasons that have partly to do with TV's capacity to reach everyone, partly to do with the accessibility of its symbolic form, and partly to do with its commercial base, TV promotes as desirable many of the attitudes that we associate with childishness: for example, an obsessive need for immediate gratification, a lack of concern for consequences, an almost promiscuous preoccupation with consumption, TV seems to favour a population that consists of three age groups: on the one end, infancy: on the other, senility: and in between, a group of indeterminate age where everyone is somewhere between 20 and 30 and remains that way until dotage descends.

A C T I V I T I E S

**Once Upon a Time
pp. 222–227**

1. Form a small group and read "Childhood through the Ages." Select two or three details you found most interesting about raising children in the past and read them aloud to the group.

2. a) Visit your local art gallery or museum or use art books from the library or the visual arts classroom for the purpose of looking at the children in pictures from the 13th-17th centuries. Make notes on the clothes they were wearing, the activities in which they are involved, their relationship to the adults in the picture, and the expressions on their faces.

   b) Compare the images of children in contemporary paintings with the images from the past.

   c) Report your findings to the class, using the illustrations from the art books to aid your talk. See the Student Handbook (page 194) for tips on making oral presentations to the class.

3. Each of these writers would have drawn up an outline before writing the article. Choose one of the articles and with a partner write the outline the author might have written. Exchange your outline with a group that worked on the other article.

4. Form a small group; discuss what idea is being communicated in each of the following passages from "Why TV Is Killing the Idea of Childhood":

   This requires very little conceptual thinking or analytical decoding. TV watching is almost wholly a matter of pattern recognition.

   TV presents information in a form that is undifferentiated in its accessibility. And that is why adults and children tend to watch the same programs.

   TV promotes as desirable many of the attitudes that we associate with childishness: for example, an obsessive need for immediate gratification, a lack of concern for consequences, an almost promiscuous preoccupation with consumption.

O WHAT VENERABLE & REVEREND CREATURES

SHARON BUTALA

"He said it was a heart attack," Meredith said. She could not find the cradle for the phone; the phone wouldn't fit. "He said she was bringing dessert to the table and she started to stagger. She sat down and then she just said, 'oh,' and fell over." Meredith suddenly let go of the receiver and balled the napkin she had been holding, pressing it against her face, trying to stifle the noise she could hear herself making. She heard Bill move, felt his arm go around her, felt his hand smoothing her hair.

"Poor girl," he said. "Poor girl."

There was a rustling in the doorway. Stacey. Stacey would have to be told. Meredith wiped her eyes with the napkin and stood back from Bill who had turned to the door. Stacey was leaning against the door frame, one hand raised to her shoulder, the thin, nicotine-stained fingers twisting a lock of thick, curly brown hair that hung uncombed in a mass around her shoulders. Her eyes glittered. The petulance of her expression made her look younger than eighteen.

"Who was that?" she asked, looking at the phone instead of at them. Even when she was in a rage or coldly withdrawn from them she could not change the startling depth and resonance of her voice. It was the voice of a great stage actress.

"Your Grandpa Robertson," Bill said. "Your grandmother is dead." Meredith put her hand on Bill's arm. These days he was often too harsh with Stacey.

"About two hours ago," she said, and tried to think of something to add that might comfort Stacey. Stacey's expression, held so carefully false for so long, had wavered and almost softened. She took a step into the room, staring at her mother.

"Oh," she said. "Oh." Meredith moved toward Stacey who, remembering herself, stiffened theatrically and made as if to back away.

Bill, watching, his voice impatient, said, "We can get the first flight west in the morning. I'll start making the arrangements." He patted Meredith's shoulder. When he reached the doorway he stopped. "You'd better start packing, Stacey," he said. "You're coming too." Meredith could see the sudden shine of sweat on Stacey's neck as she lifted her chin. They watched her, Bill indifferent, no longer even amused; Meredith sadly, seeing how beautiful she was, like some spoiled decadent rich child in the movies, her rich dark hair, her fine nose, the dark shadows around her eyes, the hysteria always just beneath her skin.

"You must be out of your mind," Stacey said. She shoved her hands into her jeans pockets, lifted her chin and turned toward the door. Bill didn't move, blocking it with his big, square body. He looked down at her. "I can't get away from school," she said. A tremor had crept into her voice as Bill stared at her and didn't move. "You were so damned anxious for me to go back and now. . . ."

"I know it's semester break," Bill interrupted. His voice was tight, his bitterness barely covered. "I know you failed all three courses. The school called my office. They can't see any point in your coming back for another semester. You're just wasting everybody's time, they said." Standing behind her, Meredith saw Stacey's shoulders quiver. Stacey was all quicksand inside and whenever she opened and the wave of her uncertainty pulsed through the air to Meredith, she remembered. Stacey, a four-five-six-year-old, screaming in terror. Smiling in the morning as if there was no blackness, no endless night. "Start packing," Bill said. "We are all going to your grandmother's funeral." Stacey twisted one shoulder and slid past him without speaking.

In the morning they boarded a plane, Bill in his grey three-piece suit, Meredith in her aging but still smart blue Chanel, and Stacey, rumpled and sleepy, her hair uncombed, wearing fraying faded jeans and a stained brown suede windbreaker. They flew west with Stacey seated several rows behind them stilting their conversation and

"You'd better start packing, Stacey, . . . You're coming too."

poisoning Meredith's grief with her hostility, which they could feel boring through the several rows of seats between them.

At Regina they rented a car and drove west for another four hours, soon leaving the wide paved highway for roads that grew narrower and more and more treacherous with snow and ice. Meredith had not been home for more than a year. She was a rancher's daughter, but she had lived the last twenty years in Toronto, and for the last fifteen she had taught chemistry at the university. Each time she returned home she was grateful that she had escaped the hardship, the male chauvinism, the ignorance.

The church was full even though outside a blizzard was blowing. Her father had begun to stoop and to move more slowly. After the service, stepping out of the church onto the snow-covered, windy step, he hesitated and looked around in a bewildered way as if he was surprised to find himself still in the town of his birth.

At the cemetery high on the hillside the wind whipped the snow across the rectangular hole in the ground and made their coats flap against their legs. Stacey had refused to get out of the car although Meredith did not notice this till after. The minister hurried through the ceremony, his words lost in the storm.

The next day Bill left to go back east, leaving Stacey and Meredith behind to look after Meredith's father for a week or two until he "could get back on his feet."

At breakfast when Meredith served him his bacon and eggs, her father put his arm around her and said, "You're a good girl, Merry. Never gave us a moment's trouble. Who'd ever think I'd have a professor for a daughter." Meredith kissed his forehead and sat down. "Your mother and me," he said carefully, as if he was trying out the sound of it, "your mother and me," he repeated, stronger this time "we . . . ." He seemed to have forgotten what he had started to say.

"Maybe now you'll think about retirement," Meredith said.

"Yeah," he said. He stirred his coffee. "You and Stacey could chase the cows around to the feed ground this morning," he said. "You know, like you used to. It's too damn cold for them to go without feed."

"All right," Meredith said. "It'll be good for Stacey to have something to do."

After her father had gone out, Meredith knocked on Stacey's door. At home she had given up waking Stacey. Usu-

ally she went off to the university and left Stacey in bed. When she came home at night Stacey was usually gone and Meredith would hear her coming in at three or four in the morning deliberately making some noise so that she and Bill would know how late it was.

"Wake up Stacey," she called. "Your grandpa needs us. We have to give him a hand." Silence. "Stacey?" she called, opening the door. Stacey was lying on her back staring at the ceiling. Her clothes were strewn on the floor. The room had a musty, closed-in smell.

Stacey threw back the covers and sat on the side of the bed. Meredith went back to the kitchen. In a few minutes Stacey came in wearing the same jeans and shirt she had worn since the funeral. Her hair needed washing and there was sleep in the corners of her eyes.

"What?" Stacey asked.

"We have to chase the cattle away from the riverbed up onto the feed grounds." Stacey was staring at the outdoor thermometer.

"It's twenty below out there!" she said. "You must be nuts!"

"I am not nuts," Meredith said, banging the coffee-pot. "When it's very cold like this, they go down into all the nooks and crannies along the riverbed looking for shelter." She poured Stacey a cup of coffee without looking at her. "And then they don't hear the tractor, or see the feed coming and they miss it." She put the coffee-pot back on the stove. "And then they can't endure the cold without good feed and they die." She tried to smile at Stacey. "So it is essential that we go out and chase them up. It's only about a mile and a half."

"Damn!" Stacey said, but Meredith saw the welling brightness in her eyes and knew nothing would stop Stacey from going, from trying the bitter air in her lungs, from testing the feel of the thigh-deep snow, from challenging a 1200-pound range cow or as suddenly grovelling in terror in front of one.

On the third morning Stacey rose without being called. She came into the kitchen where Meredith, already wearing most of her outdoor clothes, was hurrying to get the dishes washed before she went out. Stacey poured herself a cup of coffee, not answering her mother's "good morning," and stood watching at the window.

"You don't need to go out this morning," she said. Her voice sounded as if she hadn't spoken for weeks. "I know what to do."

> "... Meredith saw the welling brightness in her eyes and knew nothing would stop Stacey ..."

"I don't mind," Meredith said.

"I can do it!" Stacey said. "Meredith." She rolled the r. Meredith flushed but didn't speak. Stacey put on her parka and went outside. Meredith could hear her whistling for the dogs.

When the dishes were done, the beds made and a pie in the oven, Stacey had still not returned. I'll bet she's romping with the dogs in the snow, or maybe examining those caves along the riverbank, Meredith thought. It surprised her to think that Stacey might be having fun. It struck her now how little fun there was in Stacey's life, or that Stacey, a creature of contradictions, paradoxes and extremes, probably did not know what fun was. Whenever the police brought her back after she had run away (and then seemed not to know what to do with herself, or even why she had gone), she always looked so pale and sickly Meredith could only pity her, for the demon that pursued her and would not give her peace.

"A plastic bag full of something that looked like dried grass."

She decided to clean Stacey's room for her as a way of thanking her for saving her from the long, difficult walk along the river bottom. She stripped the bed and put clean sheets on it and put away the discarded clothes. Stacey's suitcase was still lying on the floor. Meredith picked it up by the handle intending to set it upright in the closet, but as she lifted it, it fell open spilling the contents. Oh no, Meredith thought, she'll accuse me of snooping. Quickly she bent over and began to replace the tangled underwear and shifts. Something fell out onto the floor. A plastic bag full of something that looked like dried grass. Meredith picked it up. Marijuana. No wonder the room smelled so stuffy.

I might have known, she thought. Stacey the troublemaker, the eternal embarrassment, the albatross she and Bill wore around their necks. How could she do such a thing? How could she bring this into her grandparents' house, especially at a time like this? She went to the kitchen and looked out the window. Stacey was crossing the yard toward the house, snow clinging to her pants above the knees, the dogs jumping at her side.

She came into the house stamping the snow off her boots, and throwing back her hood. Meredith stood in the doorway of the kitchen facing her, holding the bag chest-high in front of her. Stacey looked at it. For a moment she said nothing. Then she said, "Snooping again?" and grabbed for the bag. Meredith jerked it out of her reach and stepped back into the kitchen.

"How could you do this?" she asked.

"It's only grass, Meredith," Stacey said. "It's no big deal. How could you do this?" she mimicked her mother.

Meredith reached out, she did not know she was going to do this, and slapped Stacey across the face. They stared at each other. Meredith was not sorry she had hit Stacey. Stacey's face had drained white, the red slap mark standing out like a birthmark.

The bag of marijuana had fallen to the floor. Neither of them bent to pick it up. Stacey's eyes began to fill with tears. Two large drops gathered at the bottom of her eyes and as Meredith watched, they spilled over and began to run down Stacey's cheeks.

"You have caused me so much pain," Meredith said. She bent and picked up the bag, took it to the half-bath that was by the backdoor, emptied it into the toilet and flushed it. Stacey still had not moved. Meredith had begun to shake. She waited for the screams, the attack, or the fainting.

"Meredith was surprised Stacey was still there."

There was a thumping on the step outside the door and then Meredith's father called, opening the door, "Somebody give me a hand here." Meredith opened the door. He was struggling into the house pushing a slick, reddish creature ahead of him. Stacey gasped and put her hand over her mouth.

"It's a new calf, sweetheart," her grandfather said, laughing at her expression. If he saw the red mark or the tears, he gave no sign.

"Is it alive?" Stacey asked. "Ugh!" she said. "It's all slimy!" Her grandfather put the calf down on the hall floor with a thump.

"Got to get it warmed up," he said, "or it'll die."

"What are you doing, Dad, calving in January?" Meredith asked. She was surprised at how normal her voice sounded.

"Goddamn bulls must have got in with the heifers last spring. I found this one near the feed grounds, just born."

"Heifer okay?" Meredith asked, falling into the language.

"Yeah, that one's all right, but I found another dead one north. Calving too long. I didn't know they'd been bred. You can't tell with heifers. Now look at the mess. It's ears are frozen down."

"The cord's frozen too," Meredith said. Behind her, Stacey made a "yuck" sound. Meredith was surprised Stacey was still there.

"It'll be safe in the half-bath till it gets warm and dries

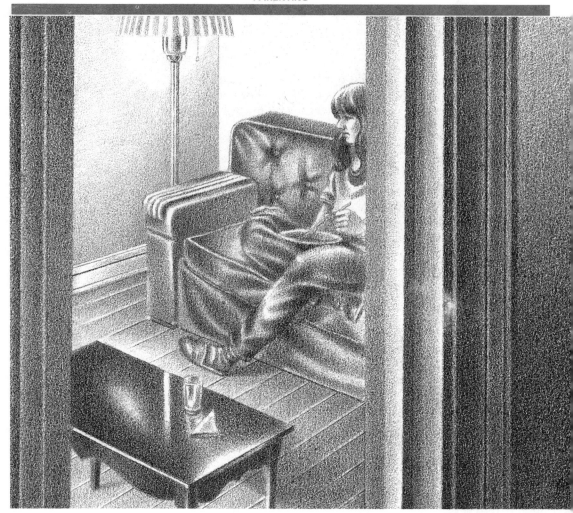

off," he said. "I didn't dare leave it for the mother to lick it off." He stood up. "There's bound to be more," he said. "I have to go check the rest of the herd. Keep an eye on it, Merry," he said. "You too, Stacey." He went outside. Stacey knelt, ignoring Meredith, cooing to the calf.

In the late afternoon Meredith's father came back to the house carrying another calf. Meredith was reading in the living-room. When she went to the kitchen she saw Stacey on her hands and knees in the half-bath trying to dry the calf off with Meredith's blow-dryer. Meredith left the room quickly before either of them saw her.

Every morning Stacey chased the cattle down the riverbed and when she finished that, she went up to the feed grounds and helped her grandfather and his hired man fork the hay off the flatdeck to the waiting cattle. After

that the three of them would come in for the noon meal
that Meredith would have ready and then, leaving the
dishes for Meredith, they would go down to the barn and
help the new calves nurse. Stacey usually didn't answer
if Meredith spoke to her. The days dragged by.

Meredith's father came hurrying in late one afternoon.

"Jim and I have to take that steer to the vet," he said.
"We should be back by seven. Got a heifer due to calve
in the barn so I have to get back as soon as I can."

Stacey ate her supper in front of the television set that
was in the living-room. Meredith ate at her place in the
kitchen.

At eight o'clock Meredith's father had still not returned.
The temperature had dropped to thirty below and the
wind was rising. She supposed he was storm-stayed some-

where. After a lifetime in this country, she told herself, he will know how to take care of himself. Remembering the heifer, she put on her parka and went down to the barn. It had begun to calve. She could see the end of one tiny hoof protruding from beneath the upraised tail. She studied the heifer nervously. She couldn't tell if it had been trying to deliver for a long time or not. Oh lord, she thought, what will I do? She decided to wait an hour before she tried to help. Maybe her father would be back by then.

At nine o'clock she went back to the barn. Now she could see both hooves. That's too slow. We'll have to help her. I wish Dad would get home. She went back to the house and said, "Stacey," to her daughter who had not taken her eyes off the television.

"What?" Stacey said.

> "Stacey's eyes, wide, bright and hard, had shifted away from Meredith to some invisible thing . . ."

"That heifer can't deliver on her own, and your grandfather's not back and . . . we'll have to pull it."

"Pull it yourself," Stacey said.

"I can't, Stacey," Meredith cried. "I'm not strong enough. You have to help me. I can't do it alone." To her amazement tears were running down her cheeks. She wiped them off and then stared at the wet streak on her hand. Stacey was watching her now, that brightness back in her eyes. "Please help me, Stacey," she said. "The heifer will die if we don't pull her calf. And the calf will die right away if we don't get it out of there." Stacey's eyes, wide, bright and hard, had shifted away from Meredith to some invisible thing; her mouth was open, she was almost smiling. She rose and went to the kitchen with Meredith following and put on her borrowed parka, her boots and mittens.

The weather had been getting steadily worse. When they opened the back door it blew out of their hands and banged against the wall. They had to walk backwards to the barn, the wind, bitterly cold now, was blowing into their faces with such force.

"Well, where is she?" Stacey asked when they were inside the barn. Meredith pointed. The cow raised her head and mooed. Stacey went to her and stared at the little pair of hooves. "How do we pull it?" she asked.

"This is all I know how to do," Meredith said. She picked a rope hanging from a nail on the wall. It had a loop on one end. She went to the heifer and set the loop over the two protruding hooves and tightened it. "Take the end." She hung onto the rope just ahead of Stacey. "Pull!" Meredith grunted. "One, two, three!" They pulled so hard that when the calf came in one whoosh, they fell backward into the straw on top of each other.

"We did it!" Stacey said, standing and staring at the calf.

"I bet it weighs close to a hundred pounds," Meredith said. They took the rope off the calf and stood back, their white breaths fading above them.

"I don't know how we're going to get it to the house, especially in that wind."

"It'll freeze to death if we don't," Stacey said. She pushed open the barn door. They each took an end of the calf and staggering with its weight, floundering in the snowdrifts, falling, being pushed off course and blinded by the wind-driven snow, they got the calf to the house. It had taken them fifteen minutes. They put the calf in the half-bath and Meredith turned up the thermostat.

"It looks okay," Stacey said dubiously.

"Well, it doesn't look any worse than the others did anyway," Meredith answered. "I'll put some coffee on. I hope Dad gets here soon."

They turned the television set on and sat drinking coffee in the warm living-room. Now and then the calf in the bathroom bleated and made a knocking noise with its hooves as it tried to stand.

"I can just imagine the mess in there," Meredith said. Stacey laughed. "I wish we'd had time to spread newspapers." Suddenly she realized that she had not been watching Stacey, she had been only looking at her as one person looks at another during a conversation. It had been years, years, since she had simply talked to Stacey, since she had been able to forget that this was her disturbed, delinquent child who couldn't be trusted, who had to be watched. Now she noticed that Stacey had put on a little weight, she was not quite so painfully, deliberately thin, and her skin was less yellowish and sickly looking. Stacey had lit a cigarette and was lounging in the chair laughing at something on the television. Her socks were not clean. Her jeans were worn out and clumsily patched, her cotton shirt faded and she wore no bra under it.

Meredith had a sense of the shadows around the edges of the room darkening, of Stacey's form taking on a depth, a richness of colour, another dimension that made her more real, like the central figure in a Rembrandt.

Do I really love her, Meredith asked herself? She remembered what the school psychologist had said when Stacey was fourteen and had been caught in the boys'

"It had been years, years since she had simply talked to Stacey . . ."

bathroom with five or six boys.

"I think, Mrs. Gilchrist, that some kids are already lost." Her hair was greying. She would soon retire. "I've been at this work a long time. I know I shouldn't say this to you. But I think some kids are lost. I mean from the moment they breathe on their own. I don't know why it should be that way." She had looked very old. Meredith could hardly believe that this was the same woman who stood up at community meetings and gave speeches on "You and your teenager." "Take her to a psychiatrist." That was all she had said.

When Meredith had asked the psychiatrist for some word, for some explanation, he had said only, "No one is responsible for what Ortega called, 'this terrible reality.' " Meredith did not know what he meant.

Do I really love her, she asked herself again?

She had been an ordinary baby, her brown eyes alert and intelligent, quick to smile, and when she could walk, she had been into everything like all babies. She was slightly underweight at birth, she cried too much, Meredith had worked all through her childhood, but none of these things, not together, not singly, accounted for Stacey. Nothing accounted for Stacey. She would be their burden all the rest of their lives.

They stayed up to watch the late movie and during it both Stacey and Meredith fell asleep. The next time Meredith looked at her watch it was six o'clock. Her father, still wearing his snowmobile suit, was looking down at her.

"Had to sleep in the truck till it cleared," he said. He sat down heavily in a chair and unzipped his suit. "I'm getting too old for this," he said. "I'm going to have to cut back on my herd come spring. I don't know how I'd have managed without you two this last couple of weeks."

He had grown older since her last visit. He was an old man. He couldn't be left alone. She was his only relative, the only one left to manage the burden of his life. It would be impossible for him to live in the city. In the city, living with them, he would die. She should stay here and look after him. He had leaned back. His eyes were closed and sadness wrapped around him like a cloak. I should stay, she thought. Snow was banked up around the picture window and the stars were still out.

"Yes, you'll have to cut back," she said. "I hate to leave you, Dad, but I have to get back to my job, to Bill."

"I know, I know," her father said. He looked across to

the window as if to hide his despair from her. One way or another, she thought, our children all break our hearts. It is the way things are.

Stacey, lying on the couch near them, stirred and they both turned to her. She sat up and they saw that she had been awake through their talk. Her expression was open, her voice heartbreakingly beautiful.

"I'm staying," she cried. Meredith and her father looked at her. Meredith opened her mouth to speak. "It's my life," Stacey said to her. She looked back at her grandfather. "I'm staying," she said.

Meredith's father drove her to town where she caught a bus to Regina, and from Regina, a plane to Toronto. It was a flight that had originated in Vancouver and the plane was full. A young mother and her four-year-old boy sat beside Meredith, the mother at the window, the child in the middle and Meredith on the aisle. The child was active, sitting on his mother's knee at the window, asking for water, asking to go to the bathroom, whining for a toy.

"I don't know what to do with him," the young woman said to Meredith, apologetically. Meredith thought, I could tell her that he's not bothering me, or that he will probably grow up to be Prime Minister, or at least a decent, normal adult. Or I could tell her that there will come a time when she will wonder whether she loves him. There will come a time when you will both have to realize that it is his life, that he will have to find his own way in the world, that he will be what he is.

Instead, she said, "He's a handsome child, and he seems quite bright." After a while she said, "I have a daughter, she's grown up now. She was a beautiful baby, lots of dark hair and big brown eyes, and always asking questions too. She used to love to throw bread to the pigeons in the park. She wasn't at all afraid of them. They would come closer and closer and she would stand still, her little arm outstretched with the bread in her hand. They would take it out of her fingers and how that delighted her. Once, one perched on her shoulder and she smiled, there was such wonder in her smile and in her eyes."

But the little boy was squirming again, he had climbed from his seat and was banging on the window with a toy car. His mother held his arm to stop him and he began to wail. The young woman was not listening to Meredith. But Meredith hardly noticed. She leaned back in her seat and closed her eyes. All the way home she thought about Stacey in the park with the pigeons.

"One way or another . . . our children all break our hearts. It is the way things are."

BREATH OF GOD

~

CLEM MARTINI

It rained all of May and the first half of June, then July baked dry as a cracker. I don't know which was worse.

Anyways, five days into summer break and the hottest day so far, I went into town for a swim and found they'd closed the municipal pool for renovations. Calem Sanderson was standing there as I read the notice and his dalmation, Dagmar, bit Rufus, so I kicked it where it was going to do the most good. "What did you do that for?" Calem asked "They were only playing." "The trouble with your dog, Calem," I told him, "is that he just doesn't know when enough is enough." "And the trouble with *your* dog" he replied "is that she isn't even a dog." And he whistled up Dagmar and off they went. Figured he's delivered quite a zinger, too. It was about then that I realized it wasn't going to be one of my more superior days, and began to have some real dark suspicions about the rest of the summer as well.

"C'mon Rufus," I said, "let's go."

Eventually, me and Rufus rounded the bend in the road and crossed the texas gate that marks the entrance to our place. Already you could begin to hear it, the soft jingle-jangling of wind chime against wind chime against wind chime. A couple more steps and we cleared the Saskatoon berry bushes and the house sprung to view.

Flat land, big old clump of cottonwoods, red cedar house set next to a small, dusty hill: that's all there is to look at. It's not much, I'll tell you. And then the three windmills out of sight on the other side of the hill that everyone talks about, turning and turning when it blows, which it wasn't for once. I remember one time Dad said he bought the place for the wind. I guess he must have, because he sure didn't buy it for the view.

Around town, Dad is kind of semi-famous for his feelings about wind. He teaches environmental design at the University in Calgary and he says that wind is just about the most important thing you can think of: "The breath of

God" he calls it. Says it's "the closest thing we have on this earth to a manifestation of divinity." When he talks like that around strangers, I just want to crawl out of the room on my belly.

Around the house, all the way round the house, we have this strip of wind chimes he's collected. There's hundreds of them, from all over the world, draped over nearly every inch of the veranda. When the wind is down, like it was that day, they just dangle and twist, but the wind can come up pretty strong and sudden, and when it does they make quite a racket. If it's really blowing, some of 'em, the ones not built for hurricane-force blows, will bust like a fire cracker exploding. I'd say about once every two weeks the front porch will be littered with shattered pieces of glass and clay.

I left Rufus cooling under the cottonwoods and went inside. Dad's office looks down from the second floor onto the living room. Right away, as soon as I entered, I knew I wasn't going to get anywhere fast with him. He was crouched over his desk, hair mussed up and glasses perched on the end of his nose.

"Hey, Dad," I said and he called back, "Hey Sandra." I flopped myself down on the couch and kinda waited for him to glance in my direction to see what I was wanting. He just kept right on drawing and erasing and calculating. I could have waited a couple of days, I think, without much success.

"Pool's closed," I announced when it didn't look like he was ever going to ask. "Still working, hey?"

"Yup," he replied and lifted a hand to nab a different pencil.

"Going to be long?" I asked, casual-like, as if it didn't matter, and tugged a magazine out of the magazine rack. I don't know why I bother around our house: *The Saturday Evening Post*. I put it back.

"Fairly,"

"I suppose you'd like it if I went back out to play, then."

He patted and brushed the paper like it was a favourite pet. "Wouldn't mind it," he allowed.

He was making it as obvious as possible that he wanted me to go out and play. The thoughtful thing to do would have been to get up, get out and let him finish his whatever. I peered out the living room window at the grass, dust, sun and no-wind.

"Dagmar bit Rufus again," I mentioned, hoping to draw him into the conversation with his familiar spiel about

the Sanderson boys. "Real hard."

It didn't phase him at all. "I've told you," he said, "*not* to bring that chihuahua into town. She's just a mouthful for most of those dogs. Like waving a sandwich under their noses."

The heat rose off the porch and shook the countryside like a bedsheet: hills, trees, clouds, everything rippled outside. Inside, Dad's head crept closer to his papers with every moment I stayed. Really, it's no good talking to him when he's at his desk. I stood up.

"Okay, Dad. I'm leaving. I'm going out for a walk now."

"Good," he said, and his fingers floated over the desk like a butterfly, hovered, and dropped like a rock on an eraser. "Much better for you than lounging around the house, anyway." Then he finally looked up. He's got nice eyes. Dad does. Blue. His best feature, I think.

"Sorry, Sandy. Work," he said and shrugged. "I shouldn't be much more than a couple of hours, then maybe you can come back and we'll find something we can do together." And then he tossed me an eraser.

"Okay," I said, and tossed the eraser back. What am I going to do with an eraser? Sometimes he's really out of it. He waved, I waved, he went back to work, I went outside. The moment I set foot on the porch, I regretted it. I felt like a small, warm puddle of water being slowly evaporated. Rufus was lying in her favourite shady spot beneath the biggest cottonwood, looking comfortable the way only a dog in dirt can. I should have just let her be, it would have been the considerate thing to do.

"Up Rufus!" I barked. She opened an eye reproachfully. "Let's go," I called, and she scrambled out of the dirt.

"No girl, there're no biscuits," I explained for about the billionth time as Rufus (again!) snuffled my empty palm. I tossed the branch, she ran to maul it before returning it, and I wiped my hand against my leg. Dog spit. If God can make anything in the universe, why didn't he make dogs with bibs attached. Anyways, like I said, she loped into the brush, the dog spit dried on my leg and I turned and saw the car drive up the road to my left.

It's not unusual for people to take a wrong turn off the highway and end up getting turned about on the gravel roads down here, so it wasn't a big surprise when it slowed to a stop beside me. People are always asking directions. I was pleased too, because it broke the monotony of the day. Besides, it was some car. The window on the passenger's side slid down like a slab of dark ice melting. I

"Sometimes he's really out of it."

looked in, trying to make out the driver.

"Hi, Mom. What are you doing here?" I asked. She just winked and grinned. "And there," she said, "hangs a tale. Hop in." When she saw I was hanging back, she added, "Just for a quick spin and a chat."

I drummed my fingers against the door and glanced back towards the house. "All right." The lock snapped up like magic and I climbed in. "But if Dad sees us, there's going to be trouble." I sat down and leaned back against the dark leather interior. The seat nearly swallowed me whole. I looked at my mother again. "You know that, eh?"

"Yes," she replied and calmly adjusted the rear view mirror. "Yes, I know that. Buckle up, will you honey." Then she turned the car the other way round and we headed in the opposite direction. "So this," I thought "is what a cruiser feels like." Dad says big cars like these are gas gluttons and only for people with nothing better to do with their money. I don't know. I waved and mouthed "go home" to Rufus as we slid away. She just barked and raced round in circles. Not the brightest breed of dog, Chihuahuas. Mom brushed a hand through her hair, smiled again, and tried to relax. "How are you?" she inquired like it was the most normal thing in the world for her to just drop by in some expensive rent-a-car.

"What the heck are you doing here? is what I wanted to ask . . ."

"Good," I replied. "Just fine." She turned right at the crossroads. "And you're looking nice too," I said because along with the fancy car she had clearly put on a new dress and a lot of make up. Truthfully though, she was looking not so terrific. Her face was pale which looked even more out of place here in all the sun than it might have in Montreal, and experienced seamen would have had trouble unravelling some of the knots she'd gotten her hair into. I could just bet she was smoking again too. And she kept smiling frantically at me. "What the heck are you doing here?" is what I wanted to ask, but she was my mother after all, so instead I said, "Go ahead and say it."

"Say what?" she asked.

"How much I've grown. You always tell me."

"Do I? Well, it's true. And you have. You're turning into a real young lady." She took a left and headed for the hill I glanced backwards to check out the rest of the car, and there, coiled on the floor, is this length of yellow, nylon rope. "Especially since I last saw you," Mom added.

"I suppose so."

"A real little lady," she repeated, and she slid a small

package across the seat to me.

"What's that?" I asked.

"Open it."

It was so carefully wrapped, I was a little reluctant to just shred the paper. But when I did, I found a gold ring with a red stone. Because it was a gift from my mother, I decided it must be a ruby. She told me to put it on, and I did, and then she asked if I liked it. I answered that it was very nice, because it was. I didn't say anything more, though, because what do you say when someone gives you something that's worth more than most of what you already own?

We were approaching the 1-A Highway at this point. The 1-A is a two-lane highway that leads south and east into Calgary.

"Mom? Where are we going?" I asked.

Her eyes didn't leave the road, as she turned right onto the 1-A. "Just for a spin," she repeated.

I watched the kilometres slowly tick away. "Not again," I said. "Tell me you're not doing it again." She didn't have to say anything. I looked out the window in disgust. "You are so stupid some times."

"And that's exactly the kind of talk your father has taught you."

"Come on!"

"Tell me it's not the truth!"

I glanced at the back seat again. "The rope!" I said with a sudden realization. "I don't believe it. You actually brought it along to tie me up, didn't you?"

"Don't be ridiculous!" she snapped, then pursed her lips. "Only," she amended and altered her grip on the steering wheel, "if it turned out to be absolutely necessary. And only until I could deprogram you."

I stared hard at her. "Deprogram me!" I repeated incredulously, but what I was thinking was, "What kind of drugs have you been taking?" She must have guessed some of my thoughts because she continued, "Well, who can tell what your father has been saying behind my back? And don't tell me he hasn't been saying anything."

The car rushed on. We passed a farm, then a fence, then another farm. I counted from twenty backwards, then took inventory of the fillings in my teeth with my tongue.

"Well, Mother," I asked after a deep breath, "how are things with *you*?"

She studied me nervously for a moment, then ran a hand through her hair. She's been doing that a lot, I thought, to put her hair in such a tangle. "Not so good," she said. "I'm lonely. The recession hurt the store. I've put on weight.

Tried to get interested in aerobics, but just can't make it stick somehow."

"Maybe swimming," I suggested half-heartedly. "It's good exercise I hear."

She nodded. "Yea, but you've got to have a pool close by, and then there are particular hours for adults."

"Yes," I agreed. I understood how pool schedules could be difficult.

She pulled two long envelopes out of her purse and displayed them the way a magician displays the rabbit you knew was hid beneath the hat. Airplane tickets. I knew that.

"I've picked up a small place in Greece," she said quietly. "It's inland, but not far inland. An hour's drive from the coast. Wonderful, eh?" She raised her eyebrows hopefully at me.

"Wonderful," I echoed and traced a design with my thumbnail in the leather seat. "Who's looking after the shop?"

"I left it with Mary."

I shook my head. "And you wonder why the business is doing lousy. Mary? *I* could run the shop better than Mary. Geez, you give me the creeps sometimes. You're my mother, part of you is supposed to be in me. I hope for my sake that it isn't the real brainy part."

It was unfair, I know, and you would have thought I'd punched her in the stomach to look at her.

"I didn't mean that. I'm sorry. But look. Look. I'll go. Anywhere you want. We'll just . . . go, you know? Simple. But do you really remember what it was like last time you did this? We flew to Mexico, you didn't let me eat anything but Big Macs, you got sick, we both never set foot out of the 'hacienda' and two weeks later the police came and that was that. After, you lost your summer visiting privileges, I didn't see you at my next birthday cause of the tonsilectomy, and now I just hope you don't mind losing Christmas, because that's what'll happen when they catch us this time for sure." I brushed my hand through my hair. Now she had *me* doing it. "I never thought you'd do this again. Never."

She kept on driving but I could see her eyes were beginning to swim. "You don't understand," she said "You don't understand." I scouted out my pockets for kleenex but couldn't come up with anything except one way too old to use. "I worked hard after the divorce to get the business going. And it's doing okay. I mean, even in this recession,

> "She kept on driving but I could see her eyes were beginning to swim."

the banks are eager to lend me money. But courts don't review their decisions. They don't say, 'Gee, you're doing all right. Maybe you deserve more time with your daughter.' They don't do that. I am fit. I have stopped drinking. I am together. And all . . .'' Her voice broke, caught and then broke again. She rubbed her nose with the back of her right hand. ''All I get is three times a year? Christmas, Birthdays and summer? That's it? What's the point?'' she concluded. The tears rolled around in her mascara, then slid down her cheek like ants on skis. ''I'm so unhappy without you,'' she whispered. ''I'm so unhappy.''

I kept my hands in my pockets and fingered the kleenex. ''Why,'' I asked, after some time, ''don't you just, forget about me? Concentrate on the business. You know. Find other interests.''

She blinked rapidly and then stared at me like I had gone crazy. The driver behind us gave her the horn, but Mom ignored him. ''Is that your Dad?'' she asked and then repeated it when I didn't answer. I said no, but she kept staring so hard that I had to turn away.

''Don't you love me anymore?''

Even with my head turned, I could still feel her staring.

I watched the countryside whiz past and felt that ancient kleenex. ''Yea,'' I said. ''Sure. I think I love you. I don't know. I guess so. I think . . . .'' The car behind revved up and tore past us. ''I think I love you less than I did when we hung around together all the time, though. I think love has something to do with who you kind of hang around with most. And I . . . .'' I trailed off. ''I hang around mostly with Dad now.''

For a long time after that we drove in silence with Mom just blinking and staring hard at the road. Then, just before we reached the Calgary limits, she pulled a left without signalling into a farmer's driveway, then turned the car back for Cochrane.

Just before we came to the fence, I said, ''You can let me out here.'' But she just shook her head and kept on over the texas gate. ''No,'' she said. ''No. I'll take you up to the house. Besides, I want to speak to your father.'' I didn't say anything about how Dad might not want to speak to her because I figured she'd know that as well as anyone.

So we pulled up in front of the house and Dad must have heard us coming because, before the dust settled, there he was.

''What the hell are you doing here?'' he asked as soon

as he laid eyes on Mom.

"I just came by to talk," she answered.

"I got nothing to talk about with you," Dad shot back, then returned to me. "Are you all right?"

"Sure, Dad, everything's fine."

"I just want to speak with you, Jim," Mom said again.

"I'm going to take Rufus for a walk," I interrupted quickly, "and leave you guys alone."

"Don't go too far," Dad told me. "This isn't going to take very long."

So, me and Rufus took the path that leads up and over the hill, and everywhere we went grasshoppers leapt up in front of us, bouncing off our chests and stuff. Dad says it's because of all the dry weather following the wet weather that there's so many, but I don't know; dry weather, wet, there's always grasshoppers. You know? Anyways, I didn't care for them so much, but Rufus went absolutely crazy— barking and snapping at them, which is the biggest reason I took off so sudden, because Rufus didn't come along until after the divorce and she's not too easy around Mom. I could see that whatever Mom had to say, she might not want Rufus running around her in circles like a mad thing.

So, we got to the crest of the hill and on one side were the windmills, still as statues, and on the other side, at the bottom of the hill, seated on a picnic table by the second biggest cottonwood, Mom and Dad. I held Rufus in my lap and put my hand over her mouth so she'd keep quiet, and between the two moving branches of that second biggest tree, I watched them. Mom was studying her nails, I think. I wasn't certain what Dad was looking at. Maybe looking for me to show up.

I keep thinking, then, that if the wind blew just a little, maybe the chimes would go at it, and they'd at least have that to talk about. But, of course, wind doesn't work that way, on demand, so they just kept sitting there, same as the chimes. Just dangling. And I thought about what it was like when they were together. It was a long time ago, I can hardly remember, really. Maybe I don't remember and only think I do. She wore her hair different, in long braids. He flew a kite with me once. We had potato salad on the grass of some park in some city out east.

Down below, my parents remained silent as ever. The branches parted and I saw them staring off in different directions, then the branches closed and they disappeared. I scratched Rufus under the chin and told her, "Never, never."

> "I wasn't certain what Dad was looking at. Maybe looking for me to show up."

ACTIVITIES

1. After reading the two stories, hold a group discussion considering these questions:

Blood Is Thicker
pp. 229–250

- What issues about being a parent does each story raise?
- Which story reveals the difficulties of parenting the most effectively? What evidence do you have for your position?
- Which story presents the difficulty of being a child most effectively? What evidence do you have for your decision?
- Which story do you feel has the most satisfying ending? Which has the least satisfying ending? Support your view.

2. a) Each of the stories is told from the perspective of one character. With a partner, select one of these characters and summarize the feelings that she has about the events and about the other members of her family.

b) Choose one of the other characters in the story and write what happens from the perspective of that character. You might include dialogue to assist in character development.

3. Each writer sets the stage for the story by describing the setting. Choose one or two descriptive paragraphs that you like and read them aloud to a partner, or draw an illustration of the setting.

4. Choose one of the parents in the stories and write a letter giving advice to him or her on how to be a more effective parent in the situation in the story. Read your letter to a partner and discuss any additions or deletions. (You might want to include the names of organizations or services available in your community that could provide help.)

5. Discuss with a partner why each author might have chosen the title. (Check the meaning of the words *venerable* and *reverend*.) Make up an alternative title for each of the stories.

Your Child's Moral Values

~

CHARLOTTE GRAY

How should you teach your child to be kind, just and responsible—to share toys, not to bully siblings and to *want* to be good? In previous generations, children generally learned moral values with the help of religious training, an extended family or widely accepted community customs. But in some cases, these influences are now weakened or absent, and from movies like *Rambo* or television programs like *The A-Team*, kids may absorb values that horrify parents.

Dr. Robert Brassington, a family therapist at the Adlerian Centre for Counseling and Education in Ottawa, says, "Kids get a lot of confusing messages about how they should behave these days. If a parent wants to trasmit her own attitudes and expectations to her child, she should start establishing lines of communication as soon as possible, even before the child has begun to talk." By being kind and fair toward the child from the start, the parent can encourage similar behaviour in the child.

New York psychologists Michael Schulman and Eva Mekler say in their book *Bringing Up A Moral Child* (Addison-Wesley) that children learn moral behaviour through three key processes: internalizing their parents' moral values, developing empathy and acquiring their own personal standards. Here is the experts' advice for guiding a child through each process:

■ Children take their cues on what is good and bad behaviour from adults. You can prevent a crisis before it arises by taking the time to explain the rules of social behaviour—"Take turns playing with the toy"—and the reasons behind the rules—"That way, everybody has a good time, which is a lot more fun than fighting." A preschooler may follow clear consistent instructions about behaviour mainly because she wants your approval. By the time she starts school, your rules may become her own rules, which she follows because they help her enjoy playtime and make her feel good.

Besides instructions, a child needs examples. "The majority of teaching comes from modeling—the child copies her parent's behaviour," Dr Brassington says. "If your child sees you being thoughtful, she is more likely to value that characteristic." For example, a preschooler may learn from you how to stroke the family cat gently; when your child is older, she will emulate your respectfulness toward elderly relatives.

■ Empathy means feeling bad about someone else's unhappiness and good about another's joy. A child may display empathy even before he is 2, and psychologists Schulman and Mekler suggest that you help develop the child's sensitivity by role-playing games. Encourage him to imagine the feelings of the child he pushed over in the playground or from whom he took a toy. A child who learns to empathize with anoth-

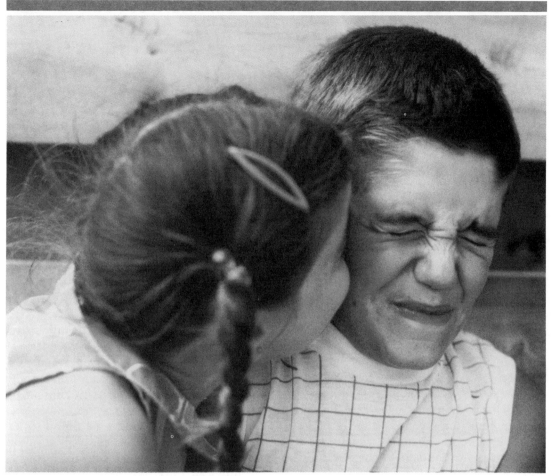

er's distress will also learn to alleviate the distress.

■ To help a child develop her own sense of what is right and wrong, Schulman suggests that you provide good reasons for moral standards—for instance, explain that morals help build a better world or that it feels good to do good.

Once a child is school-age, help her build confidence in her competence to make moral decisions. "As parents, we pamper our children too much: we don't allow them to make mistakes and live with the consequences," Dr. Brassington says. "If a child leaves a toy out, and it gets broken, don't get mad or rush to the store for a new one. Just say, 'I understand your disappointment but I'm afraid that's what happens when we don't look after our possessions.' The child then learns responsibility for his or her own actions."

By age 9, the child is capable of developing her own moral standards, and if you encourage her to make her own decisions, based on logical reasons within the moral framework you have provided, she will be better equipped to deal with moral dilemmas later in life. She will be less swayed by peer pressure when faced with the inevitable questions about sex, drugs or crime. Dr. Brassington says, "If you have good lines of communication, you can tell your child your attitude to these issues but trust her to make up her own mind."

HOUSEHUSBANDS ARE A GROWING PHENOMENON

W ide receiver James Murphy runs pass patterns six months of the year with the Winnipeg Blue Bombers of the Canadian Football League and uses his speed during the off-season to keep up with 2-year-old son Bryson.

Murphy the football player becomes Murphy the househusband, vacuum wielder and mate to wife and dancer Cheryl.

"I enjoy it," he says.

"It gives me a chance to be closer to my son. Basically, I'm his pal. When he grows up, I'll be able to say 'Hey boy, I used to change your diaper.' "

While there are no statistics on the number of househusbands in Canada, it appears to be a growing phenomenon.

"I never thought I'd be changing diapers and waking up at 5 in the morning," says Murphy, 25. "I said I'd never do that. But once I had him, those values changed."

Money may not be a problem for Murphy but economics played a factor in the decision of musician Bill Hamilton, 36, to take on the role of househusband.

When his daughter Elizabeth was born eight months ago, he says he realized that not only would he and wife Cathy no longer be "footloose and fancy-free," but she could make more as a school teacher than he could as a musician.

It was somewhat the same story for Keith Pearce, a restaurant-equipment salesman in British Columbia, whose wife Leslie landed the first job when the couple moved back to Winnipeg three years ago.

Pearce says he doesn't mind staying home to care for their daughter Alison, now 5 years old, and with another child due in May he feels he even has job security.

He doesn't believe housework is all that bad.

"It's a big sham that's been pulled over the eyes of a lot of men," he says. "It's not as bad as it's cooked up to be."

Ross Neufeld says he feels great about raising sons Ryan, 3, and Justin, 8 months.

"I don't look at this as a job," says Neufeld, who quit his job as a shipping supervisor in New Brunswick to become a photographer before returning home to Winnipeg in 1981.

His wife got a job at the University of Manitoba so he stayed home.

"This is a lot more fulfilling. The best thing about the other jobs I had were the paycheques."

Professor Hilary Lips, who teaches the psychology of sex differences at the University of Winnipeg, says she believes the slumping economy and desire of women for a career have contributed to the increasing number of househusbands.

"I think it has been happening because there is a new sense that rules don't have to be as rigidly defined as they have in the past," she says.

The Winnipeg Free Press
February 9, 1985

A C T I V I T I E S

1. a) Check the dictionary for definitions of the following key words in the article "Your Child's Moral Values": *moral, empathy*, and *responsible*.

Family Issues
pp. 252–254

   b) The writer of the article says, "You can prevent a crisis . . . by taking the time to explain the rules of social behaviour." With a partner, make a list of what you would consider to be the rules of behaviour for children below four years of age and for children over ten years of age. Decide whether or not the rules will be different for the two age groups and discuss why.

2. a) Discuss whether you would like to be a househusband or be the wife of one. Explain your reasons to a partner.

   b) After reading "Househusbands Are a Growing Phenomenon" with your partner, write a series of follow-up questions you would like to ask one of the househusbands interviewed for the article.

3. Find one other article on an aspect of parenting (see Research Skills, page 198, in the Student Handbook), read it, and prepare a short written summary of what you learned from it. Team up with three others who have read different articles and orally summarize your articles for each other. One or more of you might want to view a film or a video instead of reading an article.

TREASURES

FLORENCE MCNEIL

My father hardly noticed me
he lavished what love he had
     on a sour old vine called Isabella
ignored my mother   pinched and patted Isabella's blooms
let her crawl undisciplined over our righteous house
flaunted her green grapes under our indignant noses.

hating them both
I clung to my mother   walked with her to the fields
     in her last year of life
there was little breath in the close afternoon
like mock oranges we nodded at each other
dreamily

but when she died I understood more things

that the life surging through my father
making him move and bluster like a stormy tree
had fallen off
had been only a faint echo of my mother's gentleness

that we were orphaned by her death

and later when I opened up my father's desk
made public by his second death
I found a sketch   tucked away guiltily
     like an old billet-doux
wilting in a remote pigeonhole
that said
by Emily
age eight

MOTHER'S BISCUITS

FREDA QUENNEVILLE

In a big bowl she'd fluff in flour,
Make a fist-dent
For buttermilk and lard which she squeezed
Between her fingers
The way a child goes at a mud puddle,
Raking dry flour
From the sides until it mixed right.

She'd give the dough a pat for luck,
Nip a springy bud,
Roll it round and flat-it-down
With a motion
Continued to a grease-shined pan.
Mother's biscuits
Cooked high, crusty, with succulent middles
That took attention
At company dinners; but on kitchen-nights
They were finest
Soaked with pot liquor or gravy.

And those rich biscuits could put a shine
On Sunday patent
That let the Lord know who was there.
A panful stood
Ready as magic at dawn's light:
I'd take some
When leaving late to the schoolbus
And up the road
I'd run, puffing through biscuit crumbs
My haloed breath
Into the skin-sharp morning air.

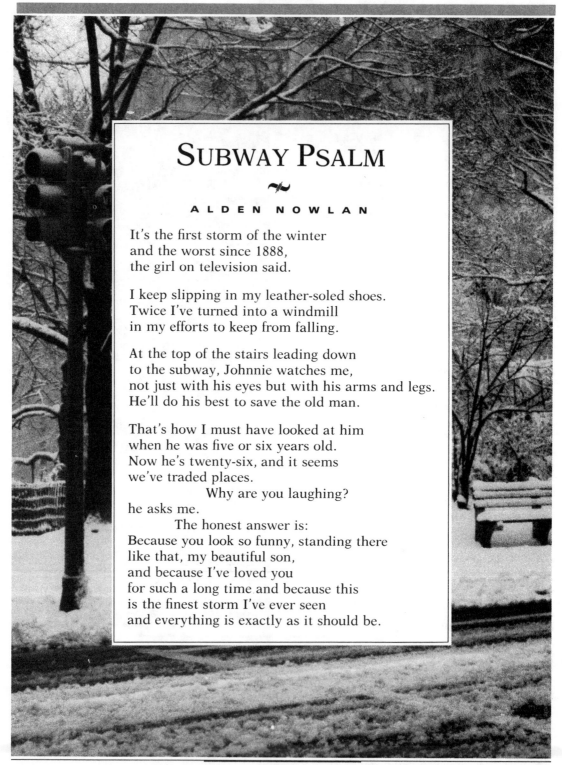

SUBWAY PSALM

ALDEN NOWLAN

It's the first storm of the winter
and the worst since 1888,
the girl on television said.

I keep slipping in my leather-soled shoes.
Twice I've turned into a windmill
in my efforts to keep from falling.

At the top of the stairs leading down
to the subway, Johnnie watches me,
not just with his eyes but with his arms and legs.
He'll do his best to save the old man.

That's how I must have looked at him
when he was five or six years old.
Now he's twenty-six, and it seems
we've traded places.
        Why are you laughing?
he asks me.
      The honest answer is:
Because you look so funny, standing there
like that, my beautiful son,
and because I've loved you
for such a long time and because this
is the finest storm I've ever seen
and everything is exactly as it should be.

DEATH OF A YOUNG SON BY DROWNING

MARGARET ATWOOD

He, who navigated with success
the dangerous river of his own birth
once more set forth

    on a voyage of discovery
    into the land I floated on
    but could not touch to claim.

        His feet slid on the bank,
        the currents took him;
        he swirled with ice and trees in the swollen water

           and plunged into distant regions,
           his head a bathysphere;
           through his eyes' thin glass bubbles

    he looked out, reckless adventurer
    on a landscape stranger than Uranus
    we have all been to and some remember.

There was an accident; the air locked,
he was hung in the river like a heart.
They retrieved the swamped body,

Cairn of my plans and future charts,
with poles and hooks
from among the nudging logs.

    It was spring, the sun kept shining, the new grass
    lept to solidity;
    my hands glistened with details.

        After the long trip I was tired of waves.
        My foot hit rock. The dreamed sails
        collapsed, ragged.

           I planted him in this country
           like a flag.

A C T I V I T I E S

Because I've Loved You
pp. 256–259

1. This is an exercise to explore the meanings of these poems. Study each poem separately and follow each step of the process below.

a) Read the poem aloud.

b) Write down three questions about the poem. Your questions should be about specific words, phrases, or ideas that you need help with in order to understand the poem.

c) Join with a partner and discuss all of your questions. Some questions you will find a satisfactory answer to. Select only three of your original questions that you still need more information about for the next step.

d) Join with another partnership to form a group of four. Again discuss all the unanswered questions. Select one question about the poem to present to the class for discussion. It should be a question your group has not been able to answer to its satisfaction.

e) As a class discuss the designated question from each group of four. If two questions seem almost identical, one group might present its second choice. During the class discussion with your teacher you will find that some questions can be answered, but others can only be discussed and don't allow for a definite answer. After you have completed this process you should understand the poems well enough to do the next two activities.

2. Work with a partner and determine what one poem says about being a parent. Be prepared to explain your ideas to the class and to support them with specific references to the poem.

3. With a partner make two lists, one on the joys of being a parent, the other on the sorrows or hardships. Write a journal entry in which you express why you look forward to being a parent or why the idea of being a parent is scary to you.

EFFECTIVE STREETPROOFING

~

T he key to effective, positive streetproofing lies in teaching children how to recognize potentially dangerous situations. Here are a few suggestions:

1. Teach children the difference between a friend, an acquaintance, and a stranger by getting them to ask themselves three questions: Do I know this person's name? Do I know where this person lives? Have I ever seen this person before? Remind children never to let a stranger into the house or to tell a telephone caller that they are alone.

2. Teach children their address and phone number (including the area code) as early as possible, then go to a phone booth with a roll of quarters and practise phoning home, Grandma's house, or the emergency police number.

3. Invest in an answering machine so that children can call home and leave a message as to their whereabouts. Make it a family rule that all kids call home to let someone know where they are.

4. Introduce your child to a police officer and get him to show her his badge. Avoid threats like "If you're bad, the policeman will throw you in jail," or she will be reluctant to go to the police in an emergency.

5. Teach your child to check with you before going anywhere with anyone, and to refuse to go with anyone who does not know the secret family code word. Encourage her or him to buddy up going to and from school.

6. Familiarize your child with your neighbourhood by walking it with her; teach her to change direction if she is being pursued by a moving vehicle. Show her the location of the Block Parent homes in her area.

7. When a child is old enough to leave home on his own, provide him with a survival kit that includes identification, parents' home and work numbers, the number of a trusted, available adult, money, bus tokens, and medical information, if necessary.

8. If you choose to fingerprint your child make sure the people running the program have been trained by the police or the prints may be useless. Never leave a copy of your child's prints with anyone.

9. Respect your children's feelings and raise them in an atmosphere where feelings can be openly discussed. Never force them to show affection, even to a relative, and avoid instructing them to do everything the sitter says. Teach them to question gifts with strings attached.

10. Start dealing with the issue of sexual abuse as soon as the child is old enough to understand. Call body parts by their proper names and reassure children that they have every right to reject touching or fondling that makes them feel uncomfortable.

11. *Believe* a child who tells you she was sexually abused. Evidence suggests that children rarely fabricate such stories.

12. Find out what films, videotapes and presentations are being made on the subject of sexual abuse and streetproofing at your child's school. These programs are often introduced to parents first and you may wish to evaluate whether the specific program is suitable for your child.

CHILDREN AND STRESS: HOW TO HELP THEM DEAL WITH IT

A dults are not the only ones who sometimes experience stress. Children, especially over-achievers, can feel stress, too.

Claire McDerment, human resources consultant says that children need time to solidify their learning. They need to establish their own rate of learning. If we hurry children, we create anxiety in them.

McDerment recommends that parents ask their children if they are feeling stress. Children, even in Grade 1, recognize words such as "tension" and "pressure."

Some of the signs of stress in children are physical pains, such as headaches and stiff necks; feeling of fear or upset; bedwetting; or increasing stress-release habits like hair-tugging, nervous laughter, and thumb-sucking.

There are simple relaxation techniques that children can be taught to relieve their stress. McDerment suggests that parents follow a five-step version of the Quieting Reflex:

- Teach children how to identify their own stress symptoms;
- Encourage them to deliberately calm down and relax their facial muscles by forming smiles;
- Have them lie down, take deep breaths, and imagine each breath as cool and refreshing. Tell them to imagine that cool air is entering their bodies through holes in the bottom of their feet and is refreshing them;
- Suggest that they exhale stale air slowly, imaging it going out through the holes. They could breathe in to the count of 4, hold for 4, exhale for 4;
- Have them imagine a place that makes them feel relaxed and happy, such a beach, Grandma's porch, or a field, and think about all the sounds they hear, and how they feel.

from THE ENEMY AT HOME

~

JACKIE SMITH

Bob Couchman, executive director of the Metro Family Services Association, says parents can take steps to ease the rivalry brought on by the arrival of a new child.

Parents should protect the rights of older children, ensuring that their toys are not ruined by younger siblings, he said. And older children should not be required to take younger siblings on outings where they will be in the way.

Most incidents of rivalry occur around a particular incident, he says. For example, a sister borrows her sibling's blouse without asking. Unless the situation is serious, parents should avoid trying to hold a court and deciding who did what.

Couchman also advises:

- The best way to mediate disputes is to say, "You are not getting along. I know neither one of you is completely innocent or completely guilty. We cannot tolerate this kind of behaviour in the household." Then separate the children and find something else for them to do, he says.
- Do not take sides. A parent who jumps into the middle of a conflict may end up escalating it and contributing to the rivalry. The ultimate aim is to have the children resolve the problem themselves. Parents can help them do that by setting up patterns for resolving conflicts.
- While parents commonly believe they should treat their children equally, it may be better to find custom-made solutions for each child. A severe, sharp reprimand may work for one child, but be totally wrong for a very sensitive child, he says.
- Parents should focus on the strengths of each child. And, he says, family meetings to talk about conflicts and of making sure that children feel they are getting the attention they want.

FIVE SUGGESTIONS FOR HEALTHY PARENTAL DISCIPLINE

~

EDWARD ZIGLER AND NANCY RUBIN

Every parent experiences exasperating moments when a child is disobedient. What is the best way to express your disapproval and correct the behaviour without becoming abusive? Here are some practical techniques:

1. Recognize that your emotions are at a peak and temporarily refrain from punishment. Don't do anything if you are livid. An angry parent is more likely to use physical discipline to correct the child and such force is likely to escalate. Allow yourself and the child a cooling-off period before you do anything.

2. Investigate the details before making any decisions. Find out what really happened with the child, the siblings, peers, teacher, or babysitter to provoke the incident. Give children an opportunity to tell their side of the story and then make sure you have a good grasp of all the details before you come to a conclusion. One of the quickest routes to emotional damage is inappropriate punishment; conversely, it is just as dangerous to dismiss a child's misbehaviour by shifting the blame to another.

3. Get perspective on your child's misbehaviour by sharing it with another. In moments of anger, we tend to lose our objectivity. Find a friend, spouse, or other trusted individual you can discuss your child's behaviour with. If people are removed from the immediate situation, they may be able to help you see the child more realistically or help you find practical ways to handle the situation.

4. Become educated about child development and the parental role. Studies show that the more you and your spouse understand about your role, and the child's normal development course, the more likely you are to parent well. Find out about courses in parent education, child development, and family relationships. Because parental consistency is a key to effective discipline, it is important to communicate your child-rearing concerns with your spouse.

5. Make your values clear to your child and be consistent in maintaining them. In order to define limits, children are likely to test their parents at each stage of development. While this is often taxing to parents, it is really a plea for parental consistency and guidance. The trick is to remain emotionally open and reasonably flexible so that the child will maintain trust in you without sacrificing the values you believe in.

ACTIVITIES

1. a) Many books full of tips and advice for parents have been written by family doctors, pediatricians, child psychologists, social workers, etc. Search the shelves of your local bookstore or library and make a list of the specific subjects the authors of these books have written about. Compare your list with those of your classmates.

   b) Ask your parent(s) or guardian(s) whether they were given any advice or whether they read any books as they were raising you. Again, compare your findings with those of others.

Bringing Up Baby
pp. 261–264

2. After reading the tips on various aspects of child raising contained in the excerpts,

   a) decide with a partner
   - which bits of advice make the most sense;
   - which you do not agree with (if any);
   - which you feel will be the most difficult to carry out.

   b) Select the five most useful tips, make up five others of your own, and prepare a one-page flyer which could be distributed to new parents. You may want to design some graphics for your flyer on a computer. If there is a parenting or family studies course in your school or if your physical education program contains a parenting unit, show your flyer to the teacher of one of those courses and ask for her or his reaction. Brainstorm a list of locations for the distribution of your flyer.

3. Many people today are concerned about good nutrition for children. Prepare a list of five or six tips based on your research into what is healthy for children to eat and what they should avoid eating. As is the case with the excerpts in this part of the unit, each tip should be a short paragraph which explains why what you are recommending is important. Ask your school nurse if she or he might have some information for you.

from THE MIRACLE WORKER

~

WILLIAM GIBSON

CHARACTERS

A DOCTOR	PERCY	ANNIE SULLIVAN
KATE	AUNT EV	VINEY
KELLER	JAMES	BLIND GIRLS
HELEN	ANAGNOS	A SERVANT
MARTHA		OFFSTAGE VOICES

ACT ONE

THE TIME *The 1880s.*

THE PLACE: *In and around the Keller homestead in Tuscumbia, Alabama; also, briefly, the Perkins Institution for the Blind in Boston.*

Doctor: Just let her get well, she knows how to do it better than we do.

(*He is packed, ready to leave.*)

Main thing is the fever's gone, these things come and go in infants, never know why. Call it acute congestion of the stomach and brain.

Keller: I'll see you to your buggy, Doctor.

Doctor: I've never seen a baby, more vitality, that's the truth.

(*He beams a good night at the baby and Kate, and Keller leads him downstairs with a lamp. They go down the porch steps, and across the yard, where the Doctor goes off left; Keller stands with the lamp aloft, Kate meanwhile is bent lovingly over the crib, which emits a bleat; her finger is playful with the baby's face.*)

Kate: Hush. Don't you cry now, you've been trouble enough. Call it acute congestion, indeed, I don't see what's so cute about a congestion, just because it's yours. We'll have your father run an editorial in his paper, the wonders of modern medicine, they don't know what they're curing even when they cure it. Men, men and their battle scars, we women will have to—

(*But she breaks off, puzzled, moves her finger before the baby's eyes.*)

Will have to—Helen?

(*Now she moves her hand, quickly.*)

Helen.

(*She snaps her fingers at the baby's eyes twice, and her hand falters; after a moment she calls out, loudly.*)

Captain. Captain, will you come—

(*But she stares at the baby, and her next call is directly at her ears.*)

Captain!

(*And now, still staring, Kate screams, Keller in the yard hears it, and runs with the lamp back to the house. Kate screams again, her look intent on the baby and terrible. Keller hurries in and up.*)

Keller: Kate? What's wrong?
Kate: Look.

(*She makes a pass with her hand in the crib, at the baby's eyes*).

Keller: What, Katie? She's well, she needs only time to—
Kate: She can't see. Look at her eyes.

(*She takes the lamp from him, moves it before the child's face.*)

She can't *see*!

Keller: [*hoarsely*]: Helen.
Kate: Or hear. when I screamed she didn't blink. Not an eyelash—
Keller: Helen. Helen!
Kate: She can't *hear* you!
Keller: *Helen*!

(*His face has something like fury in it, crying the child's name; Kate almost fainting presses her knuckles to her mouth, to stop her own cry.*

The room dims out quickly.

Time, in the form of a slow tune of distant belfry chimes which approaches in a crescendo and then fades, passes; the light comes up again on a day five years later, on three kneeling children and an old dog outside around the pump.

The dog is a setter named Belle, and she is sleeping. Two of the children are Blacks, Martha and Percy. The third child is Helen, six and a half years old, quite unkempt, in body a vivacious little person with a fine head, attractive, but noticeably blind, one eye larger and protruding; her gestures are abrupt, insistent, lacking in human restraint, and her face never smiles. She is flanked by the other two, in a litter of paper-doll cutouts, and while they speak Helen's hands thrust at their faces in turn, feeling baffledly at the movements of their lips.)

Martha [*snipping*]: First I'm gonna cut off this doctor's legs one, two, now then—
Percy: Why you cuttin' off that doctor's legs?
Martha: I'm gonna give him a operation. Now I'm gonna cut off his arms, one, two. Now I'm gonna fix up—

(She pushes Helen's hand away from her mouth.)

You stop that.
Percy: Cut off his stomach, that's a good operation.
Martha: No, I'm gonna cut off his head first, he got a bad cold.
Percy: Ain't gonna be much of that doctor left to fix up, time you finish all them opera—

(But Helen is poking her fingers inside his mouth, to feel his tongue; he bites at them, annoyed and she jerks them away. Helen now fingers her own lips, moving them in imitation, but soundlessly.)

Martha: What you do, bit her hand?
Percy: That's how I do, she keep pokin' her fingers in my mouth, I just bite 'em off.
Martha: What she tryin' do now?
Percy: She tryin' *talk*. She gonna get mad. Looka her tryin' talk.

(Helen is scowling, the lips under her fingertips moving in ghostly silence, growing more and more frantic, until in a bizarre rage she bites at her own fingers. This sends Percy off into laughter, but alarms Martha.)

Martha: Hy, you stop now.

(She pulls Helen's hand down.)

You just sit quiet and—

(But at once Helen topples Martha on her back, knees pinning her shoulders

down, and grabs the scissors. Martha screams. Percy darts to the bell string on the porch, yanks it, and the bell rings.

Inside, the lights have been gradually coming up on the main room, where we see the family informally gathered, talking, but in pantomime: Kate sits darning socks near a cradle, occasionally rocking it; Captain Keller in spectacles is working over newspaper pages at a table; a benign visitor in a hat, Aunt Ev, is sharing the sewing basket, putting the finished touches on a big shapeless doll made out of towels; an idolent young man, James Keller is at the window watching the children.

With the ring of the bell, Kate is instantly on her feet and out the door onto the porch, to take in the scene; how we see what these five years have done to her, the girlish playfulness is gone, she is a woman steeled in grief.)

Kate [*for the thousandth time*]: Helen.

(She is down the steps at once to them, seizing Helen's wrists and lifting her off Martha; Martha runs off in tears and screams for momma, with Percy after her.)

Let me have those scissors.

(Meanwhile the family inside is alerted, Aunt Ev joining James at the window, Captain Keller resumes work).

James [*blandly*]: She only dug Martha's eyes out. Almost dug. It's always almost, no point worrying till it happens, is there?

(They gaze out, while Kate reaches for the scissors in Helen's hand. But Helen pulls the scissors back, they struggle for them a moment, then Kate gives up, lets Helen keep them. She tries to draw Helen into the house. Helen jerks away. Kate next goes down on her knees, takes Helen's hands gently, and using the scissors like a doll, makes Helen caress and cradle them; she points Helen's finger housewards. Helen's whole body now becomes eager; she surrenders the scissors, Kate turns her toward the door and gives her a little push. Helen scrambles up and toward the house, and Kate rising follows her.)

Aunt Ev: How does she stand it? Why haven't you seen this Baltimore man? It's not a thing you can let go on and on, like the weather.

James: The weather here doesn't ask permission of me, Aunt Ev. Speak to my father.

Aunt Ev: Arthur. Something ought to be done for that child.

Keller: A refreshing suggestion. What?

(Kate entering turns Helen to Aunt Ev, who gives her the towel doll.)

Aunt Ev: Why, this very famous oculist in Baltimore I wrote you about, what was his name?

Kate: Dr. Chisholm.

Aunt Ev: Yes, I heard lots of cases of blindness people thought couldn't be cured he's cured, he just does wonders. Why don't you write to him?

Keller: I've stopped believing in wonders.

Kate [*rocks the cradle*]: I think the Captain will write to him soon. Won't you, Captain?

Keller: No.

James [*lightly*]: Good money after bad, or bad after good. Or bad after bad—

Aunt Ev: Well, if it's just a question of money, Arthur, now you're marshal you have this Yankee money. Might as well—

Keller: Not money. The child's been to specialists all over Alabama and Tennessee, if I thought it would do good I'd have her to every fool doctor in the country.

Kate: I think the Captain will write to him soon.

Keller: Katie. How many times can you let them break your heart?

Kate: Any number of times.

(*Helen meanwhile sits on the floor to explore the doll with her fingers, and her hand pauses over the face; this is no face, a blank area of towel, and it troubles her. Her hand searches for features, and taps questioningly for eyes, but no one notices. She then yanks at her Aunt's dress, and taps again vigorously for eyes.*)

Aunt Ev: What, child?

(*Obviously not hearing, Helen commences to go around, from person to person tapping for eyes, but no one attends or understands.*)

Kate [*no break*]: As long as there's the least chance. For her to see, Or hear, or—

Keller: There isn't. Now I must finish here.

Kate: I think, with your permission, Captain, I'd like to write.

Keller: I said no, Katie.

Aunt Ev: Why, writing does no harm, Arthur, only a little bitty letter. To see if he can help her.

Keller: He can't.

Kate: We won't know that to be a fact, Captain, until after you write.

Keller [*rising, emphatic*]: Katie, he can't.

(*He collects his papers.*)

James [*facetiously*]: Father stands up, that makes it a fact.

Keller: You be quiet! I'm badgered enough here by females without your impudence.

(*James shuts up, makes himself scarce. Helen now is groping among things*

on *Keller's desk, and paws his papers to the floor. Keller is exasperated.*)
Katie.

(*Kate quickly turns Helen away, and retrieves the papers.*)

I might as well try to work in a henyard as in this house—
James [*placating*]: You really ought to put her away, Father.
Kate [*staring up*]: What?
James: Some asylum. It's the kindest thing.
Aunt Ev: Why, she's your sister, James, not a nobody—
James: Half sister, and half—mentally defective, she can't even keep her-
self clean. It's not pleasant to see her about all the time.
Kate: Do you dare? Complain of what you can see?
Keller: [*very annoyed*]: This discussion is at an end! I'll thank you not to
broach it again, Ev.

(*Silence descends at once. Helen gropes the way with the doll, and Keller
turns back for a final word, explosive.*)

I've done as much as I can bear, I can't give my whole life to it! The
house is at sixes and sevens from morning till night over the child, it's
time some attention was paid to Mildred here instead!
Kate: [*gently dry*]: You'll wake her up, Captain
Keller: I want some peace in the house, I don't care how, but one way we
won't have it is by rushing up and down the country every time someone
hears of a new quack. I'm as sensible to this affliction as anyone else, it
hurts me to look at the girl.
Kate: It was not our affliction I meant you to write about, Captain.

(*Helen is back at Aunt Ev, fingering her dress, and yanks two buttons from
it.*)

Aunt Ev: Helen! My buttons.

(*Helen pushes the buttons into the doll's face. Kate now sees, comes swiftly
to kneel, lifts Helen's hand to her own eyes in question.*)

Kate: Eyes?

(*Helen nods energetically.*)

She wants the doll to have eyes.

(*Another kind of silence now, while Kate takes pins and buttons from the
sewing basket and attaches them to the doll as eyes. Keller stands, caught,
and watches morosely. Aunt Ev blinks, and conceals her emotions by
inspecting her dress.*)

Aunt Ev: My goodness me, I'm not decent.

Kate: She doesn't know better, Aunt Ev. I'll sew them on again.

James: Never learn with everyone letting her do anything she takes it into her mind to—

Keller: You be quiet!

James: What did I say now?

Keller: You talk too much.

James: I was agreeing with you!

Keller: Whatever it was. Deprived child, the least she can have are the little things she wants.

(*James, very wounded, stalks out of the room, onto the porch; he remains here, sulking.*)

Aunt Ev: [*indulgently*] It's worth a couple of buttons, Kate, look.

(*Helen now has the doll with eyes, and cannot contain herself for joy; she rocks the doll, pats it vigorously, kisses it.*)

This child has more sense than all these men Kellers, if there's ever any way to reach that mind of hers.

(*But Helen suddenly has come upon the cradle, and unhesitatingly overturns it; the swaddled baby tumbles out, and Captain Keller barely manages to dive and catch it in time.*)

Keller: *Helen*!

(*All are in commotion, the baby screams, but Helen unperturbed is laying her doll in its place, Kate on her knees pulls her hands off the cradle, wringing them; Helen is bewildered*).

Kate: Helen, Helen, you're not to do such things, how can I make you understand—

Keller [*hoarsely*]: Katie.

Kate: How can I get it into your head, my darling, my poor—

Keller: Katie, some way of teaching her an iota of discipline has to be—

Kate [*flaring*]: How can you discipline an afflicted child? Is it her fault?

(*Helen's fingers have fluttered to her Mother's lips, vainly trying to comprehend their movements.*)

Keller: I didn't say it was her fault.

Kate: Then whose? I don't know what to do! How can I teach her, beat her—until she's black and blue?

Keller: It's not safe to let her run around loose. Now there must be a way of confining her, somehow, so she can't—

Kate: Where, in a cage? She's a growing child, she has to use her limbs!

Keller: Answer me one thing, is it fair to Mildred here?

Kate: [*inexorably*]: Are you willing to put her away?

(*Now Helen's face darkens in the same rage as at herself earlier, and her hand strikes at Kate's lips. Kate catches her hand again, and Helen begins to kick, struggle, twist.*)

Keller: Now what?

Kate: She wants to talk, like—*be* like you and me.

(*She holds Helen struggling until we hear from the child her first sound so far, an inarticulate weird noise in her throat such as an animal in a trap might make; and Kate releases her. The second she is free Helen blunders away, collides violently with a chair, falls, and sits weeping. Kate comes to her, embraces, caresses, soothes her, and buries her own face in her hair, until she can control her voice.*)

Every day she slips further away. And I don't know how to call her back.

Aunt Ev: Oh, I've a mind to take her up to Baltimore myself. If that doctor can't help her, maybe he'll know who can.

Keller [*presently, heavily*]: I'll write the man, Katie.

(*He stands with the baby in his clasp, staring at Helen's head, hanging down on Kate's arm.*

The lights dim out, except the one on Kate and Helen. In the twilight, James, Aunt Ev, and Keller move off slowly, formally, in separate directions; Kate with Helen in her arms remains, motionless, in an image which overlaps into the next scene and fades only when it is well under way.

Without pause, from the dark down left we hear a man's voice with a Greek accent speaking:)

Anagnos: —who could do nothing for the girl, of course. It was Dr. Bell who thought she might somehow be taught. I have written the family only that a suitable governess, Miss Annie Sullivan, has been found here in Boston—

(*The lights begin to come up, down left, on a long table and chair. The table contains equipment for teaching the blind by touch—a small replica of the human skeleton, stuffed animals, models of flowers and plants, piles of books. The chair contains a girl of 20, Annie Sullivan, with a face which in repose is grave and rather obstinate, and when active is impudent, combative, twinkling with all the life that is lacking in Helen's, and handsome; there is a crude vitality to her. Her suitcase is at her knee. Anagnos, a stocky bearded man, comes into the light only towards the end of his speech.*)

Anagnos: —and will come. It will no doubt be difficult for you there, Annie.

But it has been difficult for you at our school too, hm? Gratifying, yes, when you came to us and could not spell your name, to accomplish so much here in a few years, but always an Irish battle. For independence.

(*He studies Annie, humorously; she does not open her eyes.*)

This is my last time to counsel you, Annie, and you do lack some—by some I mean *all*—what, tact or talent to bend. To others. And what has saved you on more than one occasion here at Perkins is that there was nowhere to expel you to. Your eyes hurt?

Annie: My ears, Mr. Anagnos.

(*And now she has opened her eyes; they are inflamed, vague, slightly crossed, clouded by the granular growth of trachoma, and she often keeps them closed to shut out the pain of light.*)

Anagnos [*severely*]: Nowhere but back to Tewksbury, where children learn to be saucy. Annie, I know how dreadful it was there, but that battle is dead and done with, why not let it stay buried?

Annie [*cheerily*] I think God must owe me a resurrection.

Anagnos [*a bit shocked*]: What?

Annie [*taps her brow*]: Well, He keeps digging up that battle!

Anagnos: That is not a proper thing to say, Annie. It is what I mean.

Annie [*meekly*]: Yes. But I know what I'm like, what's this child like?

Anagnos: Like?

Annie: Well—Bright or dull, to start off.

Anagnos: No one knows. And if she is dull, you have no patience with this?

Annie: Oh, in grownups you have to, Mr. Anagnos. I mean in children it just seems a little—precocious, can I use that word?

Anagnos: Only if you can spell it.

Annie: Premature. So I hope at least she's a bright one.

Anagnos: Deaf, blind, mute—who knows? She is like a little safe, locked, that no one can open. Perhaps there is a treasure inside.

Annie: Maybe it's empty, too?

Anagnos: Possible. I should warn you, she is much given to tantrums.

Annie: Means something is inside. Well, so am I, if I believe all I hear. Maybe you should warn *them*.

Anagnos [*frowns*]: Annie. I wrote them no word of your history. You will find yourself among strangers now, who know nothing of it.

Annie: Well, we'll keep them in a state of blessed ignorance.

Anagnos: Perhaps *you* should tell it?

Annie: [*bristling*]: Why? I have enough trouble with people who don't know.

Anagnos: So they will understand. When you have trouble.

Annie: The only time I have trouble is when I'm right.

(*But she is amused at herself, as is Anagnos.*)

Is it my fault it's so often? I won't give them trouble, Mr. Anagnos, I'll be so ladylike they won't notice I've come.

Anagnos: Annie, be—humble. It is not as if you have so many offers to pick and choose. You will need their affection, working with this child.

Annie [*humorously*]: I hope I won't need their pity.

Anagnos: Oh, we can all use some pity.

(*Crisply*)

So. You are no longer our pupil, we throw you into the world, a teacher. *If* the child can be taught. No one expects you to work miracles, even for twenty-five dollars a month. Now, in this envelope a loan, for the railroad, which you will repay me when you have a bank account. But in this box, a gift. With our love.

(*Annie opens the small box he extends, and sees a garnet ring. She looks up, blinking, and down.*)

I think other friends are ready to say goodbye.

(*He moves as though to open doors.*)

Annie: Mr. Anagnos.

(*Her voice is trembling.*)

Dear Mr. Anagnos I—

(*But she swallows over getting the ring on her finger, and cannot continue until she finds a woebegone joke.*)

Well, what should I say, I'm an ignorant opinionated girl, and everything I am I owe to you?

Anagnos [*smiles*]: that is only half true, Annie.

Annie: Which half? I crawled in here like a drowned rat, I thought I died when Jimmie died, that I'd never again—come alive. Well, you say with love so easy, and I haven't *loved* a soul and I never will, I suppose, but this place gave me more than my eyes back. Or taught me how to spell, which I'll never learn anyway, but with all the fights and the trouble I've been here it taught me what help is, and how to live again, and I don't want to say goodbye. Don't open the door, I'm crying.

Anagnos [*gently*]: They will not see.

(*He moves again as though opening doors, and in comes a group of girls, 8-year-olds to 17-year-olds; as they walk we see they are blind. Anagnos shepherds them in with a hand.*)

A child: Annie?

Annie [*her voice cheerful*]: Here, Beatrice.

(*As soon as they locate her voice they throng joyfully to her, speaking all at once; Annie is down on her knees to the smallest, and the following are the more intelligible fragments in the general hubbub.*)

Children: There's a present. We brought you a going-away present, Annie!

Annie: Oh, now you shouldn't have—

Children: We did, we did, where's the present?

Smallest child [*mournfully*]: Don't go, Annie, away.

Children: Alice has it. Alice! Where's Alice! Here I am! Where? Here!

(*An arm is aloft out the group, waving a present; Annie reaches for it.*)

Annie: I have it. I have it, everybody, should I open it?

Children: Open it! Everyone be quite! Do, Annie! She's opening it. Ssh!

(*A settling of silence while Annie unwraps it. The present is a pair of smoked glasses, and she stands still.*)

Is it open, Annie?

Annie: It's open.

Children: It's for your eyes, Annie. Put them on, Annie! 'Cause Mrs. Hopkins said your eyes hurt since the operation. And she said you're going where the sun is *fierce.*

A. nie: I'm putting them on now.

Smallest Child [*mournfully*]: Don't go, Annie, where the sun is fierce.

Children: Do they fit all right?

Annie: Oh, they fit just fine.

Children: Did you put them on? Are they pretty, Annie?

A. nie: Oh, my eyes feel hundreds of per cent better already, and pretty, why, do you know how I look in them? Splendiloquent. Like a race horse!

Children [*delighted*]: There's another present! Beatrice! We have a present for Helen, too! Give it to her, Beatrice. Here, Annie!

(*This present is an elegant doll, with movable eyelids and a momma sound.*)

It's for Helen. And we took up a collection to buy it. And Laura dressed it.

Annie: It's beautiful!

Children: So don't forget, you be sure to give it to Helen from us, Annie!

Annie: I promise it will be the first thing I give her. If I don't keep it for myself, that is, you know I can't be trusted with dolls!

Smallest Child [*mournfully*]: Don't go, Annie, to her.

Annie [*her arm around her*]: Sarah, dear. I don't *want* to go.

Smallest child: Then why are you going?

Annie [*gently*]: Because I'm a big girl now, and big girls have to earn a living. It's the only way I can. But if you don't smile for me first, what I'll just have to do is—

(*She pauses, inviting it.*)

Smallest Child: What?

Annie: Put *you* in my suitcase, instead of this doll. And take *you* to Helen in Alabama!

(*This strikes the children as very funny, and they begin to laugh and tease the smallest child, who after a moment does smile for Annie.*)

Anagnos [*then*]: Come, children. We must get the trunk into the carriage and Annie into her train, or no one will go to Alabama. Come, come.

(*He shepherds them out and Annie is left alone on her knees with the doll in her lap. She reaches for her suitcase, and by a subtle change in the colour of the light, we go with her thoughts into another time. We hear a boy's voice whispering; perhaps we see shadowy intimations of these speakers in the background.*)

Boy's voice: Where we goin', Annie?

Annie [*in dread*]: Jimmie.

Boy's voice: Where we goin'?

Annie: I said—I'm takin' care of you—

Boy's voice: Forever and ever?

Man's voice [*impersonal*]: Annie Sullivan, aged nine, virtually blind. James Sullivan, aged seven—What's the matter with your leg, Sonny?

Annie: Forever and ever.

Man's voice: Can't he walk without that crutch?

(*Annie shakes her head, and does not stop shaking it.*)

Girl goes to the women's ward. Boy to the man's.

Boy's voice [*in terror*]: Annie! Annie, don't let them take me—Annie!

Anagnos [*offstage*]: Annie! Annie?

(*But this voice is real, in the present, and Annie comes up out of her horror, clearing her head with a final shake; the lights begin to pick out Kate in the Keller house, as Annie in a bright tone calls back.*)

Annie: Coming!

(*This word catches Kate, who stands half turned and attentive to it, almost as though hearing it. Meanwhile Annie turns and hurries out, lugging the suitcase.*

The room dims out; the sound of railroad wheels begins from off left, and maintains itself in a constant rhythm underneath the following scene; the remaining lights have come up on the Keller homestead. James is lounging on the porch, waiting. In the upper bedroom which is to be Annie's, Helen is alone, puzzledly exploring, fingering and smelling things, the curtains, empty drawers in the bureau, water in the pitcher by the washbasin, fresh towels on the bedstead. Downstairs in the family room Kate turning to a mirror hastily adjusts her bonnet, watched by a Negro servant in an apron, Viney.)

Viney: Let Mr. Jimmy go by hisself, you been pokin' that garden all day, you ought to rest your feet.

Kate: I can't wait to see her, Viney.

Viney: Maybe she ain't gone be on this train neither.

Kate: Maybe she is.

Viney: And maybe she ain't.

Kate: And maybe she is. Where's Helen?

Viney: She upstairs, smellin' around. She knows somethin' funny's goin' on.

Kate: Let her have her supper as soon as Mildred's in bed, and tell Captain Keller when he comes that we'll be delayed tonight.

Viney: Again.

Kate: I don't think we need say *again*. Simply delayed will do.

(She runs upstairs to Annie's room, Viney speaking after her.)

Viney: I mean that's what he gone say. "What, again?"

(Viney works at setting the table. Upstairs Kate stands in the doorway, watching Helen's groping explorations).

Kate: Yes, we're expecting someone. Someone for my Helen.

(Helen happens upon her skirt, clutches her leg; Kate in a tired dismay kneels to tidy her hair and soiled pinafore.)

Oh, dear, this was clean not an hour ago.

(Helen feels her bonnet, shakes her head darkly, and tugs to get it off. Kate retains it with one hand, diverts Helen by opening her other hand under her nose.)

Here. For while I'm gone.

(Helen sniffs, reaches, and pops something into her mouth, while Kate speaks a bit guiltily.)

I don't think one peppermint drop will spoil your supper.

(She gives Helen a quick kiss, evades her hands, and hurries downstairs

again. Meanwhile Captain Keller has entered the yard from around the rear of the house, newspaper under arm, cleaning off and munching on some radishes; he sees James lounging at the porch post.)

Keller: Jimmie?

James [*unmoving*]: Sir?

Keller [*eyes him*]: You don't look dressed for anything useful, boy.

James: I'm not. It's for Miss Sullivan.

Keller: Needn't keep holding up that porch, we have wooden posts for that. I asked you to see that those strawberry plants were moved this evening.

James: I'm moving your—Mrs. Keller, instead. To the station.

Keller: [*heavily*]: Mrs. Keller. Must you always speak of her as though you haven't met the lady?

(Kate comes out on the porch, and James inclines his head.)

James [*ironic*]: Mother.

(He starts off the porch, but sidesteps Keller's glare like a blow.)

I said mother!

Kate: Captain.

Keller: Evening, my dear.

Kate: We're off to meet the train, Captain. Supper will be a trifle delayed tonight.

Keller: What, again?

Kate [*backing out*]: With your permission, Captain?

(And they are gone. Keller watches them offstage, morosely.

Upstairs Helen meanwhile has groped for her mother, touched her cheek in a meaningful gesture, waited, touched her cheek, waited, then found the open door, and made her way down. Now she comes into the family room, touches her cheek again; Viney regards her.)

Viney: What you want, honey, your momma?

(Helen touches her cheek again. Viney goes to the sideboard, gets a tea-cake, gives it into Helen's hand; Helen pops it into her mouth.)

Guess one little tea-cake ain't gone ruin your appetite.

(She turns Helen toward the door. Helen wanders out onto the porch, as Keller comes up the steps. Her hands encounter him, and she touches her cheek again, waits.)

Keller: She's gone.

(He is awkward with her; when he puts his hand on her head, she pulls

away. Keller stands regarding her, heavily.)

She's gone, my son and I don't get along, you don't know I'm your father, no one likes me, and supper's delayed.

(Helen touches her cheek, waits. Keller fishes in his pocket.)

Here. I brought you some stick candy, one nibble of sweets can't do any harm.

(He gives her a large stick candy; Helen falls to it. Viney peers out the window.)

Viney [*reproachfully*]: Cap'n Keller, now how'm I gone get her to eat her supper you fill her up wit that trash?
Keller [*roars*]: Tend to your work!

(Viney beats a rapid retreat. Keller thinks better of it, and tries to get the candy away from Helen, but Helen hangs on to it; and when Keller pulls, she gives his leg a kick. Keller hops about, Helen takes refuge with the candy down behind the pump, and Keller then irately flings his newspaper on the porch floor, stamps into the house past Viney and disappears.

The lights half dim on the homestead, where Viney and Helen going about their business soon find their way off. Meanwhile, the railroad sounds off left have mounted in a crescendo to a climax typical of a depot at arrival time, the lights come up on stage left, and we see a suggestion of a station. Here Annie in her smoked glasses and disarrayed by travel is waiting with her suitcase, while James walks to meet her; she has a battered paper-bound book, which is a Perkins report, under her arm.)

James [*coolly*]: Miss Sullivan?
Annie [*cheerily*]: Here! At last, I've been on trains so many days I thought they must be backing up every time I dozed off—
James: I'm James Keller.
Annie: James?

(The name stops her.)

I had a brother Jimmie. Are you Helen's?
James: I'm only half a brother. You're to be her governess?
Annie [*lightly*]: Well. Try!
James [*eying her*]: You look like half a governess.

(Kate enters. Annie stands moveless, while James takes her suitcase. Kate's gaze on her is doubtful, troubled.)
Mrs. Keller, Miss Sullivan.

(Kate takes her hand.)

Kate [*simply*]: We've met every train for two days.

(*Annie looks at Kate's face, and her good humour comes back.*)

Annie: I changed trains every time they stopped, the man who sold me that ticket ought to be tied to the tracks—

James: You have a trunk, Miss Sullivan?

Annie: Yes.

(*She passes James a claim check, and he bears the suitcase out behind them. Annie holds the battered book. Kate is studying her face, and Annie returns the gaze; this is a mutual appraisal, southern gentlewoman and working-class Irish girl, and Annie is not quite comfortable under it.*)

You didn't bring Helen, I was hoping you would.

Kate: No, she's home.

(*A pause. Annie tries to make ladylike small talk, though her energy now and then erupts; she catches herself up whenever she hears it.*)

Annie: You—live far from town, Mrs. Keller?

Kate: Only a mile.

Annie: Well. I suppose I can wait one more mile. But don't be surprised if I get out to push the horse!

Kate: Helen's waiting for you, too. There's been such a bustle in the house, she expects something, heaven knows what.

(*Now she voices part of her doubt, not as such, but Annie understands it.*)

I expected—a desiccated spinster. You're very young.

Annie [*resolutely*]: Oh, you should have seen me when I left Boston. I got much older on this trip.

Kate: I mean, to teach anyone as difficult as Helen.

Annie: *I* mean to try. They can't put you in jail for trying!

Kate: Is it possible, even? To teach a deaf-blind child *half* of what an ordinary child learns—has that ever been done?

Annie: Half?

Kate: A tenth.

Annie [*reluctantly*]: No.

(*Kate's face loses its remaining hope, still appraising her youth.*)

Dr. Howe did wonders, but—an ordinary child? No, never. But then I thought when I was going over his reports—

(*She indicates the one in her hand*)

—he never treated them like ordinary children. More like—eggs everyone was afraid would break.

Kate [*a pause*]: May I ask how old you are?
Annie: Well, I'm not in my teens, you know! I'm twenty.
Kate: All of twenty.

(*Annie takes the bull by the horns, valiantly.*)

Annie: Mrs. Keller, don't lose heart just because I'm not on my last legs. I have three big advantages over Dr. Howe that money couldn't buy for you. One is his work behind me, I've read every word he wrote about it and he wasn't exactly what you'd call a man of few words. Another is to *be* young, why, I've got energy to do anything. The third is, I've been blind.

(*But it costs her something to say this.*)

Kate [*quietly*]: Advantages.
Annie [*wry*]: Well, some have the luck of the Irish some do not.

(*Kate smiles, she likes her.*)

Kate: What will you try to teach her first?
Annie: First, last, and—in between, language.
Kate: Language.
Annie: Language is to the mind more than light is to the eye. Dr. Howe said that.
Kate: Language.

(*She shakes her head.*)

We can't get through to teach her to sit still. You *are* young, despite your years, to have such—confidence. Do you, inside?

(*Annie studies her face; she likes her, too.*)

Annie: No, to tell you the truth I'm as shaky inside as a baby's rattle!

(*They smile at each other, and Kate pats her hand.*)

Kate: Don't be.

(*James returns to usher them off.*)

We'll do all we can to help, and to make you feel at home. Don't think of us as strangers, Miss Annie.
Annie [*cheerily*]: Oh, strangers aren't so strange to me. I've known them all my life!

(*Kate smiles again, Annie smiles back, and they precede James offstage.*

The lights dim on them, having simultaneously risen full on the house; Viney has already entered the family room, taken a water pitcher, and come out and down to the pump. She pumps real water. As she looks offstage, we hear the clop of hoofs, a carriage stopping, and voices.)

Viney: Cap'n Keller! Cap'n Keller, they comin'!

(She goes back into the house, as Keller comes out on the porch to gaze.)

She sure 'nuff came, Cap'n.

(Keller descends, and crosses toward the carriage; this conversation begins offstage and moves on.)

Keller [*very courtly*]: Welcome to Ivy Green, Miss Sullivan. I take it you are Miss Sullivan—
Kate: My husband, Miss Annie, Captain Keller.
Annie [*her best behaviour*]: Captain, how do you do.
Keller: A pleasure to see you, at last. I trust you had an agreeable journey?
Annie: Oh, I had several! When did this country get so big?
James: Where would you like the trunk, father?
Keller: Where Miss Sullivan can get at it, I imagine.
Annie: Yes, please. Where's Helen?
Keller: In the hall, Jimmie—
Kate: We've put you in the upstairs corner room, Miss Annie, if there's any breeze at all this summer, you'll feel it—

(In the house the setter Belle flees into the family room, pursued by Helen with groping hands; the dog doubles back out the same door, and Helen still groping for her makes her way out to the porch; she is messy, her hair tumbled, her pinafore now ripped, her shoelaces untied. Keller acquires the suitcase, and Annie gets her hands on it too though still endeavouring to live up to the general air of propertied manners.)

Keller: *And* the suitcase—
Annie [*pleasantly*]: I'll take the suitcase, thanks.
Keller: Not at all, I have it, Miss Sullivan.
Annie: I'd like it.
Keller [*gallantly*]: I couldn't think of it, Miss Sullivan. You'll find in the south we—
Annie: Let me.
Keller: —view women as the flowers of civiliza—
Annie [*impatiently*]: I've got something in it for Helen.

(She tugs it free; Keller stares.)

Thank you. When do I see her?
Kate: There. There is Helen.

(Annie turns, and sees Helen on the porch. A moment of silence. Then Annie

begins across the yard to her, lugging her suitcase.)

Keller [*sotto voice*]: Katie—

(*Kate silences him with a hand on his arm. When Annie finally reaches the porch steps she stops, contemplating Helen for a last moment before entering her world. Then she drops the suitcase on the porch with intentional heaviness, Helen starts with the jar, and comes to grope over it. Annie puts forth her hand, and touches Helen's. Helen at once grasps it, and commences to explore it, like reading a face. She moves her hand on to Annie's forearm, and dress; and Annie brings her face within reach of Helen's fingers, which travel over it, quite without timidity, until they encounter and push aside the smoked glasses. Annie's gaze is grave, unpitying, very attentive. She puts her hands on Helen's arms, but Helen at once pulls away, and they confront each other with a distance between. Then Helen returns to the suitcase, tries to open it, cannot. Annie points Helen's hand overhead. Helen pulls away, tries to open the suitcase again; Annie points her hand overhead again. Helen points overhead, a question, and Annie drawing Helen's hand to her own face, nods. Helen now begins tugging the suitcase toward the door, when Annie tries to take it from her, she fights her off and backs through the doorway with it. Annie stands a moment, then follows her in, and together they get the suitcase up the steps into Annie's room.*)

Kate: Well?

Keller: She's very rough, Katie.

Kate: I like her, Captain.

Keller: Certainly rear a peculiar kind of young woman in the north. How old is she?

Kate [*vaguely*]: Ohh—Well, she's not in her teens, you know.

Keller: She's only a child. What's her family like, shipping her off alone this far?

Kate: I couldn't learn. She's very closemouthed about some things.

Keller: Why does she wear those glasses? I like to see a person's eyes when I talk to—

Kate: For the sun. She was blind.

Keller: Blind.

Kate: She's had nine operations on her eyes. One just before she left.

Keller: Blind, good heavens, do they expect one blind child to teach another? Has she experience at least, how long did she teach there?

Kate: She was a pupil.

Keller [*heavily*]: Katie, Katie. This is her first position?

Kate [*bright voice*]: She was valedictorian—

Keller: Here's a houseful of grownups can't cope with the child, how can an inexperienced half-blind Yankee schoolgirl manage here?

(*James moves in with the trunk on his shoulder.*)

James [*easily*]): Great improvement. Now we have two of them to look after.

Keller: You look after those strawberry plants!

(*James stops with the trunk, Keller turns from him without another word, and marches off.*)

James: Nothing I say is right.

Kate: Why say anything?

(*She calls.*)

Don't be long. Captain, we'll have supper right away—

(*She goes into the house, and through the rear door of the family room. James trudges in with the trunk, takes it up the steps to Annie's room, and sets it down outside the door. The lights elsewhere dim somewhat.*

Meanwhile, inside, Annie has given Helen a key; while Annie removes her bonnet, Helen unlocks and opens the suitcase. The first thing she pulls out is a voluminous shawl. She fingers it until she perceives what it is; then she wraps it around her, and acquiring Annie's bonnet and smoked glasses as well, dons the lot: the shawl swamps her, and the bonnet settles down upon the glasses, but she stands before a mirror cocking her head to one side, then to the other, in a mockery of adult action. Annie is amused, and talks to her as one might to a kitten, with no trace of company manners.)

Annie: All the trouble I went to and that's how I look?

(*Helen then comes back to the suitcase, gropes for more, lifts out a pair of female drawers.*)

Oh, no. Not the drawers!

(*But Helen discarding them comes to the elegant doll. Her fingers explore its features, and when she raises it and finds its eyes open and close, she is at first startled, then delighted. She picks it up, taps its head vigorously, taps her own chest, and nods questioningly. Annie takes her finger, points it to the doll, points it to Helen, and touching it to her own face, also nods. Helen sits back on her heels, clasps the doll to herself, and rocks it. Annie studies her, still in bonnet and smoked glasses like a caricature of herself, and addresses her humorously.*)

All right, Miss O'Sullivan. Let's begin with doll.

(*She takes Helen's hand; in her palm Annie's forefinger points, thumb holding her other fingers clenched*).

D.

(*Her thumb next holds all her fingers clenched, touching Helen's palm.*)

O

(*Her thumb and forefinger extend.*)

L.

(*Same contact repeated.*)

L.

(*She puts Helen's hand to the doll.*)

Doll.
James: You spell pretty well.

(*Annie in one hurried move gets the drawers swiftly back into the suitcase, the lid banged shut, and her head turned, to see James leaning in the doorway.*)

Finding out if she's ticklish? She is.

(*Annie regards him stonily, but Helen after a scowling moment tugs at her hand again, imperious, Annie repeats the letters, and Helen interrupts her fingers in the middle, feeling each of them, puzzled. Annie touches Helen's hand to the doll, and begins spelling into it again.*)

James: What is it, a game?
Annie [*curtly*]: An alphabet.
James: Alphabet?
Annie: For the deaf.

(*Helen now repeats the finger movements in air, exactly, her head cocked to her own hand, and Annie's eyes suddenly gleam.*)

Ho. How *bright* she is!
James: You think she knows what she's doing?

(*He takes Helen's hand, to throw a meaningless gesture into it; she repeats this one too.*)

She imitates everything, she's a monkey.
Annie [*very pleased*]: Yes, she's a bright little monkey, all right.

(*She takes the doll from Helen, and reaches for her hand; Helen instantly grabs the doll back. Annie takes it again, and Helen's hand next, but Helen is incensed now; when Annie draws her hand to her face to shake her head no, then tries to spell to her, Helen slaps at Annie's face. Annie grasps Helen by both arms, and swings her into a chair, holding her pinned there, kicking, while glasses, doll, bonnet fly in various directions. James laughs.*)

James: She wants her doll back.

Annie: When she spells it.

James: Spell, she doesn't know the thing has a name, even.

Annie: Of course not, who expects her to, now? All I want is her fingers to learn the letters.

James: Won't mean anything to her.

(*Annie gives him a look. She then tries to form Helen's fingers into the letters, but Helen swings a haymaker instead, which Annie barely ducks, at once pinning her down again.*)

Doesn't like that alphabet, Miss Sullivan. You invent it yourself?

(*Helen is now in a rage, fighting tooth and nail to get out of the chair, and Annie answers while struggling and dodging her kicks.*)

Annie: Spanish monks under a—vow of silence. Which I wish *you'd* take!

(*And suddenly releasing Helen's hands, she comes and shuts the door in James' face. Helen drops to the floor, groping around for the doll. Annie looks around desperately, sees her purse on the bed, rummages in it, and comes up with a battered piece of cake wrapped in newspaper; with her foot she moves the doll deftly out of the way of Helen's groping, and going on her knee she lets Helen smell the cake. When Helen grabs for it, Annie removes the cake and spells quickly into the reaching hand.*)

Cake. From Washington up north, it's the best I can do.

(*Helen's hand waits, baffled. Annie repeats it.*)

C, a, k, e. Do what my fingers do, never mind what it means.

(*She touches the cake briefly to Helen's nose, pats her hand, presents her own hand. Helen spells the letters rapidly back. Annie pats her hand enthusiastically, and gives her the cake; Helen crams it into her mouth with both hands. Annie watches her, with humour.*)

Get it down fast, maybe I'll steal that back too. Now.

(*She takes the doll, touches it to Helen's nose, and spells again into her hand.*)

D, o, l, l. Think it over.

(*Helen thinks it over, while Annie presents her own hand. Then Helen spells three letters. Annie waits a second, then completes the word for Helen in her palm.*)

L.

(*She hands over the doll, and Helen gets a good grip on its leg.*)

Imitate now, understand later. End of the first les—

(*She never finishes, because Helen swings the doll with a furious energy, it hits Annie squarely in the face, and she falls back with a cry of pain, her knuckles up to her mouth. Helen waits, tensed for further combat. When Annie lowers her knuckles she looks at blood on them; she words her lips, gets to her feet, finds the mirror, and bares her teeth at herself. Now she is furious herself.*)

You little wretch, no one's taught you *any* manners?
I'll—

(*But rounding from the mirror she sees the door slam, Helen and the doll are on the outside, and Helen is turning the key in the lock. Annie darts over, to pull the knob, the door is locked fast. She yanks it again.*)

Helen! Helen, let me out of—

(*She bats her brow at the folly of speaking, but James, now downstairs, hears her and turns to see Helen with the key and doll groping her way down the steps, James takes in the whole situation, makes a move to intercept Helen, but then changes his mind, lets her pass, and amusedly follows her out onto the porch. Upstairs Annie meanwhile rattles the knob, kneels, peers through the keyhole, gets up. She goes to the window, looks down, frowns. James from the yard sings gaily up to her:*)

James: *Buffalo girl, are you coming out tonight,*
Coming out tonight,
Coming out—

(*He drifts back into the house, Annie takes a handkerchief, nurses her mouth, stands in the middle of the room, staring at door and window in turn, and so catches sight of herself in the mirror, her cheek scratched, her hair dishevelled, her handkerchief bloody, her face disgusted with herself. She addresses the mirror, with some irony.*)

Annie: Don't worry. They'll find you, you're not lost. Only out of place.

(*But she coughs, spits something into her palm, and stares at it, outraged.*)

And toothless.

(*She winces.*)

Oo! It hurts.

(*She pours some water into the basin, dips the handkerchief, and presses it to her mouth. Standing there, bent over the basin in pain—with the rest of the set dim and unreal, and the lights upon her taking on the subtle color*) *of the past—she hears again, as do we, the faraway voices, and slowly she lifts her head to them; the boy's voice is the same, the others are cracked old crones in a nightmare, and perhaps we see their shadows.)*

Boy's voice: It hurts, Annie, it hurts.
First crone's voice: Keep that brat shut up, can't you, girlie, how's a body to get any sleep in this damn ward?
Boy's voice: It hurts, It hurts.
Second crone's voice: Shut up, you!
Boy's voice: Annie, when are we goin' home? You promised!
Annie: Jimmie—
Boy's voice: Forever and ever, you said forever—

(Annie drops the handkerchief, averts to the window, and is arrested there by the next cry.)

Annie? Annie, you there? Annie! It *hurts!*
Third crone's voice: Grab him, he's fallin'!
Boy's voice: *Annie!*
Doctor's voice [*a pause, slowly*]: Little girl. Little girl, I must tell you your brother will be going on a—

(But Annie claps her hands to her ears, to shut this out, there is instant silence.

As the lights bring the other areas in again, James goes to the steps to listen for any sound from upstairs. Keller re-entering from left crosses toward the house; he passes Helen en route to her retreat under the pump. Kate re-enters the rear door of the family room, with flowers for the table.)

Kate: Supper is ready, Jimmie, will you call your father?
James: Certainly.

(But he calls up the stairs, for Annie's benefit:)

Father! Supper!
Keller [*at the door*]: No need to shout, I've been cooling my heels for an hour. Sit down.
James: Certainly.
Keller: Viney!

(Viney backs in with a roast, while they get settled around the table.)

Viney: Yes, Cap'n, right here.
Kate: Mildred went directly to sleep, Viney?
Viney: Oh yes, that babe's a angel.
Kate: And Helen had a good supper?

Viney [*vaguely*]: I dunno, Miss Kate, somehow she didn't have much of a appetite tonight—

Kate [*a bit guilty*]: Oh. Dear.

Keller [*hastily*]: Well, now. Couldn't say the same for my part, I'm famished. Katie, your plate.

Kate [*looking*]: But where is Miss Annie?

(*A silence.*)

James [*pleasantly*]: In her room.

Keller: In her room? Doesn't she know hot food must be eaten hot? Go bring her down at once, Jimmie.

James [*rises*]: Certainly, I'll get a ladder.

Keller [*stares*]: What?

James: I'll need a ladder. Shouldn't take me long.

Kate [*stares*]: What shouldn't take you—

Keller: Jimmie, do as I say! Go upstairs at once and tell Miss Sullivan supper is getting cold—

James: She's locked in her room.

Keller: Locked in her—

Kate: What on earth are you—

James: Helen locked her in and made off with the key.

Kate [*rising*]: And you sit here and say nothing?

James: Well, everyone's been telling me not to say anything.

(*He goes serenely out and across the yard, whistling. Keller thrusting up from his chair makes for the stairs.*)

Kate: Viney, look out in back for Helen. See if she has that key.

Viney: Yes, Miss. Kate.

(*Viney goes out the rear door.*)

Keller [*calling down*]: She's out by the pump!

(*Kate goes out on the porch after Helen, while Keller knocks on Annie's door, then rattles the knob, imperiously.*)

Miss Sullivan! Are you in there?

Annie: Oh, I'm in here, all right.

Keller: Is there no key on your side?

Annie [*with some asperity*]: Well, if there was a key in here, *I* wouldn't be in here. Helen took it, the only thing on my side is me.

Keller: Miss Sullivan. I—

(*He tries, but cannot hold it back.*)

Not in the house ten minutes, I don't see *how* you managed it!

(*He stomps downstairs again, while Annie mutters to herself.*)

Annie: And even I'm not on my side.
Keller [*roaring*]: Viney!
Viney [*reappearing*]: Yes, Cap'n?
Keller: Put that meat back in the oven!

(*Viney bears the roast off again, while Keller strides out onto the porch. Kate is with Helen at the pump, opening her hands.*)

Kate: She has no key.
Keller: Nonsense, she must have the key. Have you searched in her pockets?
Kate: Yes. She doesn't have it.
Keller: Katie, she must have the key.
Kate: Would you prefer to search her yourself. Captain?
Keller: No, I would not prefer to search her! She almost took my kneecap off this evening, when I tried merely to—

(*James reappears carrying a long ladder, with Percy running after him to be in on things.*)

Take that ladder back!
James: Certainly.

(*He turns around with it. Martha comes skipping around the upstage corner of the house to be in on things, accompanied by the setter Belle.*)

Kate: She could have hidden the key.
Keller: Where?
Kate: Anywhere. Under a stone. In the flower beds. In the grass—
Keller: Well, I can't plow up the entire grounds to find a missing key! Jimmie!
James: Sir?
Keller: Bring me a ladder!
James: Certainly.

(*Viney comes around the downstage side of the house to be in on things; she has Mildred over her shoulder, bleating. Keller places the ladder against Annie's window and mounts. Annie meanwhile is running about making herself presentable, washing the blood off her mouth, straightening her clothes, tidying her hair. Another Negro servant enters to gaze in wonder, increasing the gathering ring of spectators.*)

Kate [*sharply*]: What is Mildred doing up?
Viney: Cap'n woke her, ma'am, all that hollerin'.
Keller: Miss Sullivan!

(*Annie comes to the window, with as much air of gracious normality as she can manage; Keller is at the window.*)

Annie [*brightly*]: Yes, Captain Keller?
Keller: Come out!
Annie: I don't see how I can. There isn't room.
Keller: I intend to carry you. Climb onto my shoulder and hold tight.
Annie: Oh, no. it's—very chivalrous of you, but I'd rather prefer to—
Keller: Miss Sullivan, follow instructions! I will not have you also tumbling out of our windows.

(*Annie obeys, with some misgivings.*)

I hope this is not a sample of what we may expect from you. In the way of simplifying the work of looking after Helen.
Annie: Captain Keller, I'm perfectly able to go down a ladder under my own—
Keller: I doubt it, Miss Sullivan. Simply hold onto my neck.

(*He begins down with her, while the spectators stand in a wide and somewhat awe-stricken circle, watching. Keller half-misses a rung, and Annie grabs at his whiskers.*)

My *neck*, Miss Sullivan!
Annie: I'm sorry to inconvenience you this way—
Keller: No inconvenience, other than having that door taken down and the lock replaced, if we fail to find that key.
Annie: Oh, I'll look everywhere for it.
Keller: Thank you. Do not look in any rooms that can be locked. There.

(*He stands her on the ground. James applauds.*)

Annie: Thank you very much.

(*She smooths her skirt, looking as composed and ladylike as possible. Keller stares around at the spectators.*)

Keller: Go, go, back to your work. What are you looking at here? There's nothing here to look at.

(*They break up, move off.*)

Now would it be possible for us to have supper, like other people?

(*He marches into the house.*)

Kate: Viney, serve supper. I'll put Mildred to sleep.

(*They all go in. James is the last to leave, murmuring to Annie with a gesture.*)

James: Might as well leave the l, a, d, d, e, r, hm?

(Annie ignores him, looking at Helen; James goes in too. Imperceptibly, the lights commence to narrow down. Annie and Helen are now alone in the yard, Helen seated at the pump, where she has been oblivious to it all, a battered little savage, playing with the doll in a picture of innocent contentment. Annie comes near, leans against the house, and taking off her smoked glasses, studies her, not without awe. Presently Helen rises, gropes around to see if anyone is present; Annie evades her hand, and when Helen is satisfied she is alone, the key suddenly protrudes out of her mouth. She takes it in her fingers, stands thinking, gropes to the pump, lifts a loose board, drops the key into the well, and hugs herself gleefully. Annie stares. But after a moment she shakes her head to herself, she cannot keep the smile from her lips.)

Annie: You *devil.*

(Her tone is one of great respect, humour, and acceptance of challenge.)

You think I'm so easily gotten rid of? You have a thing or two to learn, first. I have nothing else to do.

(She goes up the steps to the porch, but turns for a final word, almost of warning.)

And nowhere to go.

(And presently she moves into the house to the others, as the lights dim down and out, except for the small circle upon Helen solitary at the pump, which ends the act.)

A C T I V I T I E S

**The Miracle Worker
pp. 266—293**

1. Form a group of four. Each member of the group will write a letter to a doctor who is a specialist in cases like Helen's. One will write the letter as Kate would write it, another as Captain Keller would write it, and the other two from the points of view of Aunt Ev and James. Make sure your letters are consistent with the knowledge you have about each character.

Read your letter aloud in your group and decide which one gives the doctor the best understanding of Helen's problems.

2. All parents hope for healthy children, but many children are born with or develop severe handicaps. With a partner, discuss the following questions:
   a) What special problems does a disabled child present for his or her brothers and sisters?
   b) Do you think a parent is apt to love a disabled child differently from one who is not? Explain your answer.
   c) What roles should society and government play in helping parents with disabled children?

3. Write a journal entry in which you describe how a family you know copes with a child with special needs or describe how you think you would cope as a parent with a disabled child.

4. Work with a partner who is also going to read this play, and predict what you think will happen when Annie Sullivan moves in with the Keller family. Make point-form notes to refer to as you finish the story.

5. Choose two or three of the whole-book activities on page 204 of the Student Handbook to complete as you read the play or when you have finished reading it.

ACTIVITIES

1. Choose two or three magazines, a video, or a whole book on the topic of parenting (the local library or a good book store will have a selection). Using the Media Review Form from p. 191 of the Student Handbook, analyse the magazine, video, or book. Join with two or three others in your class and put together a bulletin board display or a list of your top ten recommended sources of information on parenting.

2. Develop a Parent Potential Profile. Ask the family studies teacher in your school for information on the qualities of an effective parent, read or view some of the materials suggested in activity #1 above, and interview parents who you believe are doing a good job raising their children. Once you have compiled and thought about this information, write an in-depth analysis of your own potential as a parent. You may want to use the following headings for your profile:
   - qualities that I presently possess;
   - skills that I have;
   - skills that I will have to develop;
   - what my parents have done in raising me that I consider effective;
   - what I would do differently than my parents.

3. Work with a partner and analyse several TV shows that
   a) demonstrate effective parenting skills, and
   b) demonstrate unrealistic parenting.
   You may wish to look at
   - how realistic the socio-economic situation of the family is;
   - how the parents handle conflict among siblings and between parent and child;
   - the activities the parents and children engage in together;
   - the realism of the issues dealt with in the show.
   Prepare your report and present it to a family studies class of younger students or write it up for the school newsletter that is sent to parents and the community.

C A R E E R S

These careers are related to helping families raise children.

Child Care Worker

The child care worker works with emotionally disturbed children and adolescents. Responsibilities vary with place of employment. In a treatment centre, she or he may be part of a team. In all cases, the child care worker tries to meet the emotional needs of the children in her or his charge.

Training or Qualifications

Two and three year programs in child care studies are offered at many colleges. Volunteer experience working with children is an asset for admission to these programs.

Salary

Salary varies with place of employment. The estimated starting range in 1984 was $14 000 to $16 000.

Other Careers:

- Early Childhood Educator
- Health Care Aide
- Nurse
- Day Care Worker
- Housekeeper
- Owner of a small business specializing in products for children
- Furniture Designer

R E S O U R C E S

Books

Edgar Allan—John Neufeld (Signet, 1968)
A Guide for Parents of Young Children—Ontario Ministry of Community and Social Services
Your Baby and Child from Birth to Age Five—Penelope Leach (Alfred A. Knopf, N.Y., 1986)

Films

For Keeps, Columbia Pictures 1988; 96 min
Kramer versus Kramer, Columbia Pictures 1979; 105 min
Without a Trace, 20th Century Fox 1983; 120 min
Raising Arizona, 20th Century Fox 1987; 93 min
Cradle of Violence, Magic Lantern Films
Three Men and a Baby, Buena Vista 1987; 99 min

CHILDREN'S LITERATURE

VOICES

DIRTY GEORGIE

DENNIS LEE

Georgie's face was
Never clean,
Georgie smelled like
Gasoline.

Kissing Georgie—
Mighty fine!
Just like kissing
Frankenstein!

Georgie, Georgie,
Wash your face,
Or we'll kick you out
Of the human race:

Not because you're ugly,
Not because you're cute,
Just because your dirty ears
Smell like rubber boots!

BUNDLE-BUGGY BOOGIE

DENNIS LEE

Well, way up north
On a fine bright day,
A bundle-buggy boogied
At the break of day.

It did the boogie-woogie here,
It did the boogie-woogie there,
It did the bundle-buggy boogie-woogie
Ev-er-y-where:

Calabogie,
Kapuskasing,
Espanola,
Atikokan;
Manitoulin,
Madawaska,
Mindemoya,
Moosonee!

Then another bundle-buggy
Did a boogie-woogie hop,
And another and another
In the bundle-boogie bop.

And it's boogie-woogie high,
And it's boogie-woogie low,
And it's bundle-buggy boogie-woogie
Everywhere you go:

Athabasca,
Abitibi,
Bona Vista,
Malaspina;
Bella Bella;
Bella Coola,
Batchawana,
Baie Comeau!

LOVELY MOSQUITO

**DOUG MACLEOD,
PETER THOMPSON**

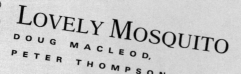

Lovely mosquito, attacking my arm
As quiet and still as a statue,
Stay right where you are! I'll do you no harm—
I simply desire to pat you.

Just puncture my veins and swallow your fill
For, nobody's going to swot you.
Now, lovely mosquito, stay perfectly still—
A SWIPE! and a SPLAT! and I GOT YOU!

NOBODY
LOVES ME

Nobody loves me, everybody hates me,
I'm going out to eat some worms.
Big fat juicy ones, long slim slimy ones,
Itsy, bitsy, fuzzy wuzzy worms.
First you eat their heads off,
Then you suck their gizzards out,
See how they squiggle and squirm!
Big fat juicy ones, long slim slimy ones,
Itsy, bitsy, fuzzy wuzzy worms.

BYE BYE

SEAN OHUIGIN

there's a creaking
in the darkness
a groaning in
the night
there are mutters
in the next
room
oh please
turn on the
light
there are footsteps
in the hallway
there's a
croaking over
there

AAAAAAAAAARRRRGGHHHHHH

an horrid
monster
has got me
by the hair
oh please don't
eat my fingers
oh please
don't bite my
nose
oh please
somebody
save me

G L U M P

301

ACTIVITIES

Voices
pp. 298–301

1. Make groups of two to four people and prepare to present one of the poems to the class. It is not necessary to memorize the poem but you should know it well enough that you only have to glance at the words every now and then. Make your reading as lively and interesting as possible. Experiment with varying the volume and tone of your voice. Remember that these poems were written for small children.

2. Once you have heard the presentations of all the poems in this section, examine the poems to discover the qualities they have which make them effective for small children. Make a list of these qualities and share it with the other groups.

3. Select a poem, rhyme, or chant you remember from your own childhood and read or recite it for the others in your group. Write in your journal about the memories this experience brought back to you and how the experience made you feel.

4. Using one of the poems as a model, write your own poem for an audience of children. Work in groups and be as creative as possible. Keep in mind the list you made in activity #2. Try your poem out on your little brothers and sisters, nieces and nephews, or any other children you know.

FOR READING OUT LOUD!

~

MARGARET MARY KIMMEL,

ELIZABETH SEGAL

any children today grow up with negative attitudes toward books and reading in any form. The media call it "a literacy crisis." The schools try new methods of teaching reading and test children more often, but nothing seems to cure the problem. Publishers bring out attractive books geared to poor readers, teachers report that these students are so turned off by books that the new formats don't entice them at all. Worried parents invest in expensive "teach your child to read" kits and high-powered electronic learning games, only to see their children growing up reading nothing on their own but an occasional comic book.

Meanwhile, research data have slowly been accumulating that suggest how we might resolve this crisis. Several studies of children from widely varied backgrounds who learned to read easily and remained good readers throughout their school years have revealed that they had something in common. They all had been read to regularly from early childhood and had as models adults or older children who read for pleasure.

In fact, reading aloud to children from literature that is meaningful to them is now widely acknowledged among experts to be the most effective, as well as the simplest and least expensive, way to foster in children a lifelong love of books and reading. The task now is to pass this word along to individual parents, school administrators,

and classroom teachers.

Many of these adults understand the importance of reading aloud to a young child who can't yet read. But too often these same adults no more think of reading aloud to the child who has learned to read than they would continue to run alongside the child's first bicycle, steadying the vehicle, after the child had learned to ride alone.

This is a sad mistake. Reading aloud should continue all through the school years, for many reasons.

■ *To stop the read-aloud sessions of the preschool years ends a rich shared experience.* A mother and father we know were concerned because their son's first-grade year was nearly over and he showed no signs of being able to read. They expressed their concern to his teacher and asked if she thought he needed special help to overcome a problem or disability. She stared at them in surprise: "Why, Jason reads quite well—and has been for several months now." It turned out that Jason had been keeping his new skill a secret, worrying that if his parents knew he could read to himself, they might stop reading him a bedtime story. Needless to say, Jason's parents reassured him that he could enjoy reading to himself *and* have his nightly story, too.

In many families now grown up, books read aloud together in childhood have become a treasured part of family history. "Remember when you read us *Five Children and It*, and we kids spent our entire week at the beach digging for a sand-fairy?" "I'll never forget when Mom was reading *Cheaper by the Dozen* in the car and Dad got laughing so hard that he had to pull over and stop."

In school, too, the shared experience that reading aloud provides creates a genuine bond in a group of diverse children that is unlikely to occur in any other way. As one teacher said after reading *A Bridge to Terabithia* to her class: "By the end of that story, we had been through so much together."

And this kind of communal experience is becoming rarer. In automobile assembly plants these days, many workers are plugged into the individual "walkaround" tape players. No doubt these help dispel the tedium of the job, but such gadgets cut off one worker from another; each is operating in his or her own world rather than sharing, as the cigar workers did, one fictional world.

■ *Being read to promotes, rather than retards, children's desire to read independently.* Contrary to some parents' and teachers' fears, listening to stories doesn't make "lazy readers." Rather, what the children hear seems to whet their appetites to read that book or others like it for themselves. One school librarian told us that when she asks children to name their favourite book, they almost always name the book she or their teacher has most recently read to them.

We all know that film and television adaptations increase interest in a book. When *The Secret Garden* was telecast on *Once Upon a Classic*, copies of the book were scarce as hen's teeth in the libraries. (We know one little girl whose popularity shot up considerably as her classmates competed to borrow the copy she owned.) Reading a story aloud is another form of book promotion and is just as effective with the children it reaches as a *Star Wars* movie or an *Afterschool Special* on television. And it has the decided advantage that the individual parent or professional—not Madison Avenue or Hollywood—can choose what book to promote to a particular child or group of children.

One reason that reading a book or story works so effectively to motivate independent reading is that learning to read is difficult and often frustrating. Going on to read more and more challenging books means repeatedly risking failure. Hearing a first-rate story read aloud makes the rewards of sticking to it clear and tangible.

■ *Being read to fosters improvement of children's independent reading skills.* Studies of first- and second-graders and fourth- through sixth-graders have demonstrated that children who are read aloud to on a regular basis over a period of several months show significant gains in reading comprehension, decoding skills, and vocabulary. The gains were greatest for disadvantaged students but not limited to them—all the children benefited significantly compared to the control groups, who were read to only occasionally or not at all.

Besides making children more eager to tackle the difficult tasks involved in learning to read, hearing stories read gets children used to the written language they will meet in books, which is different from spoken language.

■ *All through their school years, young people can enjoy listening to books that would be too difficult for them to read on their own.* How exciting it is for the first-grader, who is struggling to read brief and perhaps insipid primer stories, to share the delights and dangers of a whole prairie year when the teacher reads a daily chapter from one of Laura Ingalls Wilder's books. Similarly, seventh-graders might find *The Wizard of Earthsea* beyond their ability or ambition for independent reading yet become totally absorbed in listening to an adult read it aloud.

Listening experiences like these are especially valuable for the student whose home language is not English and for children

whose chief exposure to English comes from the television set.

■ *Wonderful books that are "hard to get into" are more accessible when read aloud.* The first few pages of an unfamiliar book usually determine whether a child reading independently will go on or give up and look for another book. In some books the reader immediately knows what's going on and is almost instantly swept up in the events of the story. Fairy tales, for example, signal in the first few sentences who the characters are, whether they are good or bad, and what their predicament is. A formula story of a

less exalted sort, like a Nancy Drew mystery or a Spiderman comic, also makes the reader feel right at home in familiar territory. But some of the richest, most rewarding books are the unconventional ones, the ones that don't fit a formula. Such books may defer gratification of the reader's curiosity in order to first establish a scene and mood; they are original rather than predictable. These books profit immensely from being read aloud. Your captive audience may be a bit restless until they get oriented, but they will soon be deep in the world of story with you if you have selected well.

■ *For the poor student whose inability to read has barred her or him from access to stimulating material in every subject, including literature, there is no substitute for reading aloud.* The attempt of publishers to be responsive to the needs of poor readers by providing high-interest/low-level-of-difficulty books is praiseworthy, but the fact is that many literary experiences that would be moving and meaningful to a fifteen-year-old reading at a third-grade level simply cannot be conveyed in simple sentence structure and vocabulary. Reading aloud is a way to be sure these students aren't deprived of their rich literary heritage.

■ *A significant number of children will always grasp material better through their ears than through their eyes.* When asked in a class, one student said he had no early memory of books. He didn't remember ever enjoying a book and doesn't read anything now except required assignments—not even the newspaper. He did recall with pleasure, however, records of stories that he owned as a child—folktales, Hans Christian Andersen stories, and the like. "Words on the page somehow come between me and the story" is the way he described his problem. He was envious of his classmates' memories of their parents reading to them. He was sure that would have been even better than the records.

There are others like this young man who may never find pleasure in reading, even if they have been read to in childhood. Is reading to such youngsters a waste of time, then? Not at all. Ideally, they should have occasional opportunities to listen to literature all their lives, so that they, too, can savor the unique pleasures of the written word.

■ *Studies have shown that reading aloud to children significantly broadens their reading interests and tastes.* Children and adolescents who tend to limit themselves to one author's books or one type of book in their independent reading—mysteries or sports stories or romances, for instance—will often be led to more challenging books and greater variety in their reading by hearing a book chosen by a knowledgeable adult.

■ *Exposing children to good literature, presented for enjoyment, will increase the chances that their reading life doesn't end with high school graduation.* A major goal of the schools should be to turn out people who not only are able to read but find enough pleasure in reading that they will actually read a book now and then after they've left school. We know that many American adults simply never read books; of these, only a small number are actually unable to read. In all likelihood, the adults who can but do not read books were once students who read only what was required of them at school. Once the assignments stopped, so did the reading. A few good books read aloud solely for the students' enjoyment could have made a difference.

■ *Seeing adults reading with enjoyment increases the chances that children will become lifelong readers.* This means that the parent, teacher, librarian, grandparent, or other adult who finds time to read to a child and does it with enthusiasm is providing a model as well as a story. Observing adults who are eager to read and are engaged in reading is more effective in making readers of children than any number of lectures on the importance of reading.

And it's important to recognize that, though the parent makes a very effective model, children whose parents have never discovered the pleasures of reading need not be left out. Any adult or older child can fill this role. By providing regular reading-aloud sessions to children who do not get that experience at home, the school or day-care centre or library can break through the cycle of illiteracy that victimizes many young people. Then when these children who have enjoyed hearing stories grow up, they may very well pass on the pleasure by reading to the children in their lives.

WHO'S AFRAID OF THE WICKED WITCH?

JANICE T. GIBSON

Once upon a time a poor woodcutter lived with his wife and two children in a cottage at the edge of a forest. The family was so poor that they didn't have enough to eat. "What's to become of us?" the man asked his wife. "How can we feed our children when there isn't enough for us?"

Most of us remember how the woodcutter and his wife sent Hansel and Gretel into the forest. And we once delighted in hearing about the children's adventures in the forest and in the gingerbread house. Even now, all of us, preschoolers included, chortle with glee when we hear how the wicked witch tried to kill the children, and how the clever youngsters succeeded in doing her in instead.

But fairy tales do far more than entertain their audiences. Their heroes and heroines teach important lessons. And scholarly devotees point out that they help children understand the world. Critics of fairy tales worry, however, that not all lessons that fairy tales teach are good for children. They point out that the messages that some fairy tales give, although possibly acceptable in earlier times, are inconsistent with what modern parents want for their children.

Just what do fairy tales teach?

■ **Fairy tales teach what life is about.** Can children really understand much about life and death, or good and evil? And can fairy tales help them? We know that young children don't have adult powers of cognitive or moral analysis. But they understand far more than most of us usually think. What they often don't understand is that their worries, problems, and conflicts are normal and natural parts of everyone's life.

Fairy tales help them by answering their timeless questions about the world and the roles they play in it. "What is the world really like? Is it a safe place, or does it contain a wolf waiting for me just like he waited for Little Red Riding Hood?" They also answer questions about the most important relationships to children: those between parents and children, and those between children and their siblings. "What will happen if I'm left all alone like Hansel and Gretel in the dark forest? Is it wrong to have bad feelings about my sister, if she's as bad to me as Cinderella's sisters were to her?"

■ **Fairy tales teach what happy and unhappy feelings mean.** Children have lots of strong feelings, happy and unhappy. Fairy tale heroes and heroines do, too, but their feelings are exaggerated so that they're easy to recognize and to understand. Exaggeration also makes them funny, so they're not so frightening. Fairy tale characters never feel rejected just because people ignore them. (That's the kind of rejection that happens in real life.) In fairy tale rejection, characters are physically separated from their peers, like Cinderella, who has to stay away from her stepsisters and sit in the ashes.

Fairy tales help children deal with their feelings too. Fairy tale characters *always* handle their emotions. And everything always works out well. Cinderella, for example, learns that crying or fighting doesn't get her what she wants. She just does her household tasks. In the end she's rewarded.

■ **Fairy tales teach what people are like.** Young children interpret everything simply and concretely. Fairy tales describe the abstract qualities of people in concrete terms they understand. Cinderella is good; we know it because she's beautiful and hardworking. Her stepsisters are evil; they're ugly and lazy.

Young children often can't understand that people can be bad and good at the same time. But they can understand fairy tale characters who are either good and beautiful (like Cinderella's fairy godmother) or bad and ugly (like her stepmother). There is no halfway in fairy tales.

In fairy tales, sometimes several characters together represent a single person with many contradictory feelings. When this happens, each fairy tale character represents a different "part" of the same person. Children deal more easily with each separate "part" than they do with a single complicated person. And they learn that they, too, can have contradictory feelings. The story of *Little Red Riding Hood* provides a good example. Little Red Riding Hood thinks of her mother as cautious. (The woman warns her daughter never to stray.) Little Red Riding Hood's grandmother represents another "part" of her, a woman so uncautious at times that some interpreters of the tale

describe her as wild. Look what the old woman does: she stays alone in a dangerous part of the forest.

■ **Fairy tales teach through inanimate objects and animals who seem like people.** Adults know that inanimate objects can't come alive and that animals can't talk. Young children "know" they can. That's why four-year-olds talk to their dolls and expect them to understand, and why they have serious conversations with squirrels or goldfish. And that's why they're not surprised when fairy-tale animals like the Ugly Duckling talk with other creatures.

When young children are still at a self-centred stage of thinking, they expect their dolls and pets to think and worry only about their owners. So they're not surprised when fairy-tale animals talk to people and care only about them, or when magic swords speak to their owners and guard them, and they're never surprised when frogs turn into handsome princes. This is the real world for children and it makes them feel comfortable.

■ **Fairy tales help children feel strong.** Fairy tale magic is very important to young children who, in real life, feel stupid and weak when compared with their parents. It gives them vicarious feelings of power. Children are delighted when a good fairy, a magic potion, or a magic sword makes the hero who is always weak in the beginning (just like children), strong. And they're delighted when a magic beanstalk makes the hero of *Jack and the Beanstalk* strong enough to get what he wants.

■ **Fairy tales teach what anger means and how to deal with it.** Children—healthy, normal children—often become angry, and they often act in hostile ways. So do fairy tale characters. When fairy tale characters behave badly (like Little Red Riding Hood, who disobeyed her mother's explicit instructions), they're usually punished. But their punishment is never permanent. And it never *really* hurts. Little Red Riding Hood learned her lesson. But she was rescued and lived happily ever after.

Fairy tale violence is usually directed against evil characters, and it succeeds.

■ **Fairy tales teach ways of dealing with dark and disturbing fears.** Fairy tales are allegorical. They describe complex and abstract problems simply and concretely, and provide thin veils for dark and disturbing fears. This hides them under the surface so that children don't have to examine them until they want to—or until they're ready.

The story of Hansel and Gretel is a delightful example of what allegory can teach. The surface tale is simple (but not the allegory): Hansel and Gretel are forced out of their home into the forest by a weak father and cruel stepmother. They're afraid to leave. But they find their way through the forest to the gingerbread house, and they destroy the wicked witch. In the end, the children return home, and, of course, live happily ever after.

The allegorical tale is more complicated. It describes what many psychoanalytic thinkers describe as the most disturbing fear of young children: fear of separation or separation anxiety.

In the allegorical tale, Hansel's and Gretel's fear of being sent into the forest is a thinly disguised description of the fear of separation. And their cruel stepmother represents for us that "part" of our mothers that forces us to separate from them and take care of ourselves.

Finally, when the allegorical Hansel and Gretel really do separate from home, they find that it isn't so bad. And when they come home at the end of the story, they bring the symbol of the witch's power—her jewels—with them. They prove they can take care of themselves, just like adults.

Are all the lessons that fairy tales teach good? Critics say, "No," and point to potentially bad lessons.

■ **Fairy tales teach violence.** Children learn by imitating. And psychologists point out that when they see people, TV characters, or fairy tale heroes and heroines rewarded for what they do, they learn to do the same things themselves. According to critics, the problem is that many fairy tale heroes and heroines commit violent acts, and they're usually rewarded. Hansel and Gretel live happily ever after because Gretel kills the wicked witch. And she does so in a particularly brutal way: by pushing her into a hot oven.

■ **Fairy tales teach dependence on magic.** According to critics, fairy tales teach another dangerous lesson: if we're good and if we want something badly enough, someone—or something—will always come along to help.

In *Cinderella*, a fairy godmother waves a magic wand and produces the coach and coachman so that Cinderella can go to the ball.

In real life, none of us can count on a fairy godmother to help. Some critics worry that children are liable to learn to wait for magic to get them what they want instead of trying more effective ways.

■ **Fairy tales teach questionable values.** Fairy tale heroes and heroines are often given rewards that many modern parents would disapprove of: power, material wealth, and physical beauty. Take the hero of *Jack and the Beanstalk*. His reward for outwitting the giant? Bags of gold, a goose that lays golden eggs, and a golden harp. In the story of *Snow White*, the heroine is rewarded by marriage to a handsome and wealthy prince. Cinderella receives the same reward, but she, in addition, first proves herself deserving by magically acquiring a coach and horsemen as well as a magnificent wardrobe in which to come to the royal ball.

Even in fables, animal heroes and heroines receive the same kinds of rewards. The Ugly Duckling, in a Hans Christian Andersen story, is rewarded with physical beauty.

Born ugly, he is good, and his good behavior leads to something that real homely children aren't likely to get: he changes (seemingly by magic for children who don't know about swans) into a beautiful creature.

Should we do anything about fairy tales or should we just enjoy them?

Some critics argue that we should remove the questionable messages. Some, like child psychiatrist Richard Gardner, M.D., have written "modern" revisions, primarily for the purpose of working with children in therapy, which are intended to teach socially acceptable values. Gardner has published some delightful examples. Look at the heroes and heroines in *Dr. Gardner's Modern Fairy Tales* (Creative Therapeutics) and *Dr. Gardner's Fairy Tales for Today's Children* (Creative Therapeutics):

In a "modern" version of *Hansel and Gretel*, "Hans" and "Greta" never kill the wicked witch. They leave her in the cage where she had kept "Hans." "Greta" tells why the two children never take the witch's treasures home: "I want people to like us for the way we are, not for how many presents we give them."

Gardner's *Ugly Duck* never grows up to be a swan. This is really impossible, the author makes clear, because, after all, he's a duck. He does, however, learn to make friends with the other ducks.

Finally, "Cinderelma" gets to the ball in Gardner's modern fairy tale, but not in a magic coach. She walks. She lives happily ever after, too, but not with the handsome prince. After living for a while in the palace, "Cinderelma" tells the prince: "I no longer wish to marry you. We're different kinds of people and are interested in different things. I don't think we'd be very happy living together for the rest of our lives." The prince's response? "I have similar feelings and sadly I agree it would be best for us not to marry." Unlike Cinderella, "Cinderelma" moves into town and lives happily ever after with a hardworking young printer.

Does "cleaning up" fairy tales make them better? And do "modern" tales convey invaluable messages that enchant children? Yes and no.

Most "modern" fairy tales get rid of violence with no problem. Hansel and Gretel, for example, certainly don't need to kill the wicked witch to make children love the story. Children would delight in any method of putting the witch out of commission, including placing her in a cage. But children are already protected from the violence of fairy tales by allegorical techniques, so that violence doesn't pose the serious danger it does when they see it in real life or on TV. And everything can't be "cleaned up" without taking away some of what is best about fairy tales.

The problem is that the same methods that "modern" fairy tales use to get rid of questionable values sometimes make the stories less relevant to children's real concerns. Hansel and Gretel, for example, don't need to *steal* the witch's jewels. But they really should *take* something home (there's nothing to eat there). Hansel and Gretel should have something tangible with them (food for the hungry family?) to symbolize the power that children know comes with adulthood.

In addition, many "modern" fairy tales replace magic with preaching. And this rarely improves them.

Finally, the delightful magic power of the heroes and heroines in the original tales gives children vicarious feelings of strength that help them deal with real problems. And it doesn't make them dependent at all. Children gradually learn the difference between make-believe and reality as they get older, anyway. And by the time they're five or six years old, their experience in the real world teaches them that fairy tale magic isn't real.

In the end, fairy tales always have delighted us and always will if we let them.

A C T I V I T I E S

Head Start
pp. 303–311

1. Write a journal entry on one or more of the following topics:
   - My favourite fairy tale was . . . because . . .
   - I think violence in fairy tales is . . .
   - Female characters in fairy tales are . . .
   - My memory of someone reading to me is . . .
   - If I ever have a child of my own, I will read . . .
   - I love it when the teacher reads aloud because . . .

2. Working with a partner, reread the article "For Reading Out Loud!" Design and make a poster to promote the importance of reading aloud to children. Discuss some good locations for displaying your poster.

3. Work in a group of four or six. Each member should bring in a fairy tale and read it aloud to the other members of the group. Discuss which were favourites in your childhood and why you liked them. Then, with a partner, and using the headings in the article "Who's Afraid of the Wicked Witch?", analyse one of the fairy tales. Make brief point-form notes under each applicable heading. Reassemble in your group and discuss your findings with the whole group.

4. Fairy tales: good or bad? Investigate this issue with a partner. Make arrangements to visit a senior kindergarten class or a grade one class to interview a number of children about fairy tales. Before you go, compose a number of questions that young children can understand. Tape the children's responses so that you may listen to them again later. Write a report summarizing your findings. Send a copy to the children's class so they may have it read to them.

MURMEL MURMEL MURMEL

~

ROBERT N. MUNSCH

When Robin went out into her back yard there was a large hole right in the middle of her sandbox. She knelt down beside it and yelled, "ANYBODY DOWN THERE?" From way down the hole something said, "Murmel, Murmel, Murmel." "Hmmm," said Robin, "very strange." So she yelled even louder, "ANYBODY DOWN THERE?" "Murmel, Murmel, Murmel," said the hole. Robin reached down the hole as far as she could and gave an enormous yank. Out popped a baby.

"Murmel, Murmel, Murmel," said the baby. "Murmel yourself," said Robin. "I am only five years old and I can't take care of a baby. I will find somebody else to take care of you."

Robin picked up the very heavy baby and walked down the street. She met a woman pushing a baby carriage. Robin said, "Excuse me, do you need a baby?" "Heavens, no," said the woman. "I already have a baby." She went off down the street and seventeen diaper salesmen jumped out from behind a hedge and ran after her.

Robin picked up the baby and went on down the street. She met an old woman and said, "Excuse me, do you need a baby?" "Does it pee its pants?" said the old lady. "Yes," said Robin. "Yecch," said the old lady. "Does it dirty its diaper?" "Yes," said Robin. "Yecch," said the old lady. "Does it have a runny nose?" "Yes," said Robin. "Yecch," said the old lady. "I already have seventeen cats. I don't need a baby." She went off down the street. Seventeen cats jumped out of a garbage can and ran after her.

Robin picked up the baby and went down the street. She met a young woman in fancy clothes. "Excuse me," said Robin, "do you need a baby?" "Heavens, no," said the woman. "I have seventeen jobs, lots of money and no time. I don't need a baby." She went off down the street. Seventeen secretaries, nine messengers and a pizza delivery man ran after her.

"Rats," said Robin. She picked up the baby and walked down the street. She met a man. "Excuse me," she said, "Do you need a baby?" "I don't know," said the man. "Can it wash my car?" "No," said Robin. "Can I sell it for lots of money?" "No," said Robin. "Well, what is it for?" said the man. "It is for loving and hugging and feeding and burping," said Robin. "I certainly don't need that," said the man. He went off down the street. Nobody followed him.

Robin sat down beside the street for the baby was getting very heavy. "Murmel, Murmel, Murmel," said the baby. "Murmel yourself," said Robin, "what am I going to do with you?"

An enormous truck came by and stopped.

A truck driver jumped out and walked around Robin three times. Then he looked at the baby. "Excuse me," said Robin, "do you need a baby?" The truck driver said, "Weeeellll . . . " "Murmel, Murmel, Murmel," said the baby.

"Did you say, 'murmel, murmel, murmel'?" asked the truck driver. "Yes!" said the baby. "I need you," yelled the truck driver. He picked up the baby and started walking down the street.

"Wait," said Robin, "you forgot your truck!" "I already have seventeen trucks," said the truck driver. "What I need is a baby . . . "

"YOU can have the truck."

PIERO'S ADVENTURE

SUE MCMILLAN

One sunny day, Piero felt quite bored. So he decided to go for a walk. Which way was he to go? The park seemed to be the best choice. So off he went to the park.

This park had a little pond, and as Piero came closer to the pond he saw some ducks. He watched the ducks for awhile, floating on the water. Watching the ducks floating on the water made Piero want to do it too.

Piero knows that he can't float on the water, like the ducks. He decided to build a raft.

Building a raft wasn't as easy as Piero thought. First of all, he needed to find some wood.

So he went into the bushes looking for twigs and stuff. After he gathered a bunch of twigs, he needed some rope. "Great, now I just have to put it all together," Piero spoke out loud.

He tried and tried. It just didn't work. Piero was just about to give up when he spotted a piece of wood. This would make a great raft, he thought to himself. Too bad he didn't notice it earlier.

So Piero dragged the piece of wood to the edge of the pond. He was quite excited by this time. Before he could go he had to find a stick to help him steer the raft. That was no trouble. There was a stick right by the edge of the pond.

Piero set off on his little trip around the pond. There was a frog on a lily pad. He waved to the frog and the frog waved back. "Hey," shouted the frog, "Can I come for a ride with you?"

"Sure, hop aboard," replied Piero. Piero, being the friendly type, was glad to have some company. "My name is Freddy," the frog introduced himself. "My name is Piero, glad to meet you, Freddy," replied Piero. They shook hands.

They floated around the pond for awhile. Freddy wanted to show Piero where his family and friends all lived. So Piero steered in the direction that Freddy was pointing.

As they approached closer and closer, Piero noticed more frogs. Their heads were peeking out of the water. Just as they reached the area where Freddy lived . . .

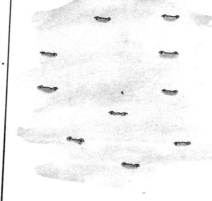

Another frog jumped on the raft. Then another frog and another frog. Soon the raft was filled with frogs. The raft was so filled with frogs that it was beginning to tip. Piero was getting nervous. Another frog jumped on the raft.

The raft tipped over. Piero swam as fast as he could to reach land. He was lucky that he wasn't too far from land. He shook himself dry.

He heard Susie calling him, from quite a distance. He was so glad to hear Susie's voice. After all this excitement, he didn't know if he had the strength to walk home.

"Piero, I'm so sorry my friends tipped over your raft," Freddy said sorrowfully. Freddy was scared Piero wouldn't be his friend anymore. Piero, being such a good natured cat, told Freddy it was alright, and that perhaps he would come down to visit Freddy again.

"Oh please do," Freddy urged. "But I don't think I'll keep this raft, " Piero said. Piero could see Susie getting closer, so he said his final goodbyes, and started walking to meet Susie.

"Piero! What happened?" Susie shouted nervously. Piero told Susie about Freddy's friends and family and about the raft tipping over. Susie carried Piero home, anxious to put a nice warm blanket around Piero.

Susie was glad to have Piero back home warm and safe.

THE END

ACTIVITIES

Read Me a Story
pp. 313–320

1. With a partner, read aloud the two children's books in this section. For each story, list what elements in the story would be entertaining and fun for a child. Make another list of what a child could learn from each story.

2. Each student should read at least two books written for children and prepare entries for an annotated bibliography. Do not select the same books as someone else. Use a separate sheet for each entry. At the top of the sheet, make a bibliographic entry using the following format:

Author. Illustrator. *Title*. City of Publication: Publishing Company, year of publication.

Examples of bibliographic entries for children's books are the following:

Gray, Robert, *Lost!* Illustrated by Barry Ross. Toronto: Macmillan, 1975.

Sendak, Maurice, *In the Night Kitchen*. London: The Bodley Head, 1971.

(In this case the author was also the illustrator.)

Below the bibliographic information, write a brief paragraph addressed to parents in which you indicate the age and interests of the child this book might appeal to. Clearly indicate whether or not you are recommending the book and your reasons. The sheets could be collected, put in alphabetical order by author, and typed up as a handy reference for parents.

3. *Piero's Adventure* was written by a grade 12 student. Working on your own or with a partner, write and illustrate a story that you think would appeal to a child in kindergarten to grade two. Use your imagination as you compose a story-line and select materials to present the text and illustrations.

4. Since the real measure of the success of your children's book is the response it elicits from children, your teacher could arrange a visit to a local elementary school so that you may read the story to your intended audience. Have fun! Your audience will love it and so will you! If you are a co-op student in a day-care placement, the audience for your book is your day-care children.

from THE IRON MAN

T E D   H U G H E S

The Iron Man came to the top of the cliff.

How far had he walked? Nobody knows. Where had he come from? Nobody knows. How was he made? Nobody knows.

Taller than a house, the Iron Man stood at the top of the cliff, on the very brink, in the darkness.

The wind sang through his iron fingers. His great iron head, shaped like a dustbin but as big as a bedroom, slowly turned to the right, slowly turned to the left. His iron ears turned, this way, that way. He was hearing the sea. His eyes, like headlamps, glowed white, then red, then infra-red, searching the sea. Never before had the Iron Man seen the sea.

He swayed in the strong wind that pressed against his back. He swayed forward, on the brink of the high cliff.

And his right foot, his enormous iron right foot, lifted—up, out, into space, and the Iron Man stepped forward, off the cliff, into nothingness.

CRRRAAAASSSSSSSH!

Down the cliff the Iron Man came toppling, head over heels.

CRASH!

CRASH!

CRASH!

From rock to rock, snag to snag, tumbling slowly. And as he crashed and crashed and crashed

His iron legs fell off.

His iron arms broke off, and the hands broke off the arms.

His great iron ears fell off and his eyes fell out.

His great iron head fell off.

All the separate pieces tumbled, scattered, crashing, bumping, clanging, down on to the rocky beach far below.

A few rocks tumbled with him.

Then

Silence.

Only the sound of the sea, chewing away at the edge of the rocky beach, where the bits and pieces of the Iron Man lay scattered far and wide, silent and unmoving.

Only one of the iron hands, lying beside an old, sandlogged washed-up

seaman's boot, waved its fingers for a minute, like a crab on its back. Then it lay still.

While the stars went on wheeling through the sky and the wind went on tugging at the grass on the cliff-top and the sea went on boiling and booming.

Nobody knew the Iron Man had fallen.

Night passed.

Just before dawn, as the darkness grew blue and the shapes of the rocks separated from each other, two seagulls flew crying over the rocks. They landed on a patch of sand. They had two chicks in a nest on the cliff. Now they were searching for food.

One of the seagulls flew up—Aaaaaark! He had seen something. He glided low over the sharp rocks. He landed and picked something up. Something shiny, round and hard. It was one of the Iron Man's eyes. He brought it back to his mate. They both looked at this strange thing. And the eye looked at them. It rolled from side to side looking first at one gull, then at the other. The gulls, peering at it, thought it was a strange kind of clam, peeping at them from its shell.

Then the other gull flew up, wheeled around and landed and picked something up. Some awkward, heavy thing. The gull flew low and slowly, dragging the heavy thing. Finally, the gull dropped it beside the eye. This new thing had five legs. It moved. The gulls thought it was a strange kind of crab. They thought they had found a strange crab and a strange clam. They did not know they had found the Iron Man's eye and the Iron Man's right hand.

But as soon as the eye and the hand got together the eye looked at the hand. Its light glowed blue. The hand stood up on three fingers and its thumb, and craned its forefinger like a long nose. It felt around. It touched the eye. Gleefully it picked up the eye, and tucked it under its middle finger. The eye peered out, between the forefinger and thumb. Now the hand could see.

It looked around. Then it darted and jabbed one of the gulls with its stiffly held finger, then darted at the other and jabbed him. The two gulls flew up into the wind with a frightened cry.

Slowly then the hand crept over the stones, searching. It ran forward suddenly, grabbed something and tugged. But the thing was stuck between two rocks. The thing was one of the Iron Man's arms. At last the hand left the arm and went scuttling hither and thither among the rocks, till it stopped, and touched something gently. This thing was the other hand. This new hand stood up and hooked its finger round the little finger of the hand with the eye, and let itself be led. Now the two hands, the seeing one leading the blind one, walking on their finger-tips, went back together to the arm, and together they tugged it free. The hand with the eye fastened itself on to the wrist of the arm. The arm stood up and walked on its hand. The other hand clung on behind as before, and this strange trio went searching.

An eye! There it was, blinking at them speechlessly beside a black and white pebble. The seeing hand fitted the eye to the blind hand and now both hands could see. They went running among the rocks. Soon they found a leg. They jumped on top of the leg and the leg went hopping over the rocks with the arm swinging from the hand that clung to the top of the leg. The other hand clung on top of that hand. The two hands, with their eyes, guided the leg, twisting it this way and that, as a rider guides a horse.

Soon they found another leg and the other arm. Now each hand, with an eye under its palm and an arm dangling from its wrist, rode on a leg separately about the beach. Hop, hop, hop, they went, peering among the rocks. One found an ear and at the same moment the other found the giant torso. Then the busy hands fitted the legs to the torso, then they fitted the arms, each fitting the other, and the torso stood up with legs and arms but no head. It walked about the beach, holding its eyes up in its hands, searching for its lost head. At last, there was the head—eyeless, earless, nested in a heap of red seaweed. Now in no time the Iron Man had fitted his head back, and his eyes were in place, and everything in place except for one ear. He strode about the beach searching for his lost ear, as the sun rose over the sea and the day came.

The two gulls sat on their ledge, high on the cliff. They watched the immense man striding to and fro over the rocks below. Between them, on the nesting ledge, lay a great iron ear. The gulls could not eat it. The baby gulls could not eat it. There it lay on the high ledge.

Far below, the Iron Man searched.

At last he stopped, and looked at the sea. Was he thinking the sea had stolen his ear? Perhaps he was thinking the sea had come up, while he lay scattered, and had gone down again with his ear.

He walked towards the sea. He walked into the breakers, and there he stood for a while, the breakers bursting around his knees. Then he walked in deeper, deeper, deeper.

The gulls took off and glided down low over the great iron head that was now moving slowly out through the swell. The eyes blazed red, level with the wavetops, till a big wave covered them and foam spouted over the top of the head. The head still moved out under water. The eyes and the top of the head appeared for a moment in a hollow of the swell. Now the eyes were green. Then the sea covered them and the head.

The gulls circled low over the line of bubbles that went on moving slowly out into the deep sea.

A C T I V I T I E S

1. With another student make a list of the elements in this first chapter of *The Iron Man* that would appeal to a young reader.

What elements in the list make the story appealing to you?

2. a) With a partner (and perhaps some help from your teacher), develop a working definition of symbolism.
b) Make a list of some symbols you are familiar with in society.
c) Discuss with your partner whether any aspects of "The Coming of the Iron Man" are symbolic. Be prepared to report to the class about any symbols you find and what the symbolism is.

3. Sometimes books for young people break the story into smaller segments and illustrate the segment of the story found on a particular page. Select one paragraph that you like from the story and draw an illustration to accompany it.

4. Work with a partner who is also going to read this book, and predict what you think will happen in the rest of the story. Make point-form notes to refer to as you finish the novel.

5. Choose two or three of the whole-book activities on page 204 of the Student Handbook to complete as you read the novel or when you have finished reading it.

ACTIVITIES

1. Working in a group, make a list of six to ten criteria for evaluating material (books, films, TV shows, toys, computer programs) prepared for children. Each member of the group should select two books, two films, two TV shows, or two toys that you think illustrate good and not so good material for children. Explain clearly, making reference to your list of criteria, why you would choose one for your child and not the other. Have a partner help you revise your piece of writing before you submit it to the teacher. You might consider sending a copy of this assignment to your community newspaper.

2. Visit a children's bookstore, the children's section of your local public library, or a storytelling, dramatic, or musical production for children with the child of your choice. Either:
   a) write up the experience in your journal, or
   b) prepare an oral report (accompanied by photographs, if you like)
   in which you describe the event, the audience's reaction, your companion's reaction, and your reaction. In your report mention the ways in which the event differed from a similar event aimed at an adult audience. In a small group, read your report or tell of your experience.

3. Children's stories vary from culture to culture. Ask your parents or guardian to tell you, or find in the library, a favourite children's story from your ethnic background or from another culture that you are familiar with. Write the story in your own words and read it to a small group of classmates.

4. Write and produce a children's play. Discuss possible story-lines with a partner and then work either at the computer or with paper and pencil and take turns creating dialogue for your script. Find classmates to play the roles you have created, arrange for someone to look after props and costumes, and present your play for the class. Then take your play "on the road." Arrange to visit local elementary schools or day-care centres. Your school's dramatic arts teacher may be willing to assist you in developing this activity.

CAREERS

These careers are related to children's literature.

Library Technician
A library technician assists in developing, organizing and maintaining a collection of library material by using a specialized knowledge of library systems and methods. The duties include recording the title, author, description, and contents of the newly acquired material on catalogue cards, computer or microfilm and preparing shelf listings. The work may include handling simple reference questions and operating or instructing library users in audio-visual equipment.

Training and Qualifications
Employment in this occupation usually requires a two-year college program in library techniques. Workers usually complete some on-the-job training under the supervision of an experienced worker.

Salary
Although each library has its own salary scale and job classifications, the starting salary in 1984 for library technicians ranged from $12 000 to $18 000 depending upon the skills required by the job.

Other Careers
- Writer of children's literature
- Illustrator
- Composer and/or Singer of children's songs
- Storyteller
- Clerk in a children's bookstore
- Actor

RESOURCES

Books
Michele Landsberg's Guide to Children's Books—Michele Landsberg (Penguin, 1985)
Alice in Wonderland—Lewis Carroll
Anne of the Green Gables—Lucy Maud Montgomery
Peter Rabbit—Beatrix Potter
The Read-Aloud Book—Jim Trelease (Penguin, 1979)
Films
Labyrinth, Tristar 1986; 101 min
Walt Disney's Cinderella, Walt Disney 1950; 75 min
The Wizard of Oz, MGM 1939; 102 min

OFF TO WORK

VOICES

As An Airplane Mechanic, My Career Has Soared

CORPORAL CHRISTINA PIDLESNY

Had my mother's plan prevailed, I'd be a registered nurse today. As things turned out, I took my own chances at 18 years old and joined the air force as an airplane engine mechanic. That was 12 years ago and in that time, this teen-age introvert has transformed into a motivated, aggressive and skilled technician who can match any male she's paired with.

Having worked both the servicing and maintenance sides of the Hercules, Boeing 707, Dash 7 and Aurora, both in and out of Canadian territory, I've experienced a wealth of cultural immersion and earned the respect of many males whose general view of female technicians is expressed in four-letter words. I guess the most important thing I want to say is that any woman out there, no matter her age, has the power to fulfil a lifetime goal. I plan to celebrate on September 25 when the red and white medal goes on my chest for 12 years of service. I believe I've earned that baby.

cathy®

by Cathy Guisewite

CATHY LESSICK, AUTOMOBILE MECHANIC
SHEILA AMATO, PAT STATON

I applied to a lot of places, but Cadillac Livery was the only place that would accept me. I've been here a little over four and a half years doing general mechanical work, alignment, tune up, brakes, exhaust, some propane work and installations. To be a mechanic you have to do a 900 hour apprenticeship. Courses or related job experience can shorten the apprenticeship time.

HOW STORYTELLER MUNSCH KEEPS HIS AUDIENCE SPELLBOUND
SHERIE POSESORSKI

When I learned to read, I disappeared into reading. One summer vacation, I read over 200 books. All I did the entire summer was go to the library, take out books, and stay home and read. I was a strange kid. A social island.

• • •

I had always wanted to work as a storyteller, but couldn't get anyone to hire me. Now that I was a published author, everybody wanted me to come and tell stories. My stories all evolve from those sessions. Usually I tell my stories for two or three years before I write them down. I get a real high from performing, a great sense of satisfaction from capturing an audience. My brain feels so alive because as I'm telling one story, I'm in the process of making up a new one, directed at a kid in the audience.

Kyte Brings Hockey to Life for Children at Deaf School

PAUL HUNTER

"I really enjoy working with kids," said Winnipeg goaltender, hearing-impaired Jim Kyte.

• • •

"With these children you have to use a lot of body expression. You have to show them things. It's like you're acting out a mime."

While communication is sometimes difficult on the ice, Kyte's impairment has presented very few problems as an NHLer.

The 6-foot-5 blueliner has developed a series of hand signals with his goalies to warn of approaching forecheckers and he has also learned to take advantage of efficient arena cleaning staff.

"In most major league arenas the glass is kept very clean so you get a reflection. If you look closely enough, you can see where the forechecker is," he said.

• • •

"I might have a disability, but it's not a handicap," he said. "I don't think anyone in this world is perfect. Everyone has their own handicaps. Some people wear glasses and they're not blind. I wear hearing aids but I'm not deaf. I don't know what it would be like to have perfect hearing."

MOST OF US ARE SCARED

INGRID BOTTING

Ingrid Botting is a 17-year-old graduate of Kelvin High School in Winnipeg.

• • •

We are very aware of problems: the threat of nuclear war, hunger, racism, and environmental pollution. Has our educational system prepared us to face them? I think that in high school we have been exposed to the problems, but we have not had enough discussion on how to deal with them—or how to solve them. And we are not acting as young people did in the past, with protests and demonstrations. Because of harder economic and social circumstances, we tend to live for today.

• • •

On the other hand, many of us work. In fact, the majority of high-school students have part-time jobs. To hold a job while attending high school is very difficult, but it is necessary in order to earn money for university. Although I know that a small percentage of other students use their money to support alcohol or drug habits, about 60 per cent of my friends are working to save money for post-secondary education. And there are other benefits to having a part-time job. I have learned to have a sense of responsibility, to work with other people—and to gain some independence.

A C T I V I T I E S

Voices
pp. 330–333

1. Form a small group and read the monologues and cartoon aloud to one another. Discuss the gratifications that people derive from their jobs.

2. You have probably held several jobs by this point in your life. Write one or two lines about each one. Try to capture a vivid memory about the job. Exchange your descriptions with a partner and read each other's.

3. In your journal write about someone who has influenced you most in regard to the job or career you are considering for your future. Explain why you think that person has had such an impact on the choice you made; how long you have thought about the job; and what jobs this one could lead to in ten, fifteen, and twenty years.

4. Collect monologues on work from people in your class, from other students in the school, and from relatives and friends outside of school. Prepare a collage of quotations and donate it to the co-op office or the guidance area in your school.

Ex-Basketball Player

~

JOHN UPDIKE

Pearl Avenue runs past the high-school lot,
Bends with the trolley tracks, and stops, cut off
Before it has a chance to go two blocks,
At Colonel McComsky Plaza. Berth's Garage
Is on the corner facing west, and there,
Most days, you'll find Flick Webb, who helps Berth out.

Flick stands tall among the idiot pumps—
Five on a side, the old bubble-head style,
Their rubber elbows hanging loose and low.
One's nostrils are two S's, and his eyes
An E and O. And one is squat, without
A head at all—more of a football type.

Once Flick played for the high-school team, the Wizards.
He was good: in fact, the best. In '46
He bucketed three hundred ninety points,
A county record still. The ball loved Flick.
I saw him rack up thirty-eight or forty
In one home game. His hands were like wild birds.

He never learned a trade, he just sells gas,
Checks oil, and changes flats. Once in a while,
As a gag, he dribbles an inner tube,
But most of us remember anyway.
His hands are fine and nervous on the lug wrench.
It makes no difference to the lug wrench, though.

Off work, he hangs around Mae's Luncheonette.
Grease-grey and kind of coiled, he plays pinball,
Sips lemon cokes, and smokes those thin cigars;
Flick seldom speaks to Mae, just sits and nods
Beyond her face towards bright applauding tiers
Of Necco Wafers, Nibs, and Juju Beads.

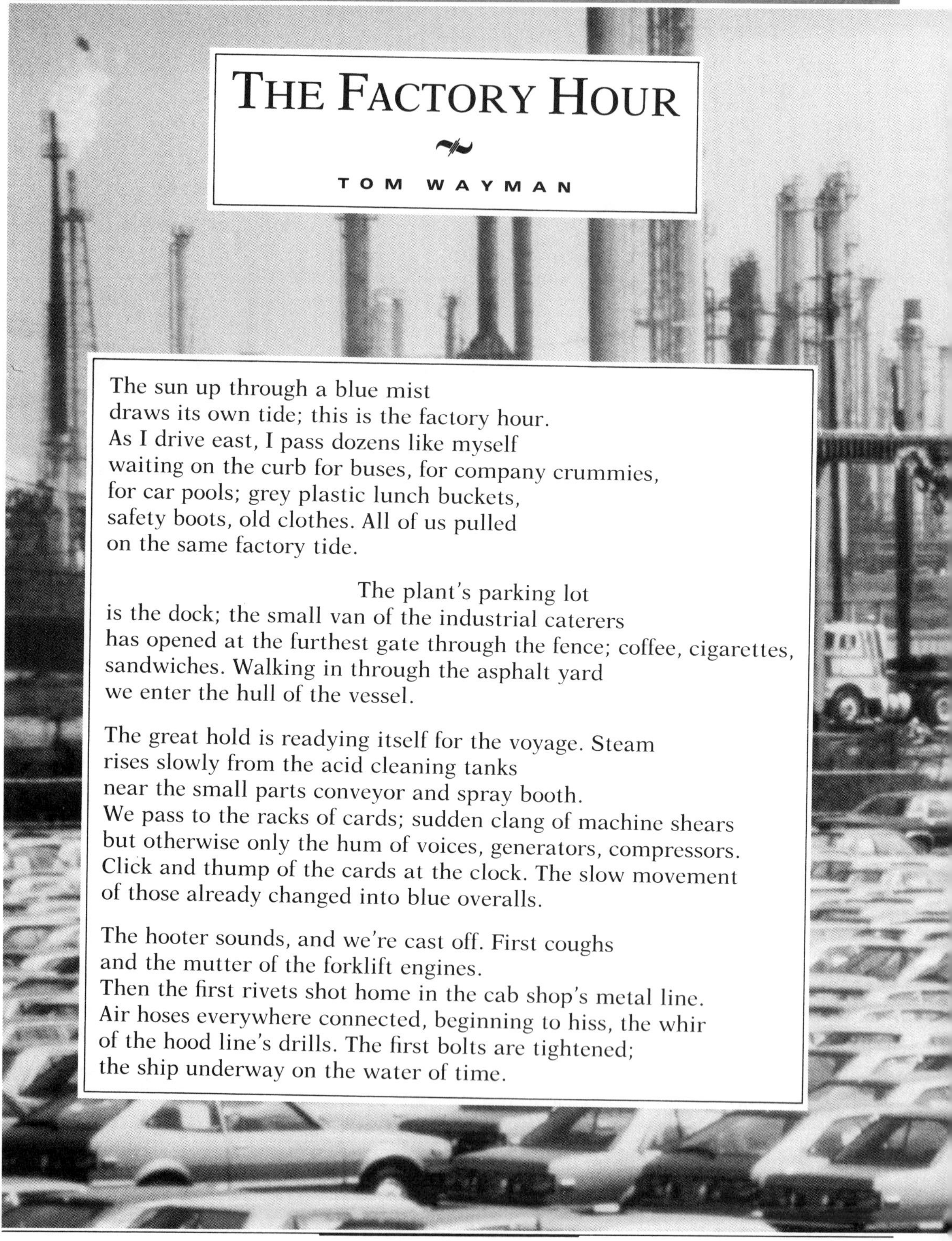

THE FACTORY HOUR

~/~

TOM WAYMAN

The sun up through a blue mist
draws its own tide; this is the factory hour.
As I drive east, I pass dozens like myself
waiting on the curb for buses, for company crummies,
for car pools; grey plastic lunch buckets,
safety boots, old clothes. All of us pulled
on the same factory tide.

          The plant's parking lot
is the dock; the small van of the industrial caterers
has opened at the furthest gate through the fence; coffee, cigarettes,
sandwiches. Walking in through the asphalt yard
we enter the hull of the vessel.

The great hold is readying itself for the voyage. Steam
rises slowly from the acid cleaning tanks
near the small parts conveyor and spray booth.
We pass to the racks of cards; sudden clang of machine shears
but otherwise only the hum of voices, generators, compressors.
Click and thump of the cards at the clock. The slow movement
of those already changed into blue overalls.

The hooter sounds, and we're cast off. First coughs
and the mutter of the forklift engines.
Then the first rivets shot home in the cab shop's metal line.
Air hoses everywhere connected, beginning to hiss, the whir
of the hood line's drills. The first bolts are tightened;
the ship underway on the water of time.

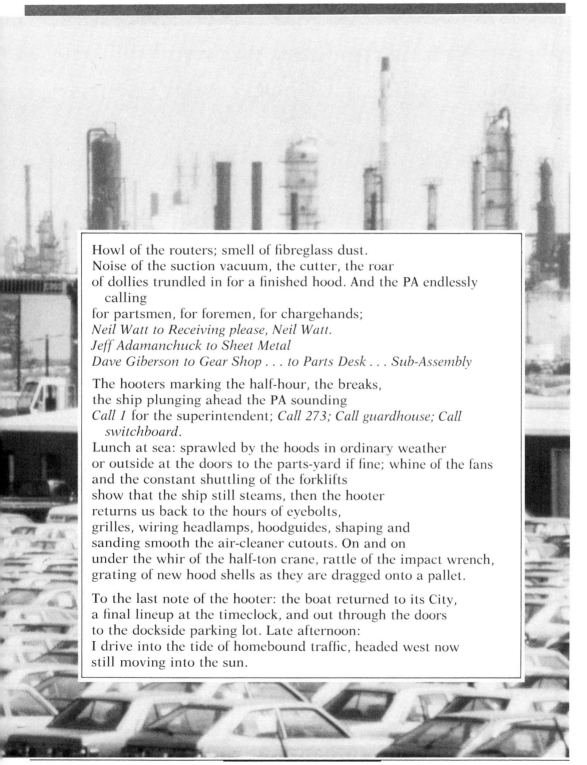

Howl of the routers; smell of fibreglass dust.
Noise of the suction vacuum, the cutter, the roar
of dollies trundled in for a finished hood. And the PA endlessly
    calling
for partsmen, for foremen, for chargehands;
Neil Watt to Receiving please, Neil Watt.
Jeff Adamanchuck to Sheet Metal
Dave Giberson to Gear Shop . . . to Parts Desk . . . Sub-Assembly

The hooters marking the half-hour, the breaks,
the ship plunging ahead the PA sounding
Call 1 for the superintendent; *Call 273; Call guardhouse; Call*
    switchboard.
Lunch at sea: sprawled by the hoods in ordinary weather
or outside at the doors to the parts-yard if fine; whine of the fans
and the constant shuttling of the forklifts
show that the ship still steams, then the hooter
returns us back to the hours of eyebolts,
grilles, wiring headlamps, hoodguides, shaping and
sanding smooth the air-cleaner cutouts. On and on
under the whir of the half-ton crane, rattle of the impact wrench,
grating of new hood shells as they are dragged onto a pallet.

To the last note of the hooter: the boat returned to its City,
a final lineup at the timeclock, and out through the doors
to the dockside parking lot. Late afternoon:
I drive into the tide of homebound traffic, headed west now
still moving into the sun.

THE SECRETARY MEETS THE ECOLOGY MOVEMENT

BRONWEN WALLACE

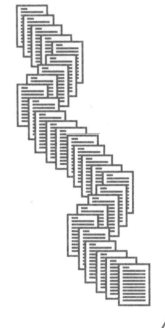

In this office
    I am accessory
   to machines.
My typewriter does everything
    except make coffee
And behind me
    are rows of machines
   ready
      to copy   to duplicate
      collate and staple
a blinding quantity of written words
   a whole forest of paper.

I am, therefore, not dismayed
   when, at 4:15
    my boss
brings me a 50-page document
  of which he wants
    a mere 100 copies;

    Without even moving from my chair
    I flick the switch on the stencil-maker
    (which makes stencils directly from typed copy)
    Check the fluid in the ditto machine
    And set up the collator . . .
    He stops me with a smile.
    "No, my dear, I want this *typed* on stencils, please.
    You see, it's double-spaced. I want it single-spaced.
    To save on paper."
    He smiles again, expansive
      with the vision
      of a dozen trees, unmutilated.

I frown.   Calculate
   that even with my
   miraculous typing machine
   the job will take
   a day and a half
(Two, if I count phone calls
   letters-that-must-go-today
   trips-to-personnel
   and coffee breaks)
   and will cost
   (in wages alone)
   $3.50 per hour $\times$ 8 $\times$ 2
   = fifty six dollars
   and will save
   5 trees @ $10
   2 trees @ $25
   1 tree @ $50   what does a tree cost?
   $^{1}/_{2}$ tree @ $100

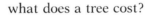

The coffee breaks will have to go   I guess
   I mean, after all
     we all want to
       do our bit
       for ecology

       don't we?

UNEMPLOYMENT

TOM WAYMAN

The chrome lid of the coffee pot
twists off, and the glass now rinsed.
Lift out the assembly, dump
the grounds out. Wash the pot and
fill with water, put everything back with
fresh grounds and snap the top down.
Plug in again and wait.

    Unemployment is also
a great snow deep around the house
choking the street, and the City.
Nothing moves. Newspaper photographs
show the traffic backed up for miles.
Going out to shovel the walk
I think how in a few days the sun will clear this.
No one will know I worked here.

    This is like whatever I do.
How strange that so magnificent a thing as a body
with its twinges, its aches
should have all that chemistry, that bulk
the intricate electrical brain
subjected to something as tiny
as buying a postage stamp.
Or selling it.

Or waiting.

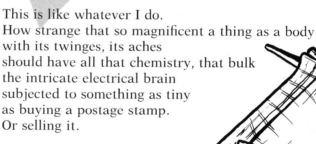

ACTIVITIES

1. The poems in this unit include *images* which allow the reader to see and experience fairly ordinary things in new and different ways. They contain images such as: "My typewriter does everything/except make coffee," " . . . The plant's parking lot/is the dock . . . Walking in through the asphalt yard/we enter the hull of the vessel," "Unemployment is also/a great snow deep around the house," " . . . His hands were like wild birds," "Flick seldom speaks to Mae, just sits and nods/Beyond her face towards bright applauding tiers/Of Necco Wafers, Nibs, and Juju Beads."

On the Job
pp. 335–340

a) With a partner or in a small group discuss the meaning of the word *image*, and discuss why each of the images above is appropriate. What does the image in each case suggest to the reader about the thing or person being described?

b) Choose one of the above images and draw it so that what is verbal becomes visual. Be sure to reread the poem to get all of the details necessary to make your visual representation of the image complete.

c) Read through other poems in other units of this book or in books of poetry in your school or local public library to find five other images. Read them to a partner or a small group and discuss each of them as you did in part a) above.

d) Create your own images and use them as the first two lines of a series of poems you may or may not complete. You might consider dreaming up some images to describe yourself or your feelings about things such as your part-time job, your school, your family relationships, your parents' or guardians' jobs. Share the lines you write with a partner, select the best ones, write them on poster paper, illustrate them, and display them in the classroom.

2. Three of the poems in this unit reveal the poet's feelings about a certain job, and one reveals feelings about not having a job. Make a chart outlining the type of job (including unemployment) and showing the advantages/satisfactions and disadvantages/difficulties of each and the personal qualities required for each.

IT'S STILL TOUGH TO WIN SEXUAL HARASSMENT CASE

~

DORIS ANDERSON

A 17-year-old starts his first job as a delivery boy in a factory. From the very first week, he is fondled, shown homosexual pictures and propositioned by a group of older men on the floor. He complains to the foreman, who ignores it as "just the boys having a little fun." Finally, he can't take it any more and he quits.

A PhD student is thrilled to be working directly under the supervision of a top scholar in his field. But he soon discovers he is expected to work late and cook intimate little dinners served with a side order of sex for the older man. He tries to get out of the situation gracefully by explaining he's engaged to be married. Soon, everything he does is being criticized and he is loaded with extra work. He asks for a transfer to another professor, but the older man, who is also head of the department, explains coldly that his work is so inferior he is being asked to leave at Christmas.

A father raising two children alone applies for a job as a salesman with a garment firm. At his interview, he is asked to take off his pants and parade across the floor because he may be required to "do some modelling." He refuses, saying he doesn't want the job under those circumstances.

"We weren't going to hire you anyway. You're too old and fat," he is told by the owner, a man in his 60s who apparently was just amusing himself.

Do these scenarios seem preposterous to you? Okay. Change the sex of the younger person to a female. Does it suddenly seem more plausible?

Two weeks ago, after four years of law suits and racking up a personal debt of $13 000, Kristina Potapczyk, who was the executive assistant of former MP Allister MacBain, had her charge of sexual harassment against him upheld by the Federal Court of Appeal. But it was a hollow victory. Due to a technicality, MacBain, as Kristina explained to me, "walks away with only court costs."

The Federal Court said even though the sexual harassment complaint was valid, MacBain would not have to pay $1500 in damages to Potapczyk. The court ruled the process under which the Canadian Human Rights Commission substantiates a complaint and then appoints a tribunal to find a remedy is biased. It said the process contravened MacBain's right to a fair hearing as guaranteed by the Canadian Charter of Rights.

Winning a court case on sexual harassment today is just about as difficult as winning a rape case was a decade ago. "Only about half the cases that go to court are being won," says Potapczyk's lawyer Mary Cornish, who did all the work on the appeal for free.

Sexual harassment has been going on since

the snake tempted Eve in the Garden of Eden. In the past, women tried to avoid it, or play ostrich and ignore it, or dress unbecomingly to discourage it, or just run away from it.

Sexual harassment occurs when anyone—man or woman—is treated like a sex object first, and a worker second. And it doesn't just happen to pretty young women. According to a survey by the National Union of Public Employees, 80 to 90 per cent of its female members had experienced some form of sexual harassment. Among university students, one in five reports harassment, according to the U.S. study, *The Lecherous Professor* (Fitzhenry & Whiteside, paperback, $13.95) by Billie Wright Dziech and Linda Weiner.

In some cases, sexual harassment is a deliberate technique to harass women out of well-paying jobs that are usually done by men—such as the recent cases at CN and Stelco.

People can't quite get it through their heads—as in the case of rape 15 years ago—that the woman hadn't "asked for it." Rape convictions used to average about 2 per cent of the number of rapes reported. In 1957,

the rape of a 5-year-old girl was dismissed by a judge because, in his opinion, the child hadn't "sustained lasting harm." In 1976, a woman who had been kidnapped and raped by two men, was incapacitated for four months, and lost her job and her fiance, was awarded the miserable sum of $2300.

Some men believe sex is just one of the side benefits of the job. "What's so terrible about a little flirtation?" they ask. Fine, if it takes place between equals. We long ago passed laws to protect minorities on the job. Now we have to extend that protection to women.

Occasionally a case of harassment is won by a man against his female employer—and that's a help, because everyone can understand that kind of harassment more easily.

Kristina Potapczyk is tired, and even this may not be the end. The Canadian Human Rights Commission over the next 90 days is going to decide whether to appeal the case to the Supreme Court of Canada.

"But I'm glad I did it," says Kristina. "I only hope other men won't be encouraged by the verdict to think they can get away with it on a technicality, too."

THE CHANGING FACE OF WORK

DIAN COHEN

idway between elections every voter starts to think that our politicians are way behind the people. What is harder to evaluate is the way our institutions keep up with the times. Some recent statistics are profoundly disturbing in their implications. The bulk of the people affected are older men.

Most of the jobs being created are going to women and part-timers, many of them young. And, in terms of long-term trends, what we are seeing is a weaker participation rate in the labour force for men and a growing one for women. That in itself should set off some alarm bells. Our employment policies, tax policies, de facto credit ratings and retirement policies are generally based on the idea that men are more "seriously" attached to the labour force than women. Though this is patently no longer true, it is taking a lot of time for that fact to trickle through the consciousness of governments, lenders and employers.

For example, women are not treated as employers for tax purposes when they employ others to take care of their children or clean their houses when they work. The reason given for this is that it would cost too much money. But if women didn't have to pay taxes on the money they pay as wages to others, they might be able to pay better. In turn, a lot of people who now work only for cash under-the-table might come out into the above-ground economy. I'm not so sure that it wouldn't be a positive exercise in the end.

Nobody knows these things for certain, just as nobody knows what would happen if we actually had equal pay for jobs of equal value. It has become the fashion in business circles to raise cries of alarm at the very idea of such a thing. The assumption is obviously being made that equity means bringing women's wages up to where men's are. But since women's employment role is increasing and men's decreasing, men are much more vulnerable to seeing their wages cut. This is even truer because men are in the dying smokestack industries and women are in the burgeoning service fields.

The fact is that it is very hard to determine what equal pay for work of equal value means because women have not been doing the same jobs as men have. That may be changing. We are now starting to hear male voices when we dial directory assistance. Younger men may begin to care more about

having a job—any job—than about the stereotypes attached to it, and pay equity may come to mean a kind of levelling of wages and stereotypes.

The area of the economy that is growing is small business and, in the employed sector, part-time work. Women may be better equipped in many ways to respond to the needs of our changing economy. They are used to being fragmented—to answering the phone while braiding a child's hair and watching the soup pot and thinking ahead to what the family needs next week. They are used to working out of their kitchens, which is where many small businesses are started. And because it has always been harder for them to borrow money (this too is changing) they know how to plan and spend carefully. Women are also taught to expect to serve others, and see no stigma in doing so. All of these qualities are the ones that are needed to survive in the new economy. Men, on the other hand, are taught to believe that they deserve a long-term job. They may find it very hard to adjust to the new reality.

Our governments have traditionally thought in terms of short-term job creation, despite reams of evidence that it doesn't do any good. As well, in recent years 100 per cent of net job creation in Canada has been in the small-business sector, yet only a tiny part of the department of regional industrial expansion's job creation budget is devoted to it.

Most small-business people will tell you they don't really want direct government subsidies. They would prefer to have life made easier for them, with perhaps limited grants available for testing completely new ideas.

In Quebec, where I live, half of the small businesses are run by women. But they are in the micro businesses.

Women have a long way to go before they hold the levers of established power in Canada. But they are extremely productive, and getting more so every day. If the treatment of travelling businesswomen in hotels and restaurants is any indication, many businesses have a lot to learn about how to adjust to some new realities. Women are only just beginning to wake up to the clout that they have in this area, and we will see changes in the way many services are marketed in the years to come.

Women and young people are still the sources of cheap labour, but young people will be a much smaller proportion of the population in the next few years, and nothing is being done about the problems of the burgeoning elder class.

The one area where we can see some real changes being made is in retirement options. It is not enough, and it is not quick enough, but it is becoming easier for part-timers, for women and for young people to make pension arrangements. Because nobody can count on the same job for 10 years, let alone a lifetime career, it has become vital to have earlier vesting and portability in pensions, and this is now beginning to happen. We still need to find ways within the system to allow older people with productive years still in them to bow out of jobs that are desperately needed by younger people. If we were smart, we would find ways to use those older people and all their experience to help fix some of our problems, and we would find a way of financially bridging their way to retirement.

In large companies, the fashionable and necessary concept of flattening the management structure—reducing the number of top-level managers—has led to a soggy middle of young, ambitious middle managers with no place to go but sideways. We have to find ways of making breadth of experience just as valuable as ascension in the pyramid, and many of the most energetic of these people may well start their own businesses. When will our institutions catch up?

THE LOST GENERATION

~

J A N I C E   T U R N E R

They're caught between distorted teenage fantasies and the "heavy" demands of the adult world. Across Metro, they rank in the thousands.

Unemployed and under the age of 20, they're frequently homeless, poorly educated and largely unskilled. And unlike the older jobless, their lives seem more complex as they struggle with the quirks and pains of adolescence.

They're the "lost generation," lamented a $200,000 Senate report, released in February.

Nearly two years in preparation, the study called for a national war against youth unemployment, warning that otherwise some young Canadians may never hold a job in their lives. A committee of 12 senators toured 11 cities and interviewed more than 300 high school students, dropouts and others to prepare the report.

The Star talked to some members of this "lost generation."

■ "I left (school) because they were going to kick me out, and I didn't want to give them the satisfaction," said Allan Johnston.

■ Jim Morrow, 19, sits on a bench in the Eaton Centre dreaming of making it big in a heavy metal band. Maybe not *real* big, but big enough to not have to worry about money.

Morrow said he has worked in more than half a dozen fast-food restaurants, never staying for more than two months at a time. He only works to keep clothes on his back. His real love is his music.

"All I want is $5 an hour, nothing great—I'm not going to cut my hair for that," added the grinning blond teen, who has quit and been fired with amazing regularity. "I was a good worker, but I was late all the time," he said of one pizza shop job.

Of his two-month stint at a well-known hot dog emporium, he commented: "I got tired of working constantly at night. I had no social life."

Morrow has only a men's hostel to call home. Despite the "mindless" jobs he takes, he said he won't go back to school. "I couldn't handle the head games. Music's my thing. Security doesn't mean anything. I want fun; I want adventure."

■ Neil Richardson, 18, dropped out of high school when he was 16.

"School was like a bad job for me," said the teen, who sometimes stays at the same hostel as Morrow. "I couldn't walk in with a smile."

Recently laid off as a security guard, he is now between jobs. "There's work," he told The Star. "You just have to look for it."

Richardson tries to find jobs that pay at least a dollar above minimum wage, but usually has to lie about his experience.

"I look for something that's a little permanent," he said. "If I don't think I'm going to be there a couple of months, I don't bother with it."

■ Shawn Brown, 17, said nobody will give him a job. Tugging on his collar-length hair, he said he will wash dishes, "but I couldn't even get that."

"McDonald's wouldn't even have me because I didn't have experience," he said.

"I'm looking for something artistic, even social work."

It was "stupid" to quit school in Grade 9, he admitted, "but I had a lot of problems at home. I just couldn't concentrate." Although he said he has applied for work in "every store on Yonge St.," nothing has turned up.

He has enrolled in a new provincial job-creation scheme and wants one day to have his own apartment. "It's taken me six months to be where I thought I'd be in two weeks," he said.

■ Kim Selzer, 21, said "goodbye" to high school when she was 15.

The Thunder Bay woman moved to Toronto last fall and worked as a bar waitress until she'd "had it" and quit in March. At $4 an hour plus tips, it was "impossible" for her to afford an apartment. She spends most nights in a hostel.

Selzer said it's harder for unskilled women

to find work then it is for men. "It's an attitude problem. (Employers) don't think you can do (manual labour)."

"You're working largely with a population (those under 18) that isn't ready to work yet," said Rick Stubbert, program manager with Mercury Youth Services, a publicly funded youth counselling agency.

"Gradually, they begin to cope with a working environment. They find a lot of jobs boring, and when they're offered minimum wage, they're quite insulted."

Michael Knight of Covenant House, a crisis centre for young people under 21, concedes there is no shortage of jobs. "If a kid is really serious about getting a job, there isn't a problem. It just isn't a very good job."

Knight said that because Covenant House rules force youngsters to get a job within two weeks, most do. But that is no guarantee they will stick with it.

"More than half of our kids come from middle-class families," he said. "They're used to Walkmans (portable stereos) and coloured TVs, highly materialistic living."

To them, working for a $4-an-hour minimum wage is like taking from the "bottom of the barrel," he said.

The prospect of quick money and a more glamorous lifestyle lures some into street prostitution, Knight noted.

Stubbert said youngsters who have quit high school face a tough dilemma. "They're between a rock and a hard place. Without wanting to destroy them, you tell them they aren't worth much in the marketplace."

Many such youngsters are "predisposed to fail," according to Knight. Faced with low pay or no money at all, they often cannot afford such basic needs as housing and food.

Employers "have to teach them more than how to do the job," and to be reliable, added Knight, contending that television has helped to distort their views of reality.

"You get a kid who thinks he can do anything, and he ends up washing dishes," he said. . . .

Barbara Atlas, acting supervisor with Employment Canada's Specialized Youth Unit for "severely disadvantaged" unemployed, said the problem is finding jobs that hold promise.

The service sees about 100 new clients a month and is "swamped" by young people trying to find satisfactory work.

"Very few" describe themselves as happy on welfare, Atlas added. Most will take minimum wage jobs "if they think it will mean something to them in the future."

For her clients, trying to survive is a "struggle . . . if they need a pair of jeans, it just blows the budget."

Blanche MacDonald, supervisor of Toronto's Inner City Youth Program for street kids, which sees about 6000 clients a year, called some minimum wage jobs "pretty revolting."

Many do not provide youngsters with enough hours for them to survive, and there is "an enormous prejudice" against hiring adolescents in the first place, she said.

She denied that youngsters prefer welfare—most do not have enough work experience to qualify for unemployment insurance—over a job. "You can live better on minimum wage than you can on welfare."

"There are some kids who are lazy in the world," MacDonald said, "but part of the problem is their adolescence. They have a lot of fantasies about work and a lot of fantasies about their own skills. That's normal."

"It's typical to blame the victim," said Peter Crosby of Huntley Youth Services, a publicly aided counselling agency.

"The kids are not lazy. Many are demoralized and find it very difficult to have a positive attitude."

Government job-creation programs "aren't much of a solution," in his view. "They don't have a great reputation among kids. They're viewed somewhat cynically."

At Covenant House, some clients are "sec-

ond-generation welfare," and getting a job is not always a priority, Knight acknowledged. "They've seen how to use and abuse the system," he said. "It's so easy for them to do. If they put as much effort into getting a job as they did into getting out of working, they would really do well."

Bruce Martin, director of the Peanut Employment Centre for Youth said youngsters who turn down minimum wage jobs are usually hoping to "luck into" those that pay more.

After seeing their parents work for $7 and $8 an hour, they regard $4-an-hour jobs as leading nowhere. Disillusioned, they give up hope, he said.

"The concept of competing for a job has waned over the years. There doesn't seem to be that drive."

He said society is sending young people mixed messages about education; many school drop-outs cite cases of university graduates doing $5-an-hour-jobs that they themselves could get.

Colour Does More Than Brighten Your Day

~

ARDEN GAYMAN

ou have perhaps never considered mauve to be a neutral shade—more of a neutral, say, than beige or gray. Get ready to change your mind; and if you work at a terminal with its bright green images and cursor, to be thankful for mauve.

When you lift your eyes for momentary relief from the terminal, you see an after-image of red, which is disturbing, says Kay Stephenson-Wrack. A noted design and colour consultant, she heads her own Montreal-based company, Creative Services.

The red component in mauve cancels the after-image, she says. It is much more restful than beige or gray in a hi-tech office. Mauve as an office colour has been around for about five years, by the way.

But yes, your office walls and big ticket items may still be beige, long considered "safe". It was, in fact, so successful that consumers were afraid to choose a colour, says Stephenson-Wrack. Seeming safe, beige obviously was right for big ticket items that had to last and last and last.

Colour accepted

But now, the idea of colour as part of a workplace is an accepted fact. It's no longer "will we have colour," but "which colour will we have?" she says.

Consumers have conquered their chromophobia, the fear of colour, she says. Gray is the neutral of the 1980s, replacing beige. Shades of rose, blue and gray all go with mauve, now being widely specified, she says.

"You can no longer talk about contract fashion, or residential fashion or fashion-fashion," says Stephenson-Wrack. "It's all fashion."

And colour doesn't just happen. There is an industry devoted to developing colours in England, Europe, the United States. In Canada there is a colour service for the fashion industry.

The relationships of colours in cars, in women's and men's fashions (note the number of mauve golf shirts you see), and contract colours are not accidental. Car colours are developed five years ahead of the fact, and, incidentally, are geared to women, who now buy half of all new cars. And, when a husband decides on the model of car, he brings along his wife to choose the colour.

Women shine

An important element in the introduction of colour in the office is the fact that women increasingly are in positions of authority, says Stephenson-Wrack. And, women can perceive colour more clearly than men, she adds. An interesting aside: blue-eyed people can perceive colour more clearly than those with brown eyes.

Given the new soft palette of colour, what can you do with long-term office renovations? Your office is strong on beige and brown. Shades of apricot, peach and nectarine can work with brown for an updated look, Stephenson-Wrack suggests. You can work with fabrics to give a fresh look. But, if you are going to get rid of anything, the first colour to go should be brown, she says. And adds, "there's a lot of brown carpet around."

Soft grayed desert colours of the U.S. southwest are now a strong influence, she says. Next year, colours will virtually be the same, but in clearer, stronger tones. In a year or two, brighter colours may be added to existing colour schemes, and in three years, there will be very dark accents, she predicts.

Good design and colour are not just for fantasy. They have a marked although unmeasurable effect on productivity, says Stephenson-Wrack. People have pride in their workplace, and she can cite instances when an updated office has resulted in staff dressing better, arriving at work on time and feeling more comfortable. "When people are more comfortable, they're not twitching," she says.

Is there a no-no? "Navy blue," says Stephenson-Wrack without hesitation. People in navy blue environments are sick more often. It's a cold, authoritarian colour, the colour of police and airline pilot uniforms.

And, mustard-coloured walls have a low acceptance rate.

Health-care officers are moving away from white, which is threatening, a pain colour. Apricot has become the beige of health care facilities, she says. It's combined with sand, turquoise and dark gray.

What about the future? "Expect to see black and white with brights," says Stephenson-Wrack.

Regarded as one of North America's leading contract colour consultants, Stephenson-Wrack has just completed generic seminars on colour for the design community, presented by Haworth Office Systems, Ltd. in Toronto, Ottawa and Montreal.

A C T I V I T I E S

**In the Workplace
pp. 342–351**

1. There have always been issues related to the workplace. With two or three other students prepare a bulletin board display on WORK ISSUES—PAST, PRESENT, AND FUTURE. (Some issues to explore are child labour, pay equity, robotics, and working at home rather than with other people in an office.) The librarian, history, and geography teachers will be able to assist you in researching this topic.

2. You have been asked to design a work environment (perhaps an office or a bank). Reread "Colour Does More Than Brighten Your Day" for ideas. As the designer, you may decide on the colours and accessories but you must have energy-efficient windows, which means they cannot be opened. You must also take into consideration by-laws regarding smoking in the workplace. Prepare drawings for the project and present them to another group that did a similar project, explaining why you made the design decisions you did.

3. Work in a group of three. Find out the original use of the phrase *the lost generation*. Discuss whether the people mentioned in "The Lost Generation" article are similar to those of the original lost generation.

    Role-play an interview with one of the people interviewed in the article, expanding on the ideas that it includes.

    Write a newspaper article on "The Found Generation." Interview two young people you know who are successful and write up their stories.

4. a) Work with a partner and after rereading "It's Still Tough To Win Sexual Harassment Case," make a list of the techniques Doris Anderson used in writing this article
    - to catch the reader's attention;
    - to demonstrate that the issue is widespread;
    - to elicit an emotional response;
    - to individualize the topic.
    b) Interview someone who has suffered sexual harassment in the workplace and play the interview for another group of students or take it to your co-op, law, politics, or history class.

So You're Applying for a Job . . .

Help yourself out by following these few simple tips.

1. Be Prepared
Know why you want the job
and what the job involves.

2. Complete an Application
Make sure it's neat.
Fill it out completely.
Take your time.
Be sure to print.

3. Go Alone
Leave your friends and family
at home.

4. Be on Time
Know the correct time and location
of your interview.

5. Dress Neatly
Be clean and tidy.
Don't chew gum.
Don't smoke.

6. Speak Clearly
Answer and ask questions carefully.
Use proper grammar.

7. Make a Good Impression
Be polite.
Listen carefully.
Sit upright.
Be confident and sincere.

8. Follow-up
Check back with the employer
to see if you have the job.

HOW YOU SHOULD WRITE A JOB APPLICATION LETTER

~

GARY DESSLER

hat's the most common error job seekers make when answering help-wanted ads? According to Jack Erdlen of the Massachusetts-based Employment Management Association, the biggest mistake is using the same standard cover letter for every reply, a tactic that gives the (often accurate) impression that you're sending the same letter to hundreds of other employers.

The best approach, he says, is to be more selective and to zero in on what the employer is seeking. Then, construct your letter to address those needs.

Here's what a consensus of other experts in the field suggest you do:

■ Cite accomplishments. Underline the qualifications requested in the ad. Then select your one accomplishment that most nearly corresponds to the qualification that's of greatest importance to the job advertised.

Include this accomplishment in the first sentence of your letter.

Also, in this sentence, express a genuine interest in the job. Give a specific reason for your interest, based on accomplishments.

■ Respond to the advertised needs. For each, underscore the need at the start and provide a paragraph to show you're qualified for the job. In a separate paragraph, describe a relevant accomplishment.

■ Summarize your experience. In a separate paragraph at the end of your letter, summarize other experience you consider relevant, including your education.

■ Request an interview and indicate how you can be reached.

25 THINGS YOUR BOSS WANTS YOU TO KNOW

~

S H I R L E Y   S L O A N   F A D E R

When you report to work those first days and weeks of your new job, your boss doubtless will mention the visible, mechanical portions of your responsibilities. She or he probably will say almost nothing about the crucial, invisible parts. You'll be told about hours, meetings, reports, general performance goals. Beyond vague clichés like "We all work together as a team," who will tell you what attitudes and behaviour separate the also-rans from those who win promotions?

Usually no one. You are supposed to be aware of these guidelines. It is essential because, although no one will educate you in the Dos and Don'ts, people will notice when you violate unspoken performance expectations. Then your superiors' private reaction will be, "She ought to know better" and "She doesn't have what it takes."

Beyond our basic 25 expectations, your boss may have additional, personal behaviour expectations for you. Listen and watch. Soon you'll recognize your boss's pet behaviour criteria. Some bosses, for example, value an employee only if she comes early and stays late. Other bosses interpret such long work hours as incompetence—an inability to complete your work in the allotted time. These are variations you have to search out about your individual supervisor. Add your boss's expectations to the 25 below and you'll be well along to standing out as a valued performer. If you're the boss, you can help your staff members do the best job possible by informing them of these business axioms.

1 Forget about excuses. With rare exceptions, such as true life-and-death crisis, no boss hears or cares why an assignment wasn't done. It's your job to get it done on time.

2 Don't aim for perfection. Getting it done well and on time is much more important than doing it "perfectly." To your boss, absolutely perfect performance counts against you if it interferes with your carrying your share.

3 Simply carrying your share is not enough. Doing only what is expected of you and no more sets you among the expendable mass of performers. Bosses value people who do their job and look around for or create or ask for more real work, not busy work.

4 Follow through on your own. Pick up the pieces; tie the loose ends of your assignments. Don't wait to be reminded, particularly by a supervisor.

5 Anticipate problems. Ask yourself what could go wrong? When your responsibilities depend on input from others, check their plans and understanding of what you're requesting. There is no substitute for having your projects come out right.

6 Be resilient about foul-ups. Part of carrying your responsibilities is understanding that commotions, mistakes, "unforeseeable" failures by others (supplies or contributions) are a normal, routine part of work

life. When foul-ups occur, no one is picking on you and you can't excuse it as "bad luck". You are supposed to know that Murphy's Law—"If something can go wrong, it will and at the worst possible time"—operates everywhere. Realize this, and it won't be so hard to adapt to unfavourable conditions and make your projects successful. Pass on to your staff the same expectations.

7 Take care of problems, don't take them to your boss. (Bosses have enough of their own.) If you lack the authority, come prepared with solutions when you broach the problem. Even though your boss may not use your solutions, you've made your point as a problem solver—not as a problem collector.

8 Punctuality counts. No amount of staying late makes up for your not being available when other people need you in order to do their work. And, as a boss, set an example: let your staff know when you'll be late or have to leave early.

9 Attendance counts. People quickly become aware of who makes an effort to be there and who uses any excuse to miss a day.

10 Don't be a squeaking wheel. As a daily work style, this approach is self-defeating. Don't be seen as "Here comes a problem."

11 Don't carry grudges over routine losses. You cannot win them all. No one can. Even Babe Ruth, Roger Maris, Hank Aaron, and the other home-run champions were out at bat about 65 per cent of the time. Expect to lose some. So don't squander your energy, the goodwill of your allies, and the patience of your boss by turning every issue into a crusade. Concentrate on winning some of the big ones, and you'll be ahead of most people.

12 Choose your battles carefully. To decide if something is worth fighting for, ask yourself: How much difference does this problem really make in my job? Is it permanent or transitory? Is it worth making an enemy (enemies)? and most important, do I have a realistic chance of winning? Don't be among the astonishing number of people who fling themselves into no-win job situations.

13 Deal directly with the person who can make the decision. This is the way to get action (and thus be an effective employee). Dealing with people with less authority may be easier on your nerves, but you'll be wasting time and effort. Your most elaborate and smashing presentation may be passed on to the real power reduced to something feeble, such as "Riva thinks we ought to change this procedure". When you're in charge, set aside time to have your staff members present their ideas directly to you.

14 Whenever possible, keep control of solving your own problems. This is another essential to being effective and valuable. Let's say you need a new machine or some special work done for you. Don't stop with getting approval. If the other person doesn't follow through, you're left looking inept with your explanation of how John promised to take care of it. Make it happen: "OK, thanks, I'll let them know to start on it and what's involved." Then do it.

15 Learn to translate boss language. "If it's not too much trouble" means, "Do it . . . and the sooner the better."

16 Learn what other people in the organization are doing. What were last year's big triumphs and failures? What is being planned? What are the organization's major goals and fears? How does your job intertwine with all this? Then you'll understand when, how and where to press for your goals.

17 Get along with your co-workers. No boss is ever interested in who is "right" in a co-worker squabble. Internal battles mean less production. To your boss, if you're involved, you're automatically wrong.

18 Protect the organization's reputation and privacy. Never discuss organization business and people in detail or by name in a public place where strangers can overhear. Even in private, be reticent about organization politics, problems, business.

19 Let others win sometimes—even when you have the power. "Sounds like a good idea. We'll do it that way." If you don't, people will resent you and give you grief.

20 Learn timing. This often involves developing the patience to wait for an appropriate occasion.

21 Don't lie. Nothing is so serious that lying won't make it worse. If you're caught in a lie, you lose your credibility. Then you're dead.

22 Read your business's professional and trade publications. Indicating that you haven't the time or money to read or subscribe will shock your bosses. When they were at your career stage, they were ravenous for trade information. To them, your lack of interest indicates no real career goals on your part. Or worse yet, they may think that you are ignorant of the importance of professional/trade news. Let your staff know which publications apply to your industry.

23 Get to know your peers in your industry. Be active in one or more professional/trade organizations. The contacts you make and information you glean aid you on a personal level whenever you change jobs—while improving your status with your current boss.

24 Never assume other people are operating from your premises, your standards, your goals or your rules. When you find yourself thinking, "I never would have expected such behaviour from her," you know you've made the mistake of projecting your outlook onto others' behaviour. That's a narrow, problem-generating attitude that irritates bosses.

25 Use common sense in applying these and all business-behaviour rules to your own situations. For instance, the rules of timing and controversy obviate "making waves" when you're brand new on a job. But one MBA reported to her new executive position to find the other newly hired MBAs all had work stations while her boss had forgotten to prepare for her. The absent-minded boss gave her a makeshift table and chair in a supply closet. After a week of vague promises, the MBA decided that this was a situation worth reacting to. New job or not, she made some genteel but effective waves and obtained a suitable work setting. She was right, of course.

ACTIVITIES

Getting Your Act Together
pp. 353—358

1. With a partner, research several different résumé formats. Be prepared to explain to your class the different formats you found and indicate what you feel are the best points of each. Prepare a résumé for yourself using one of the formats you found most useful. If you have access to a computer, put your résumé on a disk for future reference.

2. With a partner, prepare a collage of help wanted advertisements that specifically mention one of the following:
   - educational level required
   - the need for team or group communication skills
   - personality type required (aggressive, energetic, friendly, etc.)
   - investment capital required
   - experience necessary
   - part-time positions
   - salary, benefits, or job satisfaction

   You may find that you and your partner can think of another heading to base your collage on. Explain your collage to the rest of the class and explain why these jobs require special qualifications.

3. Write an application letter for one of the jobs that appeals to you. If you are presently applying for a job, write your letter as an application for the position you are interested in.

4. Role-play job interviews for some of the jobs you came across in the newspaper.
   - Begin by formulating questions and answers.
   - Videotape the interview.
   - Play back the videotape and, focussing on the person being interviewed, make two positive comments and two suggestions for improvement.
   - Switch roles and repeat the process.

5. Make a job-related How To . . . chart. For example, you might make a chart on 10 Ways to Anger Your Boss; 10 Ways to Get a Promotion; 10 Ways to Impress Your Boss; 10 Ways to Ask for a Raise. Be creative. Post your chart on the classroom bulletin board.

BREAKING TRADITION

~

JACKIE SMITH

Karen Morrison is a rookie firefighter with 18 months' experience behind her and the only woman fighting blazes for the Windsor Fire Department.

Packing 19 kg of equipment on her 180 cm 58 kg frame, Morrison spent her first day as a trained firefighter beating back a blaze at a local lumber yard. "We were there 13 hours," she says. "I couldn't believe you could put as much water on something and it wouldn't go out."

Six months ago, the 28-year-old native of Prince Edward Island—who has been a Royal Canadian Mounted Police officer and a Parks Canada warden—toppled head first from a second-floor balcony after a railing gave way as she and another firefighter tried to toss a burning couch over it. . . .

Five weeks in hospital and six weeks off work didn't dampen Morrison's enthusiasm for firefighting, despite the fact she's still being treated for ear problems resulting from the fall. Her partner wrenched his knee in the fall and was off the job for two weeks.

Morrison admits she gets nervous when she goes to a fire. But she says she doesn't become frightened. "I wouldn't want to follow anyone who wasn't nervous," she says, "because you don't know what they might do. You don't know what's going to be around the next corner."

She remembers a fire at a tire company where the smoke was so dense she couldn't see. "If you have to get out, you just follow the hose back," she says.

One of at least 12 firefighters on each shift, Morrison works two 24-hour shifts a week, from 8 a.m. to 8 a.m., and earns about $28 000 a year.

To get the job she passed aptitude and physical tests, including being able to do 18 reverse chinups, 10 pushups and 25 situps. She had to carry a 45 kg dummy, carry a pack with a heavy hose up two stories, go up another flight on a ladder and use a 15 kg sledge hammer to hit a metal and rubber pad 56 times with enough strength to go through a roof.

The tests were tough, but they were tough for everyone, says Morrison, who was in shape before she took them because of her jogging and exercise routine. She had also done some weight training while with the RCMP.

"It wasn't in my mind that because I was a woman I wouldn't get the job."

To a visitor, Morrison seems to fit right in at the Windsor Number 2 firehall where she is stationed. It's a home away from home, complete with television and games room, dining area and kitchen and bedroom—a home in which the firefighters play cards to decide who will do the dishes.

"I imagine some people thought a woman couldn't do the job as well as a man, but she's a good worker . . . She's just like one of the guys," says lieutenant Glenn Zimmerman.

Windsor Fire Chief Rene Cecile says there were never any real reservations about hiring a woman, though there were rumours that the wives of the other firefighters didn't like the idea.

"We always had a standard and we felt that anyone who met it would have to be considered," says Cecile. The city across the river, Detroit, "had women firefighters long before we had (women) applicants," he says.

Morrison says that once she started as a firefighter it was just a matter of the men getting used to her, though a few eyebrows were raised when she brought in her knitting and needlepoint. She had already worked for the department as a dispatcher following five years with the RCMP, mostly on drug duties. . . .

She performs the same duties as the men—including cleaning the firehall windows, floors, trucks, fridge, stove and bathroom. Because she's the junior member, she does the washrooms.

When not fighting fires, Morrison wears blue fatigues like the men, which have been tailored to fit her smaller frame. She has her own washroom at the firehall because a single one is available. When she worked at headquarters, she shared one with the men, who went outside until she had showered and dressed.

At night she bunks in the same room as the men, wearing underclothes so she'll be ready for a fire.

During the afternoons there are training sessions in procedures like cardiopulmonary resuscitation, search and rescue and high-rise drill.

Morrison doesn't feel like a pioneer for women. "I'm doing this for me," she says. "If anyone else wants to try it, I wish them all the luck."

Morrison doesn't think anything should be changed to make it easier for women to get firefighting jobs. "It is a hard job," she says.

"The main thing is the heavy lifting and the guts to do the job. The worse thing is putting in hours waiting for something to happen and not knowing what's coming up. You can spend hours where you are not really doing too much and then you might spend a half-hour where you are really going."

The best thing about the job is the guys. "They're great," she says.

DRIVE, HARD WORK HELPED MAKE IT IN SKILLED TRADES

~

TRISH CRAWFORD

Cathy Lessick, 24, could have chosen any career. So why did she decide to battle her way into an almost all-male world of motor vehicle mechanics? There are only 24 women in her field in the entire province.

"I planned to go to university but I worked in a gas station pumping gas and I started talking to the mechanic. I had helped my older brothers fix their motorcycles and I decided I wanted to be a mechanic instead.

"It means long hours. You don't go home at 5 p.m. There are no lunch breaks, no coffee breaks. You have to know everything about everything from Ford to General Motors to Japanese to Cadillacs.

"I'll never get my nails clean and I've got scars on my hands. When you dress to go to work, you've got to put coveralls on or pants and shirt and baseball cap. I've had people call me 'son'.

"I have always been treated like a younger sister. Sometimes girls feel they have to be pushy to fit in but you don't. You can't be really feminine but you don't have to spit and wear tattoos either.

"Looking for an apprenticeship was the hardest part. After lots of searching, I was hired by Cadillac Livery. My dad didn't like it, he refused to believe it. A lot of people have a low opinion of mechanics. You've really got to want it.

"But a top mechanic can earn $17.80 an hour. The pay can be very good. And I also like working with machinery. You know whether it's right or wrong. You can have a car come in that's really sick and make it like brand new.

"My ultimate goal is to work in a racing pit, that would be incredible."

As a general machinist, Susann Haw, 32, helps run a training program at West End Machining, a federal government-sponsored machine shop that teaches women a trade in a real manufacturing plant geared to profits and products. There are only 41 women machinists making metal (and sometimes plastic) parts for the machines that drive Ontario's manufacturing industry.

"I can make all the parts that fit on a machine, follow a blueprint and work to tolerances. I took my training at George Brown College—Machine Shop 107. I worked for three different small companies trying to get my apprenticeship and then I ended up at the University of Toronto's mechanical engineering department.

"It was very interesting. We were involved in research work with thermal energy machines, wind tunnels and test items. But it is hard to get an apprenticeship. I ended

up knocking on 60 different doors until I was accepted at U of T.

"For women who go into this field, they have to have tough skin, a sense of humour and be very focussed on their goals. Or else they'll give up. Many times she is the only woman in the shop. Rough language and dirty pictures—it's all nonsense. On the good side, machinists make $14 an hour and up.

"I took math all through high school. I went into the Armed Forces. I wanted to try something different. I drove a truck. I ended up leaving after $5\frac{1}{2}$ years when I was injured in a jeep accident. The main reason more women aren't in non-traditional jobs is that young women are unrealistic about their life.

"My father died when I was growing up. Our lives and financial situation went from okay to not okay. I vowed then I'd never, never, never let happen to me what happened to my mother. I vowed I would be able to provide for myself and my family."

WORKING CLASS HEROES

~

PAUL HOWARD

GREIG CLARK,
FOUNDER, COLLEGE PRO PAINTERS LTD.

In 1971, summer evenings would find Greig Clark dripping with paint. Now he's drenched in success. What began as a means of paying for his university tuition has blossomed into a North American franchise with more than 400 outlets employing over 5000 students and boasting yearly revenues in excess of $28-million.

Banking on a conviction that college students could be trained and organized into house-painting crews that could hold their own in the trade, Clark was earning $12 000 by his third summer. He continued to develop his fledgling firm, College Pro Painters, even after he graduated from the University of Western Ontario's business program in 1975, and joined General Foods' marketing department. By 1978, he had accumulated $50 000 in capital and shifted into the trade full-time, opening 19 Ontario franchises whose sales quickly topped the million-dollar mark. "My original goal was to establish 30 Ontario outlets," says the softspoken 34-year-old. "But I had many good people coming up in the organization, which made continuing expansion seem like the route to go."

PENNY NOBLE,
PRESIDENT, NOBLE TALENT MANAGEMENT INC.

Penny Noble typifies the spirit and commitment of the new breed of entrepreneurial women, who form new businesses at three times the rate that men do—and, indeed, are nearly twice as successful at making them long-run successes. The 31-year-old former model set up Noble Talent Management Inc. seven years ago and now represents 150 actors, including Barbara Hamilton and Barry Morse. In addition to this flagship enterprise, which garners "close to seven digits" in annual earnings, she also represents models and last year opened a modelling school. "That way, you can really groom them," Noble says.

Noble ventured into business with $2000 and a firm belief in networking. "Right from the beginning I concentrated on contacting as many people as possible who might use my service." This involved considerable travelling across the continent attending theatre and film auditions in search of fresh talent. She still travels extensively—to her New York office, which she opened three years ago, and elsewhere, to meet with clients and affiliate agencies. Often, her working day doesn't wind down until theatre is out at 11:30 p.m.

She'd love to be able to travel on an actual vacation, but, she says, "I'm on call a lot. If anything goes wrong, I have to accept responsibility." On the upside, she notes, "One of the joys of having your own business is seeing it grow, and actually being in control. Being your own boss lets you aim higher and higher."

JOB IS LOTS OF FUN FOR VIDEO PRODUCER

LESLIE FRUMAN

A few years ago, Allan Weinrib says, he was just a step up from the space between the cigarette butt and the floor.

He was a production assistant at Shultz Productions, where he did all the go-for jobs for the staff involved in making rock videos and commercials. He got coffee, swept the floor, and did all the things no one else wanted to do.

Today, at 25, Weinrib is a rock video producer at the company, deeply involved in the growing new industry. He's happy to get on with his business until, who knows, he may get that "call from the coast" someday.

His work involves making sure the production of the videos runs smoothly. That means keeping directors, musicians, record company officials, and editors happy while maintaining the budget. It can mean making what might seem like brutal decisions at times. It can also be a lot of fun.

"It's an ideal blend of creative sources," Weinrib says. "I always loved film, and because of a close relative of mine who is involved in the music industry, I love music. Sometimes I think I'm having too much fun."

After high school, Weinrib thought he'd like to explore several different areas before settling on a career. He worked as a bond carrier, as a driver, and for a while, he worked for an insurance company.

He went to college where he studied creative advertising, which was what got him started in the film industry.

He worked for Shultz Productions as a production assistant, then started doing some freelancing for that company and others. He was eventually hired as a full time production co-ordinator at Shultz Productions, and then given a job as a producer.

"I took every opportunity to learn about the industry," Weinrib says. "A lot of production assistants come and go, but the ones who make it are the ones who have a real interest in the work going on around them."

The first video he produced was Parachute Club's *Dancing At The Feet Of The Moon*. Critics think it's outstanding and Weinrib is pleased with the result.

Not only was it his first effort, but it was Toronto fashion photographer Deborah Samuels first directing effort as well.

Weinrib's days are spent going over all aspects of production. When the videos are at the shooting stage, Weinrib is on the set. It's an exciting job, never 9 to 5.

Being so young, Weinrib sometimes feels odd when he has to tell people who have more experience what to do. But he steers away from trouble and does his work well.

"If the finished product isn't right, in any way, it's my fault," Weinrib says. "If I tell someone they can't spend x number of dollars on something, and it turns out it would have been the right thing to do, then I'm in trouble. But so far so good. I think everyone is happy with what we've done. I am."

JOBS AND OCCUPATIONS, 1986–1995

20 TOP JOB OPENINGS 1986–1995	
Number of new jobs	
95 000	Salespersons
82 000	Food serving occupations
56 000	Bookkeepers
55 000	Secretaries and stenographers
47 500	Cashiers and tellers
47 000	Chefs and cooks
44 000	Janitors and cleaners
37 000	Truck drivers
29 000	Sales managers
29 000	Barbers and hairdressers
26 000	Motor vehicle mechanics
25 000	Nurses: registered, graduate and training
24 000	Financial officers
21 000	Sales supervisors
19 000	Supervisors: food and beverage
18 000	General office clerks
17 500	Manual labor, services
17 000	Service managers
16 000	Receptionists and information clerks
16 000	Carpenters

Source: Employment and Immigration Canada
Note: Numbers are approximate

FASTEST GROWING OCCUPATIONS
1986–1995

Aircraft fabricating and assembling		4.7%
Supervisors in food and beverage serving and in accommodation services	Cafeteria supervisor, Bell captain, Lodge keeper	3%
Managerial occupations in services and social sciences	Chief librarian, Art gallery manager, Hotel manager, Restaurant manager	2.5%
Occupations in sports and recreation	Coach, Instructor, etc.	2.1%
Geologists and occupations in physical sciences	Geologist, Oceanographer, Geophysicist, etc.	1.9%
Engineering	Chemical, Metallurgical, Petroleum and Aerospace	1.9%
Occupations in the performing and audio visual arts	Producer, Director, Performer, Stagehand, etc.	1.8%
Health diagnosing and treating	Physician, Surgeon, Dentist	1.7%
Other occupations in medicine and health	Pharmacist, Optometrist, Optician, Dental Hygienist and Assistant	1.7%
Sales occupations in insurance, real estate, securities	Adjuster, Investor, Real estate agent, Bond dealer, etc.	1.6%

Source: Employment and Immigration Canada
Note: Numbers are approximate

ACTIVITIES

**Job Satisfaction
pp. 360–367**

1. After reading the selections, work with a partner to discuss and make point-form notes on the following:
   - education and/or training necessary for each job;
   - on-the-job qualities and attitudes necessary for success;
   - "secrets of success" for these jobs.

2. Write a journal entry on one or both of the following:
   - Which of these jobs appeals to you most? Why?
   - What do you consider to be the "secrets of success" for any job?

3. After looking over the two charts "20 top job openings in 1986–1995" and "Fastest growing occupations 1986–1995", each person in a group of five should choose a different one of the occupations and, using the resources of your guidance department, career centre (if one is available), or your school or public library, research the following aspects of the occupation chosen:
   - education/training required;
   - starting salary;
   - best things about the job/drawbacks to the job;
   - other jobs this one prepares you for;
   - any other aspect of the job you found interesting.

4. Make up a board game called *Success*, based perhaps on Snakes and Ladders or Trivial Pursuit. If you base your game on Snakes and Ladders, you will want to identify things that will allow the players to advance towards success in a job and things that will set them back. For example, taking a training course will be an advance, and being late for work three days in a row will set the player back. If you base your game on Trivial Pursuit, make up a series of questions which will test the players' knowledge of what it takes to be successful in a job.

from THE EDIBLE WOMAN

~

M A R G A R E T   A T W O O D

I know I was all right on Friday when I got up; if anything I was feeling more stolid than usual. When I went out to the kitchen to get breakfast Ainsley was there, moping: she said she had been to a bad party the night before. She swore there had been nothing but dentistry students, which depressed her so much she had consoled herself by getting drunk.

"You have no idea how soggy it is," she said, "having to go through twenty conversations about the insides of peoples' mouths. The most reaction I got out of them was when I described an abcess I once had. They positively drooled. And most men look at something besides your *teeth*, for god's sake."

She had a hangover, which put me in a cheerful mood—it made me feel so healthy—and I poured her a glass of tomato juice and briskly fixed her an alka-seltzer, listening and making sympathetic noises while she complained.

"As if I didn't get enough of that at work," she said. Ainsley has a job as a tester of defective electric toothbrushes for an electric toothbrush company: a temporary job. What she is waiting for is an opening in one of those little art galleries, even though they don't pay well: she wants to meet the artists. Last year, she told me, it was actors, but then she actually met some. "It's an absolute fixation. I expect they all carry those bent mirrors around in their coat pockets and peer into their own mouths every time they go to the john to make sure they're still cavity-free." She ran one hand reflectively through her hair, which is long and red, or rather auburn. "Could you imagine kissing one? He'd say 'Open wide' beforehand. They're so bloody one-track."

"It must have been awful," I said, refilling her glass. "Couldn't you have changed the topic?"

Ainsley raised her almost non-existent eyebrows, which hadn't been coloured in yet that morning. "Of course not," she said. "I pretended to be terribly interested. And naturally I didn't let on what my job was: those professional men get so huffy if you know anything about their subject. You know, like Peter."

Ainsley tends to make jabs at Peter, especially when she isn't feeling well. I was magnanimous and didn't respond. "You'd better eat something before you go to work," I said, "it's better when you've got something on your stomach."

"Oh god," said Ainsley. "I can't face it. Another day of machines and mouths. I haven't had an interesting one since last month, when that lady sent back her toothbrush because the bristles were falling off. We found out she'd been using Ajax."

I got so caught up in being efficient for Ainsley's benefit while complimenting myself on my moral superiority to her that I didn't realize how late it was until she reminded me. At the electric toothbrush company they don't care what time you breeze in, but my company thinks of itself as punctual. I had to skip the egg and wash down a glass of milk and a bowl of cold cereal which I knew would leave me hungry long before lunchtime. I chewed through a piece of bread while Ainsley watched me in nauseated silence and grabbed up my purse, leaving Ainsley to close the apartment door behind me.

We live on the top floor of a large house in one of the older and more genteel districts, in what I suppose used to be the servants' quarters. This means there are two flights of stairs between us and the front door, the higher flight narrow and slippery, the lower one wide and carpeted but with stair-rods that come loose. In the high heels expected by the office I have to go down sideways, clutching the bannister. That morning I made it safely past the line of pioneer brass warming-pans strung on the wall of our stairway, avoided catching myself on the many-pronged spinning-wheel on the second-floor landing, and sidestepped quickly down past the ragged regimental flag behind glass and the row of oval-framed ancestors that guard the first stairway. I was relieved to see there was no one in the downstairs hall. On level ground I strode towards the door, swerving to avoid the rubber-plant on one side and the hall table with the écru doily and the round brass tray on the other. Behind the velvet curtain to the right I could hear the child performing her morning penance at the piano. I thought I was safe.

But before I reached the door it swung silently inward upon its hinges, and I knew I was trapped. It was the lady down below. She was wearing a pair of spotless gardening gloves and carrying a trowel. I wondered who she'd been burying in the garden.

"Good morning, Miss McAlpin," she said.

"Good morning," I nodded and smiled. I can never remember her name, and neither can Ainsley; I suppose we have what they call a mental block about it. I looked past her towards the street, but she didn't move out of the doorway.

"I was out last night," she said. "At a meeting." She has an indirect way of going about things. I shifted from one foot to the other and smiled again, hoping she would realize I was in a hurry. "The child tells me there was another fire."

"Well, it wasn't exactly a fire," I said. The child had taken this mention of her name as an excuse to stop practising, and was standing now in the velvet doorway of the parlour, staring at me. She is a hulking creature of fifteen or so who is being sent to an exclusive private girls' school, and she has to wear a green tunic with knee-socks to match. I'm sure she's really quite normal, but there's something cretinous about the hair-ribbon perched up on top of her gigantic body.

The lady down below took off one of her gloves and patted her chignon. "Ah," she said sweetly. "The child says there was a lot of smoke."

"Everything was under control," I said, not smiling this time. "It was just the pork chops."

"Oh, I see," she said. "Well, I do wish you would tell Miss Tewce to try not to make quite so much smoke in future. I'm afraid it upsets the child." She holds Ainsley alone responsible for the smoke, and seems to think she sends it out of her nostrils like a dragon. But she never stops Ainsley in the hall to talk about it: only me. I suspect she's decided Ainsley isn't respectable, whereas I am. It's probably the way we dress: Ainsley says I choose clothes as though they're a camouflage or a protective colouration, though I can't see anything wrong with that. She herself goes in for neon pink.

Of course I missed the bus: as I crossed the lawn, I could see it disappearing across the bridge in a cloud of air pollution. While I was standing under the tree—our street has many trees, all of them enormous—waiting for the next bus, Ainsley came out of the house and joined me. She's a quick-change artist; I could never put myself together in such a short time. She was looking a lot healthier—possibly the effects of makeup, though you can never tell with Ainsley—and she had her red hair piled up on top of her head, as she always does when she goes to work. The rest of the time she wears it down in straggles. She had on her orange and pink sleeveless dress, which I judged was too tight across the hips. The day was going to be hot and humid; already I could feel a private atmosphere condensing around me like a plastic bag. Maybe I should have worn a sleeveless dress too.

"She got me in the hall," I said. "About the smoke."

"The old bitch," said Ainsley. "Why can't she mind her own business?" Ainsley doesn't come from a small town as I do, so she's not as used to people being snoopy; on the other hand she's not as afraid of it either. She has no idea about the consequences.

"She's not that old," I said, glancing over at the curtained windows of the house; though I knew she couldn't hear us. "Besides, it wasn't her who noticed the smoke, it was the child. She was at a meeting."

"Probably the W.C.T.U.," Ainsley said. "Or the I.O.D.E. I'll bet she wasn't at a meeting at all; she was hiding behind that damn velvet curtain, wanting us to think she was at a meeting so we'd *really* do something. What she wants is an orgy."

"Now Ainsley," I said, "you're being paranoid." Ainsley is convinced that the lady down below comes upstairs when we aren't there and looks round our apartment and is silently horrified, and even suspects her of ruminating over our mail, though not of going so far as to open it. It's a fact that she sometimes answers the front door for our visitors before they ring the bell. She must think she's within her rights to take precautions: when we first considered renting the apartment she made it clear to us, by discreet allusions to previous tenants, that whatever happened the child's innocence must not be corrupted, and that two young ladies were surely more to be depended upon than two young men.

"I'm doing my best," she had said, sighing and shaking her head. She had intimated that her husband, whose portrait in oils hung above the piano, had not left as much money as he should have. "Of course you realize your apartment has no private entrance?" she had been stressing the drawbacks rather than the advantages, almost as though she didn't want us to rent. I said we did realize it; Ainsley said nothing. We had agreed I would do the talking and Ainsley would sit and look innocent, something she can do very well when she wants to—she has a pink-and-white blunt baby's face, a bump for a nose, and large blue eyes she can make as round as ping-pong balls. On this occasion I had even got her to wear gloves.

The lady down below shook her head again. "If it weren't for the child," she said, "I would sell the house. But I want the child to grow up in a good district."

I said I understood, and she said that of course the district wasn't as good as it used to be: some of the larger houses were too expensive to keep up and the owners had been forced to sell them to immigrants (the corners of her mouth turned gently down) who had divided them up into rooming houses. "But that hasn't reached our street yet," she said. "And I tell the child exactly which streets she can walk on and which she can't." I said I thought that was wise. She had seemed much easier to deal with before we had signed the lease. And the rent was so low, and the house was so close to the bus stop. For this city it was a real find.

"Besides," I added to Ainsley, "they have a right to be worried about the smoke. What if the house was on fire? And she's never mentioned the other things."

"What other things? We've never *done* any other things."

"Well . . . " I said. I suspected the lady down below had taken note of all the bottle-shaped objects we had carried upstairs, though I tried my best to disguise them as groceries. It was true she had never specifically forbidden us to do anything—that would be too crude a violation of her law of nuance—but this only makes me feel I am actually forbidden to do everything.

"On still nights," said Ainsley as the bus drew up, "I can hear her burrowing through the woodwork."

We didn't talk on the bus; I don't like talking on buses, I would rather look at the advertisements. Besides, Ainsley and I don't have much in common except the lady down below. I've only known her since just before we moved in: she was a friend of a friend, looking for a room-mate at the same time I was, which is the way these things are usually done. Maybe I should have tried a computer; though on the whole it's worked out fairly well. We get along by a symbiotic adjustment of habits and with a minimum of that pale-mauve hostility you often find among women. Our apartment is never exactly clean, but we keep it from gathering more than a fine plum-bloom of dust by an unspoken agreement: if I do the breakfast dishes, Ainsley does the supper ones; if I sweep the living-room floor, Ainsley wipes the kitchen table. It's a see-saw arrangement and we both know that if one beat is missed the whole thing will collapse. Of course we each have our own bedroom and what goes on in there is strictly the owner's concern. For instance Ainsley's floor is covered by a treacherous muskeg of used clothes with ashtrays scattered here and there on it like stepping-stones, but though I consider it a fire-hazard I never speak to her about it. By such mutual refrainings—I assume they are mutual since there must be things I do that she doesn't like—we manage to preserve a reasonably frictionless equilibrium.

We reached the subway station, where I bought a package of peanuts. I was beginning to feel hungry already. I offered some to Ainsley, but she refused, so I ate them all on the way downtown.

We got off at the second-last stop south and walked a block together; our office buildings are in the same district.

"By the way," said Ainsley as I was turning off at my street, "have you got three dollars? We're out of scotch." I rummaged in my purse and handed over, not without a sense of injustice: we split the cost but rarely the contents. At the age of ten I wrote a temperance essay for a United Church Sunday-school competition, illustrating it with pictures of car-crashes, diagrams of diseased livers, and charts showing the effects of alcohol upon the circulatory system; I expect that's why I can never take a second drink without a mental image of a warning sign printed in coloured crayons and connected with the taste of tepid communion grape-juice. This puts me at a disadvantage with Peter; he likes me to try and keep up with him.

As I hurried towards my office building, I found myself envying Ainsley her job. Though mine was better-paying and more interesting, hers was more temporary: she had an idea of what she wanted to do next. She could work in a shiny new air-conditioned office-building, whereas mine was dingy brick with small windows. Also, her job was unusual. When she meets people at parties they are always surprised when she tells them she's a tester of defective electric toothbrushes, and she always says, "What else do you do with a B.A. these days?" Whereas my kind of job is only to be expected. I was thinking too that really I was better equipped to handle her job than she is. From what I see around the apartment, I'm sure I have much more mechanical ability than Ainsley.

By the time I finally reached the office I was three-quarters of an hour late. None commented but all took note.

A C T I V I T I E S

1. With a partner, make a list of the differences between the requirements of Marian McAlpin's (the narrator) job and those of Ainsley Tewce's job. The narrator says that she found herself envying Ainsley her job. Make a journal entry in which you explain which job you would prefer and why.

The Edible Woman
pp. 369–374

2. This first chapter is taken from the novel *The Edible Woman*. The narrator feels that her life and her person are being "eaten up" by the demands of society. In a group of four, discuss how each of the following adds to our life and "devours" us at the same time. In each case, explain why the positive or the negative qualities are more important to you.
a) a job
b) marriage and children
c) an apartment or home of your own
d) societal expectations

3. Work with a partner who is also going to read this novel, and predict what you think will happen as the story develops. Make point-form notes to refer to as you finish the story.

4. Choose two or three of the whole-book activities on page 204 of the Student Handbook to complete as you read the novel or when you have finished reading it.

ACTIVITIES

1. Interview a person who is doing the job that you see yourself doing within the next five years. See page 189 of the Student Handbook for tips on interviewing. Tape-record your interview, play it for a small group, and tell the group what you learned and whether or not you are still interested in that job; or write an article for a local newspaper based on your interview.

2. Keep a "Reflections on Work" journal over the next few weeks. You may wish to include some of the following:
   - a description of your present job, how you got it, what you like/dislike about it, and interesting experiences you have had;
   - how your present job compares with past jobs and why you changed jobs;
   - jobs your family members have;
   - your dream job;
   - getting along with others—your strengths and weaknesses;
   - job skills you have developed and would like to develop;
   - your ambitions/aspirations (what you would like to be doing in five, ten, twenty, etc. years);
   - sources of conflict—co-workers, boss, clients, customers, etc.;
   - experiencing prejudice on the job because of youth, race, religion, sex, values, ethnic or cultural background, etc.;
   - what encourages you to do a good job;
   - why you work (other than for money);
   - non-traditional jobs: are there jobs that men/women cannot do?/why are there more women seeking non-traditional jobs than there are men doing the same?
   - the effects of unemployment—how it feels to be unemployed;
   - good and bad working conditions;
   - maintaining your own integrity.

3. Work with a partner and view two or three films that deal with the topic of people and their work. Some movies you might consider are the following:
   - *Good Morning, Vietnam,*
   - *Norma Rae,*
   - *Wall Street.*

   As you are viewing the film, make notes on the dilemma, problem, or situation facing the main character; the impact this situation has on his or her working and personal relationships; the decisions he or she made and the cost to him or her.

   Make a brief presentation based on your notes to another group or to the class.

4. Create a scrapbook titled *Work in the 1990s* that students studying history in 2090 could use to understand the labour situation today. With a partner brainstorm various subtopics such as salaries, Sunday work, blue/white collar work, future employment trends, youth employment. Collect newspaper and magazine articles, list TV programs and films, interview workers, and write brief descriptions of issues. Ask a history teacher for a published history scrapbook that you could use as a model.

CAREERS

These are a few careers in the wonderful world of work.

Industrial Safety/Occupational Health Technologist
The industrial safety-occupational health technologist is concerned with protecting the health and safety of industrial workers on the job. She or he inspects the job site to identify hazards to life, health and property, develops plans to protect workers and then discusses with labour and management ways to put these plans into effect. A large part of each day is spent talking to employers, managers and union representatives to ensure that the plans are being carried out and to check their effectiveness.

Training and Qualifications
Several colleges offer three-year courses in Safety Engineering Technology or related subjects. It is helpful to have a knowledge of first aid.

Salary
Industrial safety/occupational technologists earned a starting salary of $16 000 to $27 000 in 1984.

Other Careers:
- Driver
- Office Equipment Repairer
- Telephone Installer
- Florist
- Special Effects Technician
- Dental Assistant
- Retail Store Manager

RESOURCES

Books
Death of a Salesman—Arthur Miller
Fantasy Summer—Ruth Beth Pfeffer (Pacer Putnam, 1984)
That Gentle Touch—Beverly G. Warren (Doubleday, 1984)
Pay Cheques and Picket Lines—Claire MacKay (Kids Can Press, 1987)
Films
Tin Men (Touchstone Home Video) Buena Vista 1987; 111 min
Here Today . . . Where Tomorrow? Ontario Women's Directory
Office of the Future (W5 Segment, CTV) International Telefilm 1980; 15 min

ACKNOWLEDGMENTS

I'm Black, She's White: By David McKie. David McKie is an Ontario-based free lance print and broadcast journalist. **Friends:** Music and lyrics by Sharon Newman for York Memorial C.I. Graduation 1988. **Greta:** From *Growing Up Dead*, ed. Brenda Rabkin. Used by permission of The Canadian Publishers, McClelland and Stewart, Toronto. **Mum Always There When I Need Her:** By Donna Yawching. Taken from the *Toronto Star*. Reprinted by permission of the author. **To Be In Love:** By Gwendolyn Brooks. From *Blacks* 1987 by Gwendolyn Brooks. The David Company, Chicago. **Words** and **Now That Our Love:** By Waring Cuney. **At Seventeen:** By Janis Ian. Copyright © 1974 Mime Music Ltd. All rights reserved. **For Anne:** By Leonard Cohen. From *The Spice Box of Earth* by Leonard Cohen. Used by permission of The Canadian Publishers, McClelland and Stewart, Toronto. **Benny, the War in Europe, and Myerson's Daughter Bella:** By Mordecai Richler. From **The Street** by Mordecai Richler. Used by permission of The Canadian Publishers, McClelland and Stewart, Toronto. **Thanks for the Ride:** By Alice Munro. From *Dance of the Happy Shades*. Copyright © Alice Munro 1968. Reprinted by permission. **Man-Woman Talk:** By Deborah Tannen. **Salt-Water Moon:** By David French. Copyright David French, Talon Books Ltd., Vancouver. **Health Administrator or Supervisor:** Amended excerpt adapted from *Career Selector: Health Care, 1986*, a publication of the Ontario Women's Directorate. **Metamorphosis:** By David Suzuki. Excerpts from *Metamorphosis* by David Suzuki. Reprinted with permission of The Colbert Agency, Inc. 303 Davenport Road, Toronto, Ont., M5R 1K5. Copyright © 1987 New Data Enterprises Ltd. **Letters: Our Policy:** Reprinted from *The Telegraph Journal*, Saint John, N.B. **Leila Heath Radio Reporter:** Excerpt from *Making Choices: Women in Non-Traditional Jobs* by Sheila Amato and Pat Staton, Green Dragon Press, 135 George Street S, #902, Toronto, Ont., M5A 4E8. **Olympic Stories Irk Readers:** By Ron Goodman. Reprinted with permission—The Toronto Star Syndicate. **Lunar Module Lifts Off Moon:** By G. Brimmell & Bob Cohen. Reprinted from *The Calgary Herald*. **Turk's Plight Moves People of Quebec:** Reprinted with permission The Canadian Press. **Sexual Awakenings in the 1980's:** A cartoon by Jim Borgman. Reprinted with special permission of King Features Syndicate, Inc. **Polls:** A cartoon by Aislin. Reprinted with permission—The Toronto Star Syndicate. **Pollution:** A cartoon by Raeside. Reprinted with permission—The Toronto Star Syndicate. **And The CUPW:** A cartoon by Aislin. Reprinted with permission—The Toronto Star Syndicate. **Reginald Featherstone:** Reprinted courtesy of the *Chronicle Herald*, Halifax. **Arrogant Officialdom:** Reprinted with permission the *Winnipeg Free Press* — February 1988. **Put

PHOTOGRAPHS

pp. 90 (left) Tony Stone Worldwide/Masterfile,
(right) Eastern Canada Towing Limited
pp. 92-93 Canapress Photo Service
pp. 105 Canapress Photo Service
pp. 108 Toronto Star
pp. 110 Calgary Herald
pp. 112-113 Canapress Photo Service
pp. 114 Canapress Photo Service
pp. 116 Canapress Photo Service
pp. 160-161 Masterfile
pp. 253 A. Sandron/Focus Stock Photo Inc.
pp. 258 Arnold Winterhoff
pp. 259 Masterfile
pp. 305 A. Sandron/Focus Stock Photo Inc.
pp. 336-337 The Image Bank
pp. 348 Daniel Dutka
pp. 349 Daniel Dutka
pp. 360 Windsor Star
pp. 363 Toronto Star

ILLUSTRATIONS:

pp. 13, 71, 123, 144-145, 185, 215, 297, 329 by Nicholas Vitacco
pp. 19, 129, 133 by Andrea Lawson
pp. 20-21 by Susan Leopold
pp. 22-23 by Barb Sommer
pp. 24, 140, 222, 223 by Henry van der Linde
pp. 29, 30, 34, 298, 299 by Laurie Lafrance
pp. 37, 40-41, 44, 47, 308-309 by John Dawson
pp. 53, 338-339 by Janice Goldberg
pp. 98-99 by Jill Chen
p. 109 by Marcia Masino
pp. 128, 226, 335 by Frank Viva
pp. 96, 100-111, 139, 203 by Thom Sevalrud
p. 141 by Avril Orloff
pp. 149, 152-153, 156, 158 by Wojtek Gorczynski
pp. 166-167, 168, 300, 301 by Clive Dobson
pp. 94, 100, 172, 263 by Emmanuel Lopez
pp. 229, 231, 232, 236-237 by Michael Reinhart
pp. 243, 246-247, 249 by Sandra Dionisi
pp. 256, 257 by Jirina Marton
pp. 262, 351 by Val Fraser
p. 323 by Scott Cameron
p. 340 by Martin Gould
pp. 91, 343 by Lori Langille
p. 345 by Rick Frieze
pp. 353, 354, 355, 357 by Dan Hobbs